IMAGES
of America

EASTERN SEVIER COUNTY

On the Cover: Eva McCarter works at a loom weaving cloth to make bed linens and towels. These products were a source of income for local craftsmen who sold their wares at retail outlets in neighboring Sevierville. (Courtesy of Carolyn Large Whaley.)

IMAGES
of America

EASTERN SEVIER COUNTY

Michael Williams

ARCADIA PUBLISHING

ISBN 978-1-4671-1429-5

Published by Arcadia Publishing
Charleston, South Carolina

Printed in the United States of America

Library of Congress Control Number: 2014959970

For all general information, please contact Arcadia Publishing:
Telephone 843-853-2070
Fax 843-853-0044
E-mail sales@arcadiapublishing.com
For customer service and orders:
Toll-Free 1-888-313-2665

Visit us on the Internet at www.arcadiapublishing.com

To my wife, Renee, and to the people of eastern Sevier County who labored and toiled in often difficult conditions to build a community and a way of life.

Contents

ACKNOWLEDGMENTS

Special thanks go to many who contributed photographs for inclusion in the book. They are Pete Owens of Dollywood, Carroll McMahan, Stephanie Postlewaite, Carolyn Large Whaley, and Jackie Underwood. I am also grateful for my wife, Renee, who has been a part of my life for more than 30 years.

INTRODUCTION

The story of eastern Sevier County is one that is rich in history and steeped in tradition, legends, and lore. The region has survived a tumultuous history predating the forced eviction of its native inhabitants. The region was torn and divided by the War Between the States, which split the inhabitants and pitted neighbors against one another. In the ensuing years, the residents of the region answered the call for arms during the 20th century when the nation was swept into two world wars and two wars in Asia. Tragedy marred the area on several occasions, including an Indian attack and a flood that took several lives.

Eastern Sevier County, Tennessee, is in the foothills of the Great Smoky Mountains National Park. The largest of the six communities that comprise eastern Sevier County is Pittman Center. The area surrounding the community, within a 50-mile radius, was the home of many interesting persons, among them a man known as "the hanging judge," a country music legend, a US president, a legendary frontiersman, and a nationally renowned naturalist. The area holds its secrets, including the story of lost treasure. Numerous churches and industries dot the landscape, surrounding the mountains and set against a bucolic backdrop.

Pittman Center and the surrounding region were originally inhabited by Native Americans, who first arrived in the region as many as 20,000 years ago. Numerous artifacts, such as arrow points found in the area dating back 10,000 years, give researchers a clue as to how the indigenous natives lived. During the mid-16th century, Spanish expeditions led by Hernando de Soto, in 1540, and Juan Pardo, in 1567, passed through the region now known as Sevier County. At the time, the area was part of the domain of Chiaha, a Muskogean chiefdom located on a now submerged island just upstream from modern-day Douglas Dam. The Muskogean village was inundated beneath the waters of Douglas Lake during the late 1930s with the creation of the Tennessee Valley Authority.

By the late 17th century, the Cherokee, whose ancestors lived in the mountains at the time of the Spaniards' expedition, had become the dominant tribe in the region. The Cherokee planted corn on the mountain and hunted bear, deer, turkey, and turtles. Although they used the region primarily as hunting grounds, the Chickamauga faction of the Cherokee vehemently fought white encroachment on their lands, frequently leading raids on households and settlements. Various peace treaties brought short periods of tranquility, frequently interrupted by violent upheavals.

Most of the region that comprises eastern Sevier County has always been densely wooded, with magnificent forests that stretched for many miles. The forests, teeming with wild game, were often the hunting ground for many settlers. One of the most famous people who may have hunted in the surrounding forests was the noted "King of the Wild Frontier" himself, Davy Crockett. Born in present-day Greene County, which lies almost 70 miles to the north, Crockett often stayed in Dandridge, located 25 miles west of Pittman Center. Founded shortly after the end of the American Revolution, Dandridge was named after Martha Washington and is the second-oldest city in Tennessee. Crockett had met the woman he intended to marry and traveled to Dandridge, where the marriage bond was drawn up. But the future famed frontiersman was jilted by his betrothed. The marriage bond is still on display at the county courthouse.

Sevier County was formed on September 18, 1794, from part of neighboring Jefferson County, and has retained its original boundaries ever since. The county was named in honor of John Sevier, governor of the failed state of Franklin and first governor of Tennessee, who fought in the American Revolution and played a prominent role during the early years of the settling of the region. Since the founding of the county, the county seat has been situated at Sevierville, the eighth-oldest city in Tennessee, which was also named for Governor Sevier.

The creation of ironworks in East Tennessee in 1809 paved the way for mining in Sevier County, although it would be 11 years before iron was discovered on Foxfire Mountain in 1820. With the help of the Cherokee, the iron was mined, and the Native American workers were paid with the sparse amounts of silver by-product of the mining operation. The miners usually hid their silver in the mine for safekeeping. In 1838, the Cherokee were forced to relocate to Oklahoma in what is known as the Trail of Tears and were driven out of East Tennessee and Foxfire Mountain. Many never recovered the silver they had stashed in the mine, and thus the legend of lost treasure was born. After the departure of the Cherokee, Isaac Love and his sons created a partnership with the Shields Iron Co. to continue mining at Foxfire Mountain.

Sevier County remained staunchly pro-Union during the War Between the States. On June 8, 1861, Tennessee held a vote on the state's Ordinance of Secession. Sevier Countians voted resoundingly 1,528 to 60 in favor of remaining in the union. The war was highly divisive, inciting public officials such as Sevier County sheriff William Pickens, who led a failed attempt to destroy the railroad bridge in Strawberry Plains, outside of Knoxville, in November 1861, as part of the East Tennessee bridge-burning conspiracy.

During the Civil War (1861–1865), the Confederate army built a camp at the bend in the river near the area of Richardson's Cove. The natural resources in the area and access to iron, sulfur, and saltpeter made the area strategic to the creation of much-needed war materials. As the war encroached into Tennessee, Union soldiers were reported in the area near Pearl Valley. One afternoon, a Union soldier killed a local man, William Thomas, near his home. They reportedly believed Thomas was a Confederate sympathizer providing food and supplies to Southern forces. It was soon determined that he was a moonshiner hauling ingredients for his liquor to his still, which was hidden in the crevices of the old iron mine.

The East Tennessee region was ravaged by the war when Confederate general James Longstreet battled Union general Ambrose Burnside in the counties surrounding Sevier County during the battles of Knoxville, Fort Sanders, and Dandridge.

Naturalist Wiley Oakley, known as the "roamin' man of the Smokies," became nationally renowned for his knowledge of every nook and cranny of the Great Smoky Mountains and all the flora and fauna that grows in the mountain range. Oakley was a true mountaineer who spent much of his life exploring the hills.

With the creation of the Great Smoky Mountains National Park in 1934, the dynamics of the Sevier County economy changed dramatically, from one sustained by agriculture to one driven by tourism. Sevier County contains 30 percent of the total area of the national park.

Numerous attractions drive the tourism trade in Sevier County, including Dollywood, an amusement park created by country music legend Dolly Parton, who was born on Locust Ridge, less than five miles from Pittman Center. Parton's is a classic rags-to-riches story. She was the fourth of twelve children of Robert Lee Parton, a tobacco farmer, and his wife, Avie Lee. Parton has often described her family as being "dirt poor." Her father paid the doctor who helped deliver her with a bag of oatmeal, and they lived in a rustic, two-room cabin. A replica of the cabin stands in the theme park that bears her name.

One

People and Families

Settlers of Europeans descent began migrating into the eastern Sevier County region in the 18th century. Several families proved instrumental in carving out the communities from the dense, untamed wilderness. The earliest families to settle the area were the Whaleys, McMahans, Dennises, Cardwells, Partons, Reagans, and Ogles. The descendants of these early pioneers still occupy modern-day eastern Sevier County.

William Richardson settled the area now known as Richardson's Cove in 1792. The encroachment of white settlers brought conflict with the Cherokee, who carved out war paths from the dense foliage. The Cherokee inhabiting Richardson's Cove were forced out with the Indian Removal Act of 1838, also known as the Trail of Tears.

The so-called queen of country music, Dolly Parton, was born into grinding poverty in a tiny two-room house on Locust Ridge in eastern Sevier County. She was one of 12 children born to Robert and Avie Lee Parton. After making her mark in country music, Dolly returned to her home and opened a theme park that bears her name. Her business ventures have created more than 3,000 local jobs.

Present-day Pittman Center lies in the shadows of the Great Smoky Mountains. Among the first settlers to arrive in the area was Frederick Emert, who came with his family in 1785. The area was soon known as Emert's Cove.

The region remained largely isolated throughout the 18th and 19th centuries. Most of the inhabitants worked as farmers and lived off the land. In 1919, Dr. John Burnett, a Methodist minister, visited Emert's Cove and discovered that education and health care were deficient. Burnett envisioned the establishment of a large-scale school that would serve the needs of the children of all of eastern Sevier County with virtually no tuition charged. Later that year, Burnett presented his missionary plan to the Methodist Episcopal Church, at the annual meeting in New York, which approved his plan to create a community school in the remote area of Emert's Cove. That school became known as Pittman Community Center and was established in 1921.

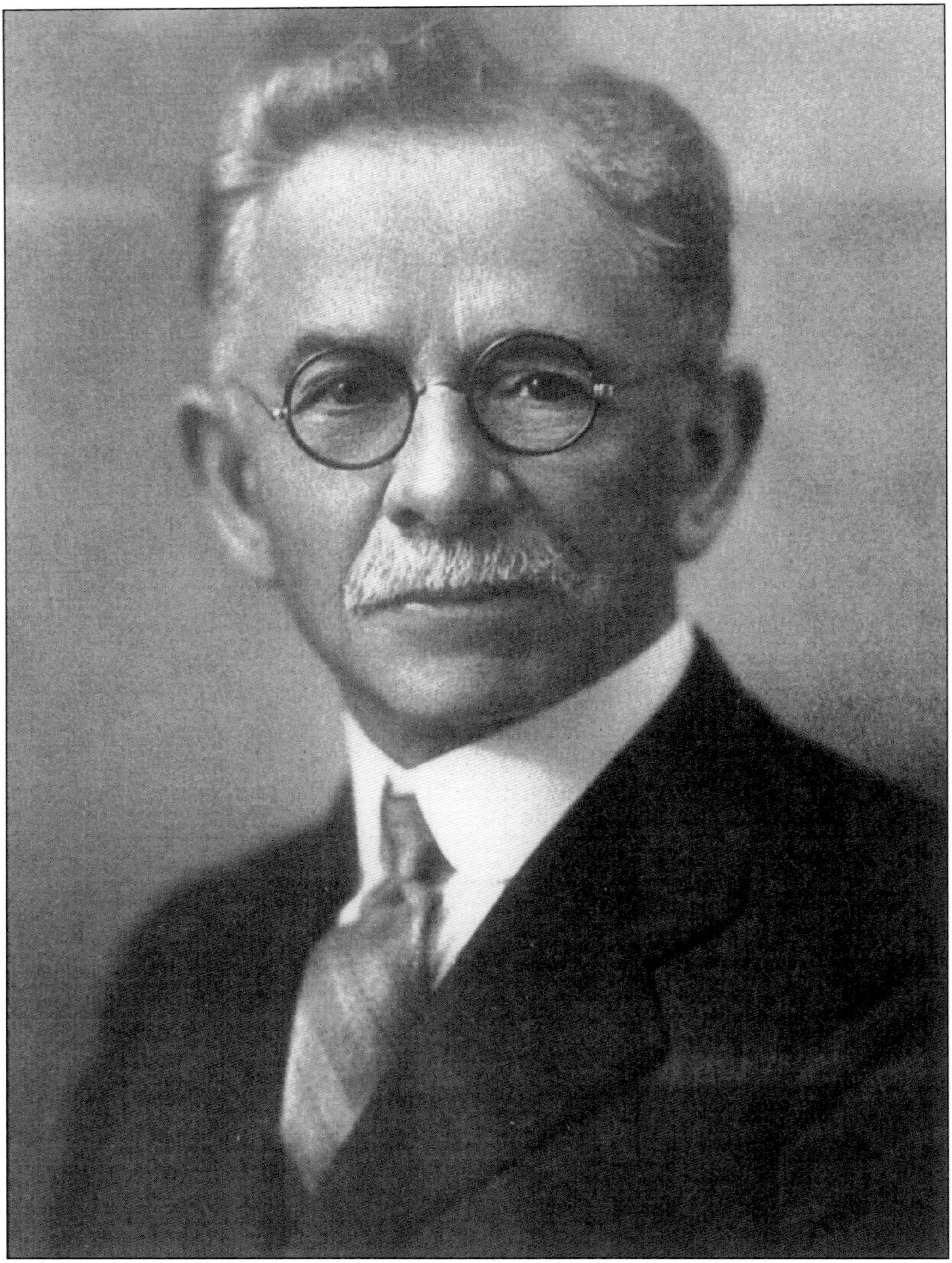

The town of Pittman Center bears the name of Rev. Eli Pittman from Elmira, New York. Pittman had numerous affluent friends in New York. His friends provided funding for the construction of a school with 16 buildings on a 1,500-acre plot of land. Once completed, the campus was referred to as Pittman Community Center. (Courtesy of Glen Cardwell.)

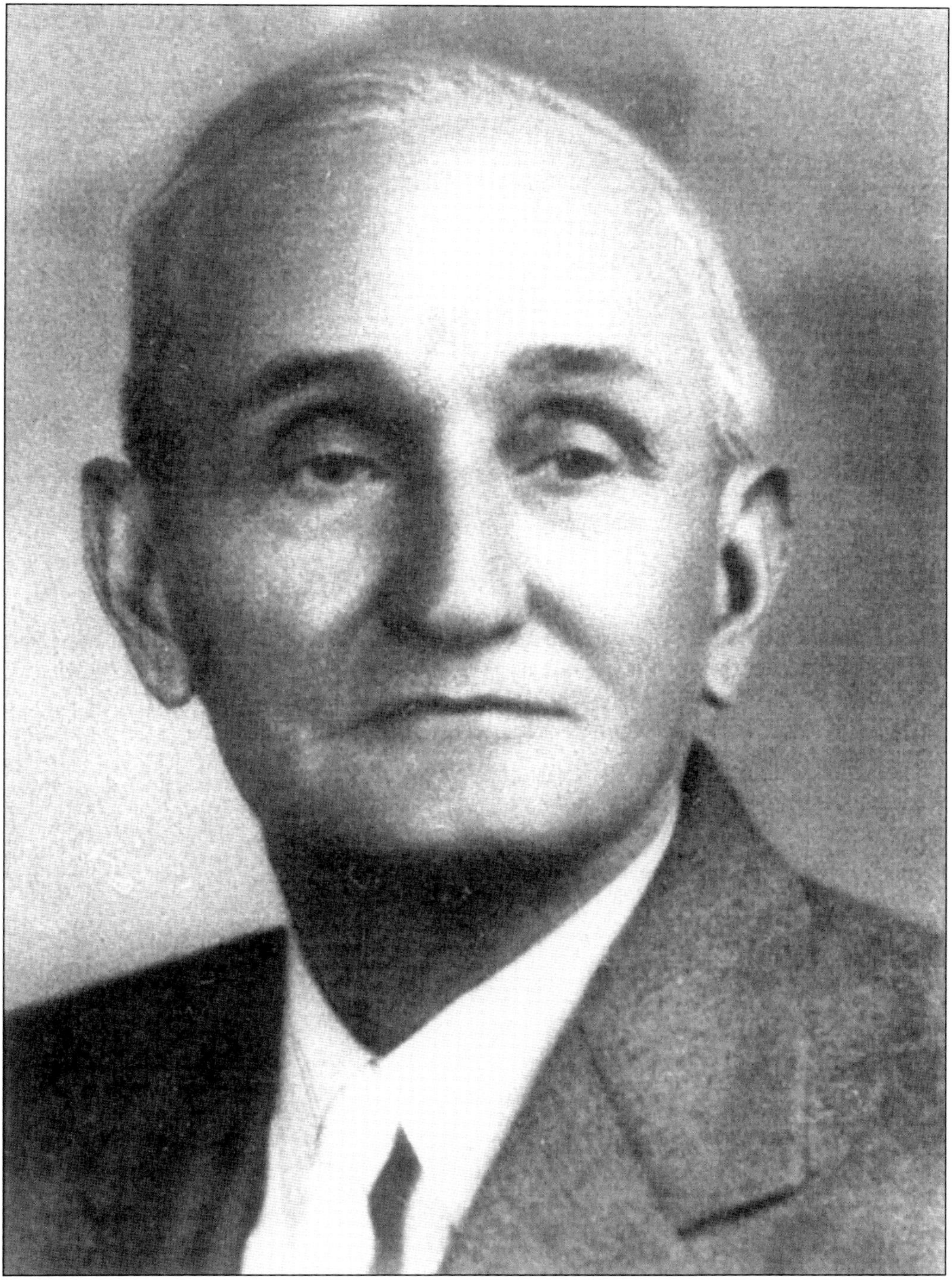

Dr. John Sevier Burnett was a Methodist minister who visited the area, which was then known as Emert's Cove. Witnessing the poverty in the area, Burnett realized that education and access to improved health care was desperately needed. Burnett attended the national meeting of the Methodist Episcopal Church in 1919 and asked the church to perform missionary work in the area. The church endorsed the mission and appointed Burnett to supervise construction of the needed buildings. (Courtesy of Glen Cardwell.)

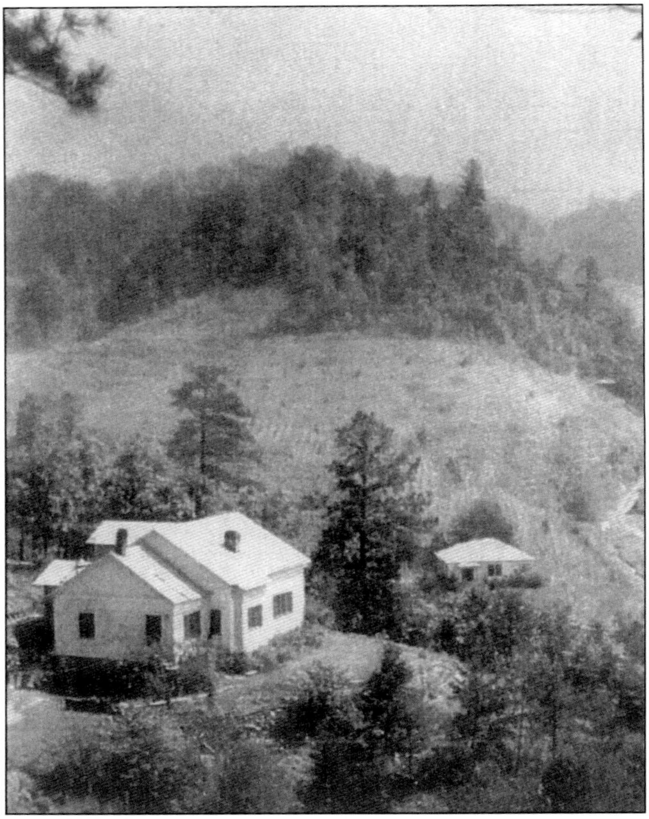

Pictured at left is the home of Dr. R.F. Thomas in the 1930s. Dr. Thomas came to Sevier County in 1926 with plans to serve the county in dual roles as a physician and a minister. He traveled the rough-and-rugged roads of Sevier County, making as many as 1,000 house calls a year. He traveled to these appointments by jeep, on foot, and on horseback. Below, Dr. R.F. Thomas and his wife, Eva, entertain guests in their new home in Emert's Cove in 1938. Dr. Thomas was known as the mountain missionary. (Left, courtesy of Glen Cardwell; below, courtesy of Carolyn Large Whaley.)

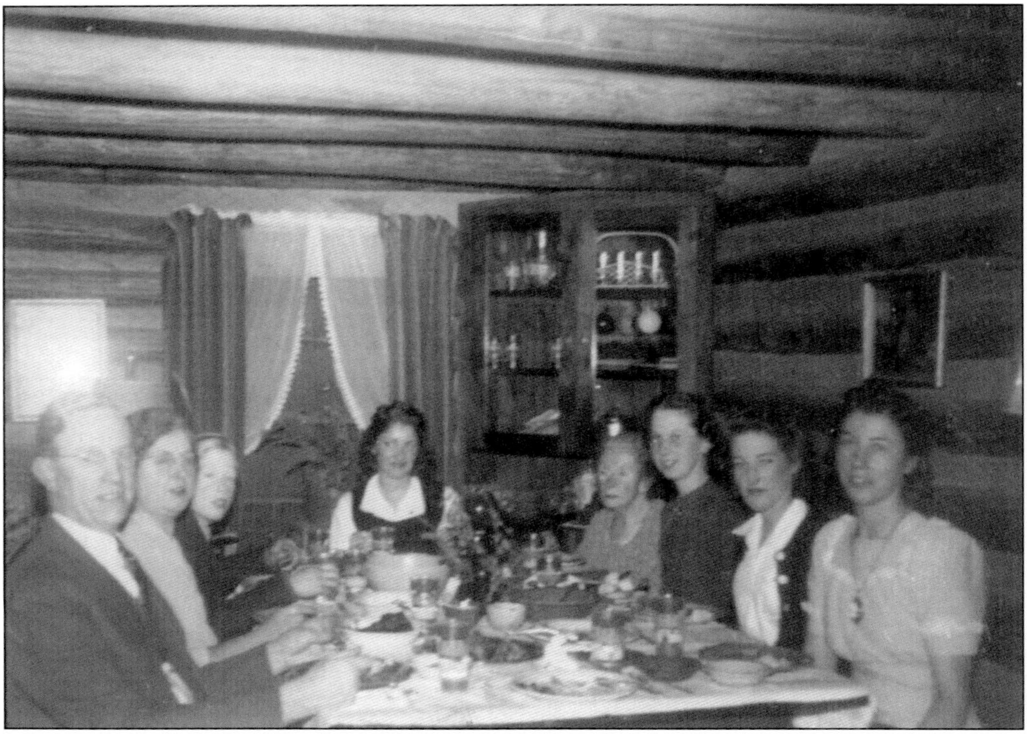

Judge Benjamin Owens served as a criminal court judge in Sevier County during the 1880s, and he frequently held court on his personal property. Known as "the hanging judge," Owens was said to have hanged at least two convicts on his property. He occasionally rode an ox to town to hold court at the Sevier County Courthouse. He is buried on Foxfire Mountain in the Owens Family Cemetery with his wife, son, and 20 unidentified people. Owens's picture hangs in the Sevier County Courthouse and in a small museum on Foxfire Mountain. (Courtesy of Stephanie Postlewaite.)

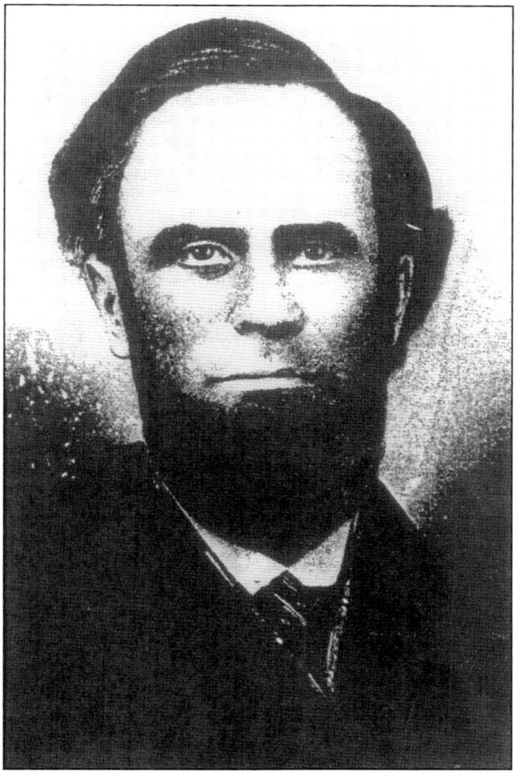

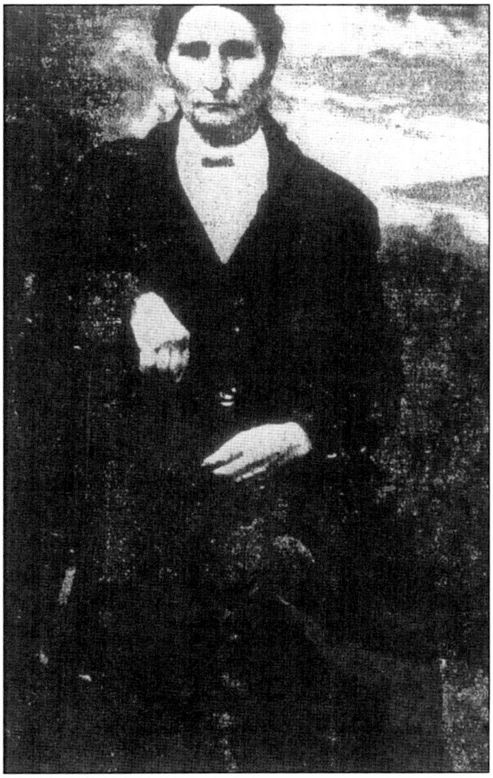

Annie Oakley Owens, the aunt of Wiley Oakley, married Judge Owens. A midwife for more than 30 years, she helped deliver many. She was an excellent herb doctor and almost always carried a little satchel stuffed with various types of plants. Annie once healed a wounded Cherokee man after he had fallen on rocks in the woods. As a token of appreciation, his fellow Cherokees celebrated with a great feast. Annie is buried next to her husband on Foxfire Mountain. (Courtesy of Stephanie Postlewaite.)

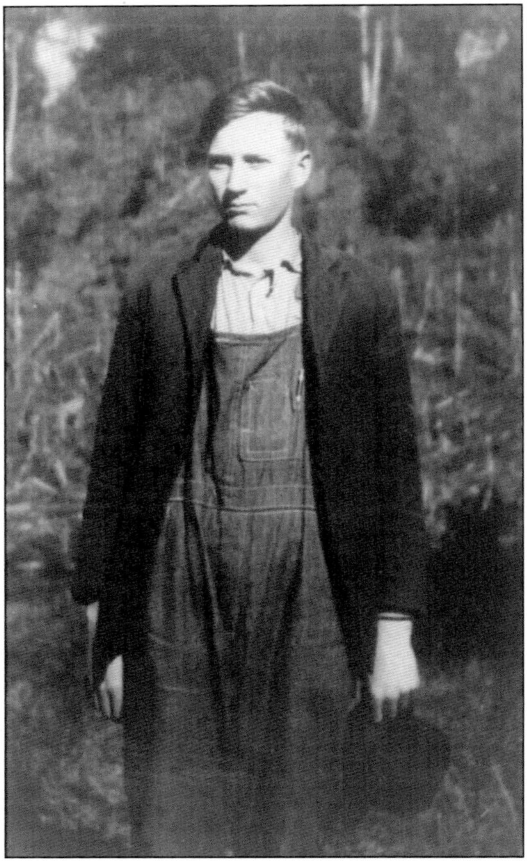

Oliver Huskey was a student at Pittman Center. Like most teens his age, Huskey worked on the family farm when not in school. He is pictured in 1922. (Courtesy of Glen Cardwell.)

Dr. Richard Guinn Wright was the dentist at Tunis Creek. He was the grandfather of Pittman Center's first mayor, Conley Huskey. During the early years, doctors and dentists bartered for services, trading dental or health care for livestock or any implement the patient could spare. (Courtesy of Glen Cardwell.)

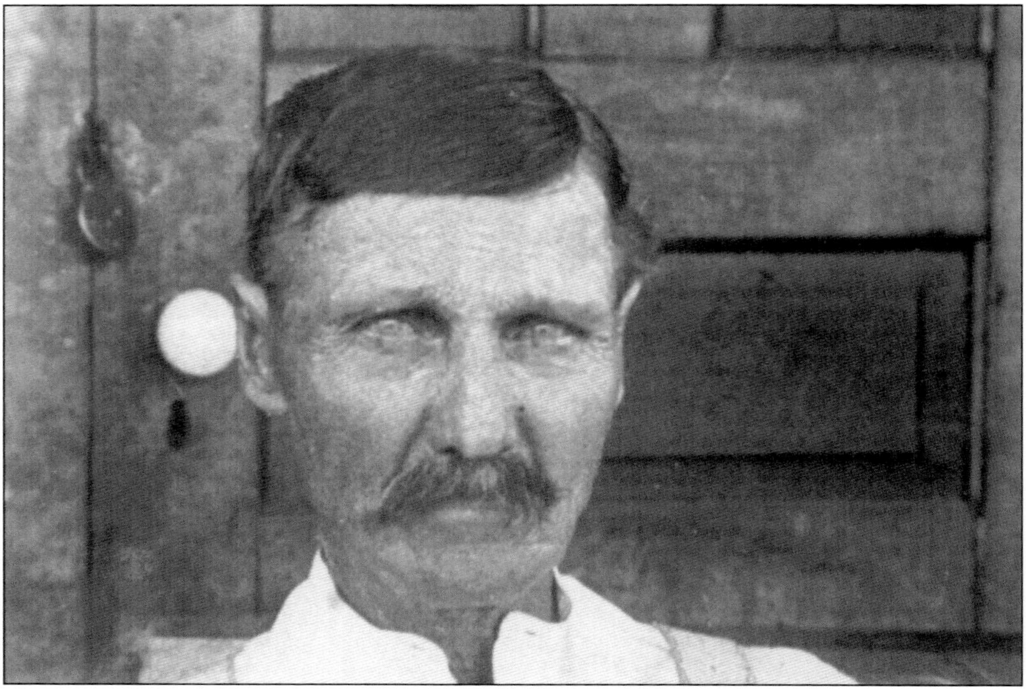

Jim Maples, pictured, owned a farm in addition to his business ventures. (Courtesy of Jackie Underwood.)

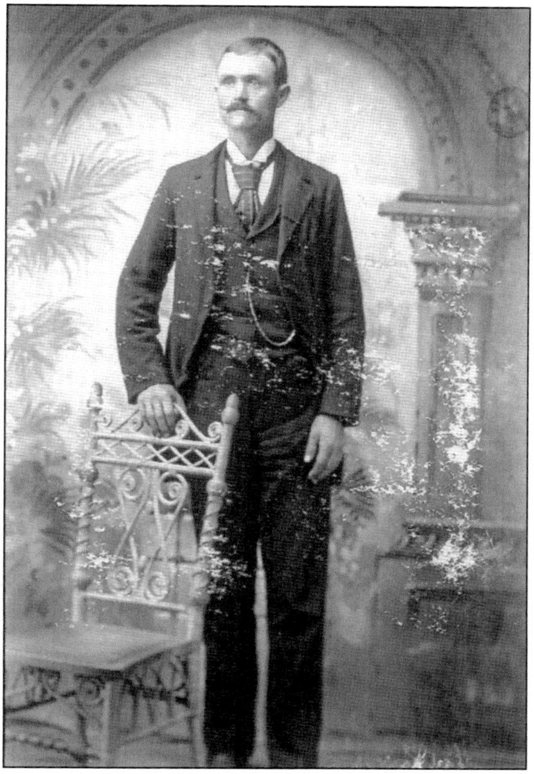

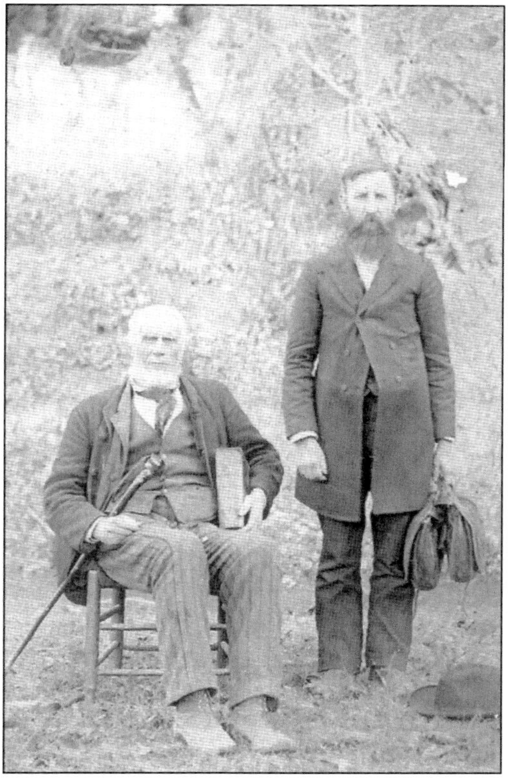

John Shields, born September 27, 1825, is pictured with Rev. G.W. Glendenson. Shields was the grandfather of Tiny McMahan, who wrote that when she was a child she frequently accompanied her grandfather when he walked over English Mountain to visit relatives on Chestnut Hill. (Courtesy of Jackie Underwood.)

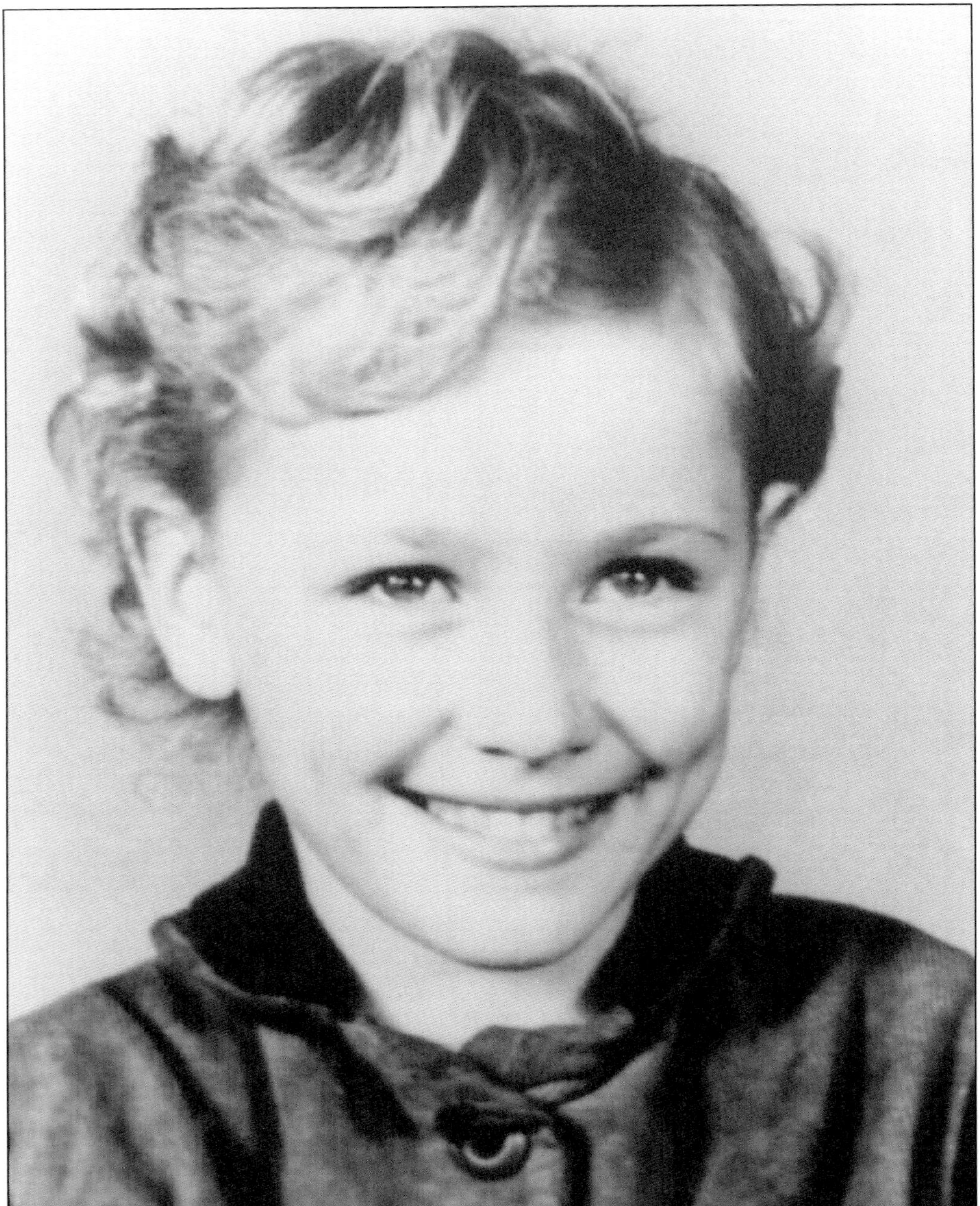

The most famous of all Sevier County residents is Dolly Parton, who was born on Locust Ridge. Her father, Robert Lee, paid the doctor who delivered her with a bag of cornmeal. Dolly left Sevier County and rose to international stardom and became known as the queen of country music. She later recounted that bag of cornmeal was the best investment her father ever made. Parton has given back to the Sevier County community by helping to build the area's hospital, creating a popular theme park that bears her name, and establishing the Imagination Library, which provides free books to children born in Sevier County for the first five years of their lives. Parton's theme park, Dollywood, and her Dixie Stampede attraction provide jobs to more than 3,000 people. (Courtesy of Dollywood.)

Dolly's parents Robert Lee Parton and Avie Lee Parton were the parents of 12 children. They raised their burgeoning brood in a tiny two-room home on Locust Ridge. (Courtesy of Dollywood.)

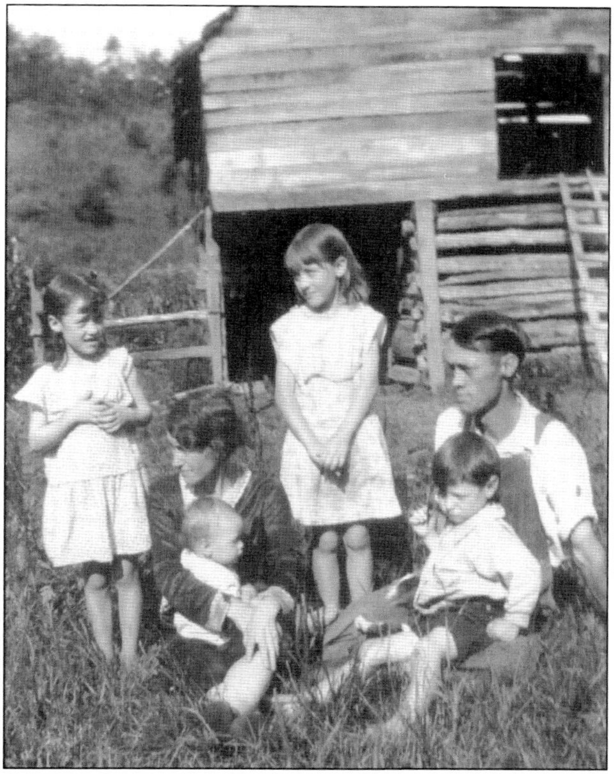

Dolly (far right in the second row) is pictured with her third-grade class in Pittman Center. A former classmate remembers Dolly coming to school for the first time. According to Glen Cardwell, Dolly wore no shoes and no jacket on her first day of school and wore a dress made from an old flour bag. (Courtesy of Dollywood.)

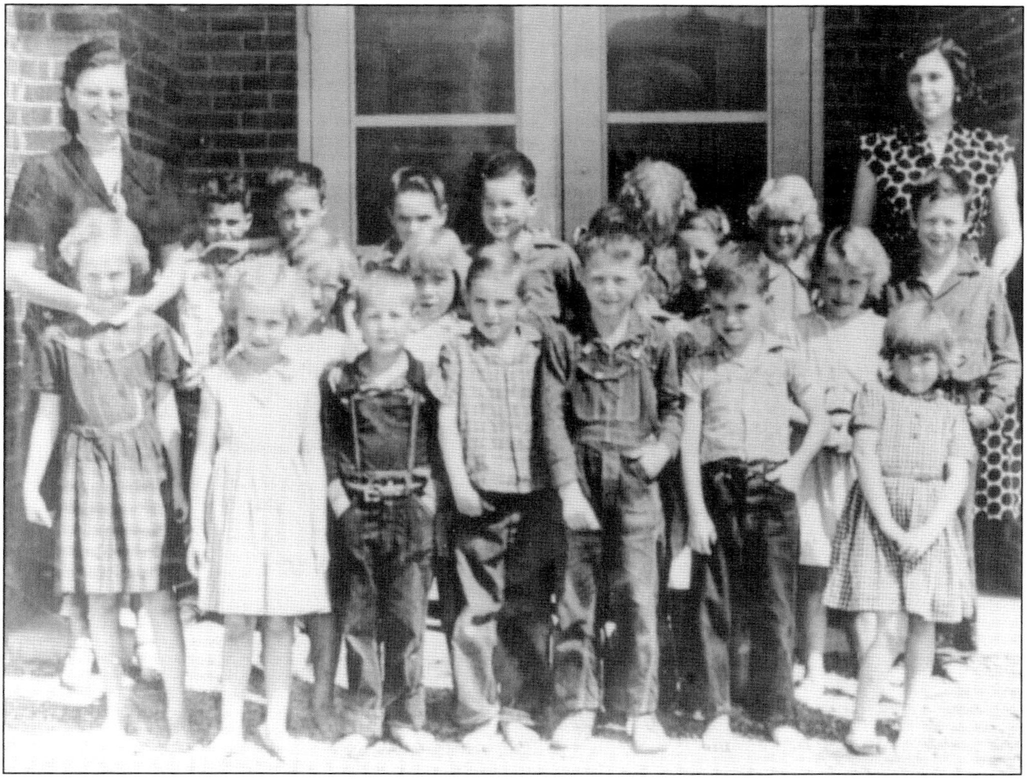

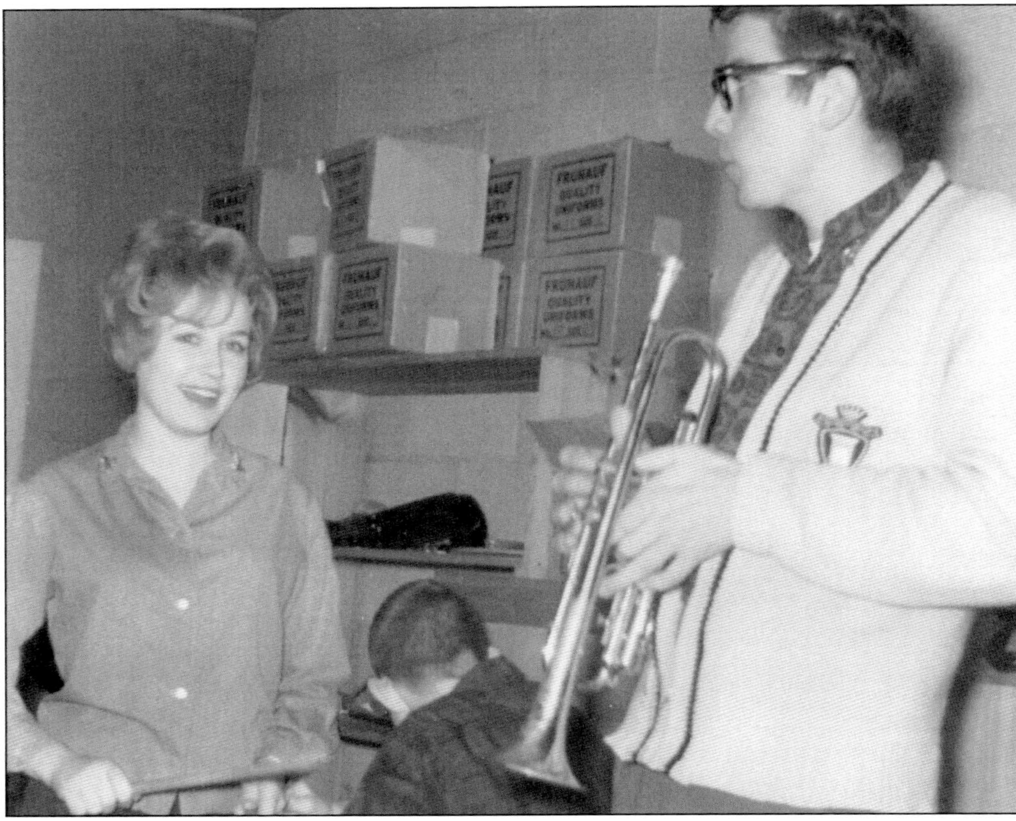

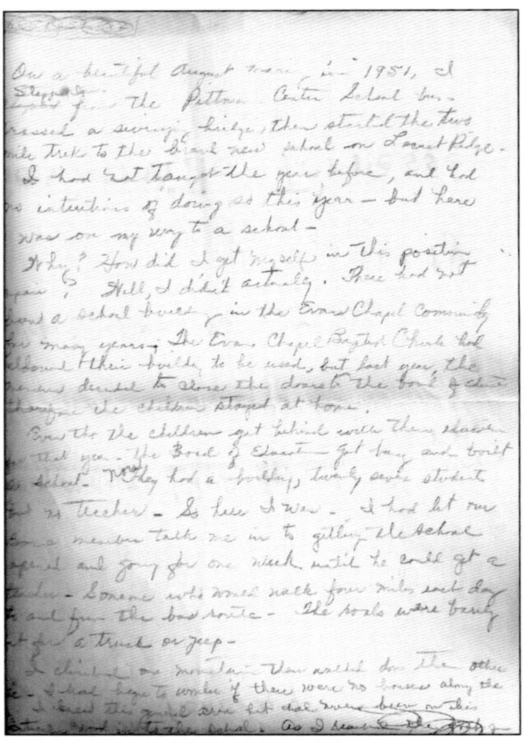

On a beautiful August morn in 1951, I stepped down from the Pittman Center School bus, crossed a swinging bridge, then started the two mile trek to the brand new school on Locust Ridge. I had not taught the year before, and had no intentions of doing so this year — but here was on my way to a school —

Why? How did I get myself in this position? Well, I didn't actually. There had not been a school house in the Evans Chapel Community for many years. The Evans Chapel Baptist Church had allowed their building to be used, but last year the members decided to close the doors to the board of [illegible] therefore the children stayed at home.

Even tho the children got behind with their education that year. The Board of Education got busy and built a school. Now they had a building, twenty seven students but no teacher. So here I was. I had let one [illegible] member talk me in to getting the school opened and going for one week until he could get a teacher. Someone who would walk four miles each day to and from the bus route. The roads were [illegible] for a truck or jeep.

I climbed one mountain then walked down the other [illegible]. I had begun to wonder if there were no houses along the [illegible] [illegible] [illegible] [illegible] [illegible] been on this [illegible] [illegible] to the school. As I [illegible] [illegible]

Dolly studied music at Sevier County High School in Sevierville. In the years after her graduation, she was named to the school's wall of fame, and her picture now hangs next to several other notable graduates of the high school, including Gary Wade, a justice on the Tennessee Supreme Court. (Courtesy of Dollywood.)

This photograph is of a letter written by a Mrs. McMahan, one of Dolly Parton's teachers growing up. The letter describes Dolly as a studious and attentive child. As an adult, Dolly was instrumental in creating the Imagination Library, which provides free books to children born in Sevier County for the first five years of their lives. (Courtesy of Carroll McMahan.)

Lester McCarter left Pittman Community Center and joined the Navy. He later went to college at Lincoln Memorial University on the GI Bill. McCarter became an educator and coach and taught at Harrison Chilhowee and the Baptist Academy. (Courtesy of Glen Cardwell.)

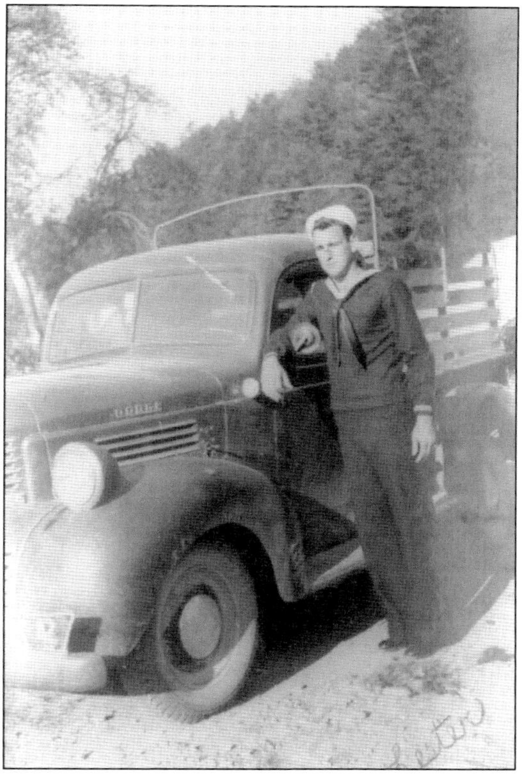

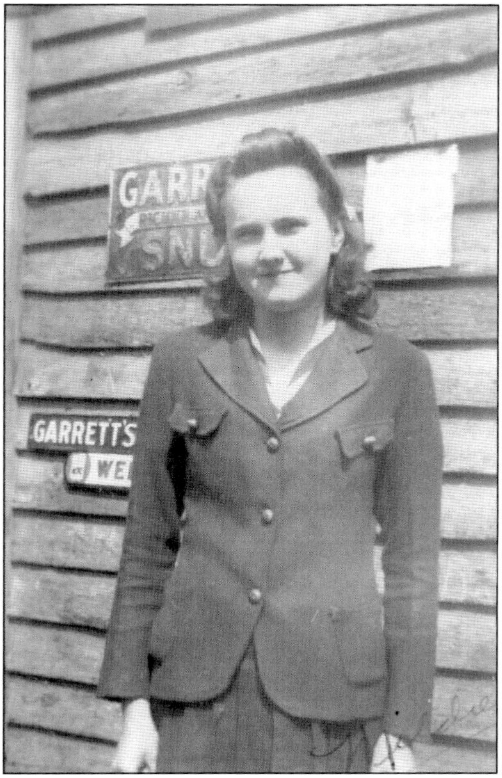

Mildred McCarter is pictured in 1944. After high school graduation, she went to work for Dr. Ralph Shilling. There were no nursing schools in the area, and Dr. Shilling hired young women with no medical experience as nurses. He gave them on-the-job training, teaching them everything they needed to know about nursing. (Courtesy of Glen Cardwell.)

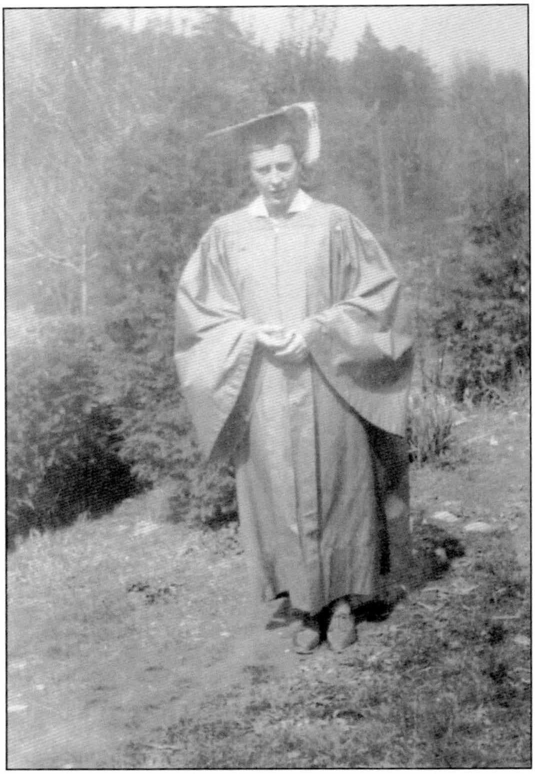

Vivian McCarter Branam graduated from Pittman Center High School in 1946. Like her mother, Eva Ramsey, she learned the craft of making clothes. Her self-sufficiency served her well. Soon after high school, Vivian married and had children. Sadly, her husband was killed in an accident, leaving her to care for the children alone. She later remarried. (Courtesy of Glen Cardwell.)

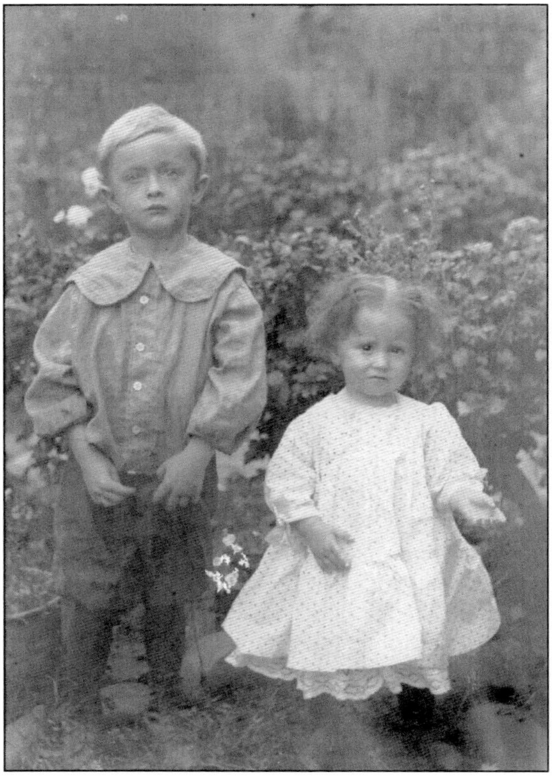

Roy McCarter and Jenny McCarter are pictured around 1905. The two attended Webb's Creek School. The school was a small one-room facility that was later renovated and became the Webb's Creek United Methodist Church. (Courtesy of Glen Cardwell.)

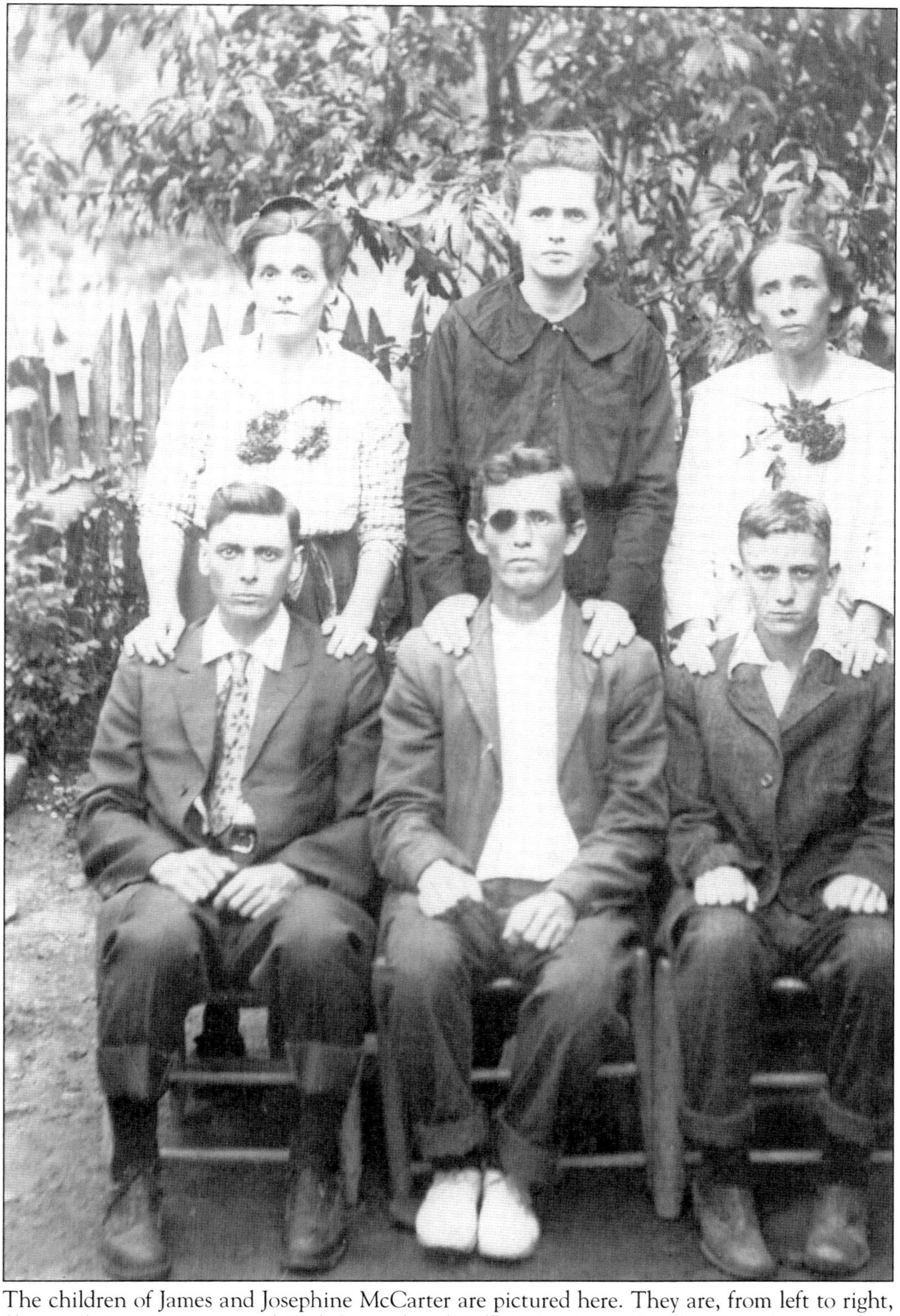

The children of James and Josephine McCarter are pictured here. They are, from left to right, (first row) Horace, Steve, and Carl; (second row) Polly, Winnie, and Lindie. Steve lost an eye in a sawmill accident. (Courtesy of Carolyn Large Whaley.)

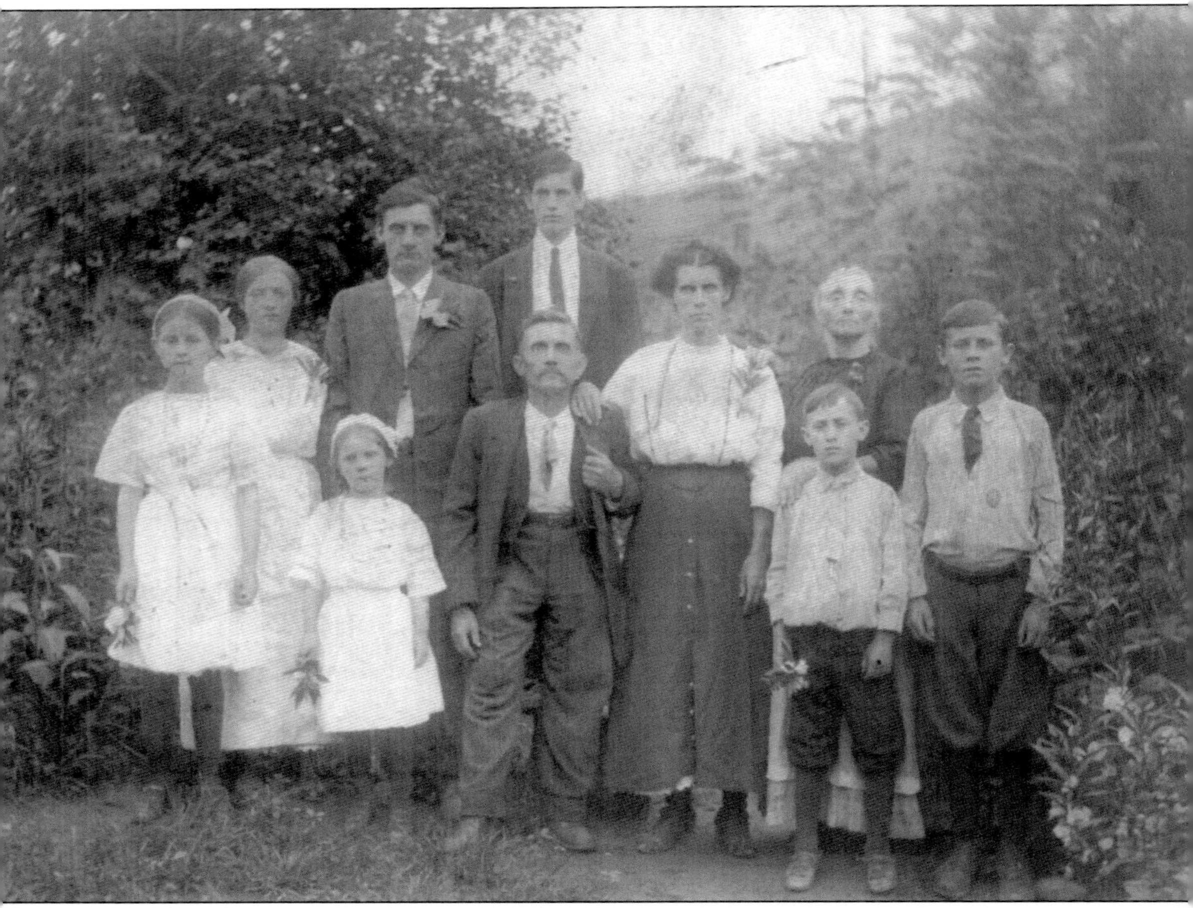

The family of Johnny Proffitt is all decked out for a wedding in the early 1930s. Pictured are, from left to right, (first row) Myrtle, Hazel, Johnny, Rachel, Bruce, and Glenn; (second row) Zettie McCarter Proffitt, Elmer (Zettie's husband), Ellis, and Laurence. (Courtesy of Carolyn Large Whaley.)

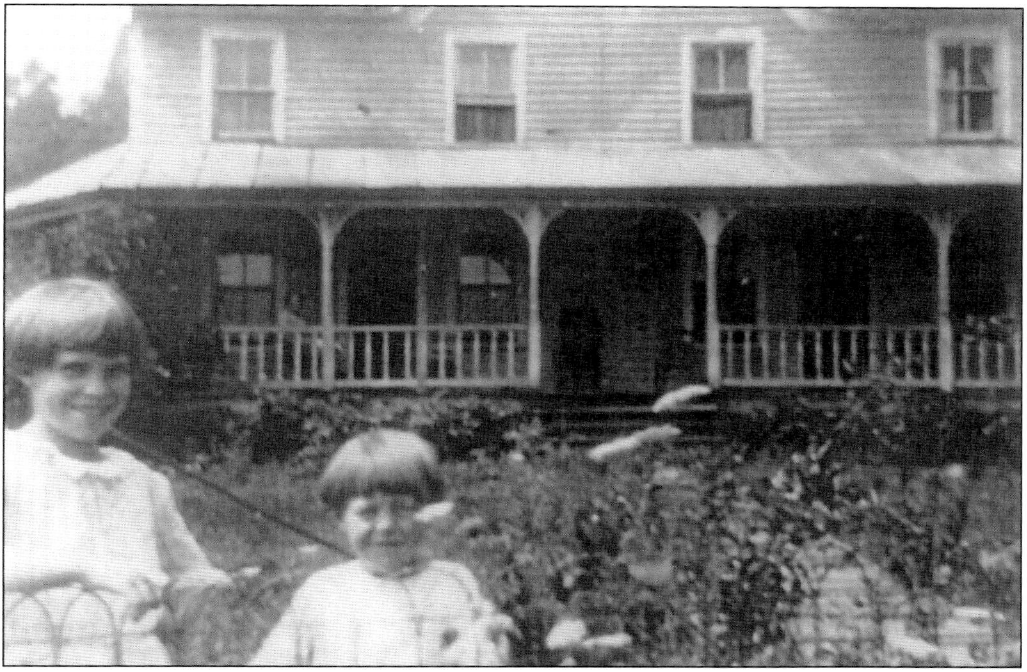

Beulah Dennis McCarter and Archie Ray Dennis McMahan are shown at their grandfather's home in Pearl Valley. The area was also known as "Mac Cove." (Courtesy of Jackie Underwood.)

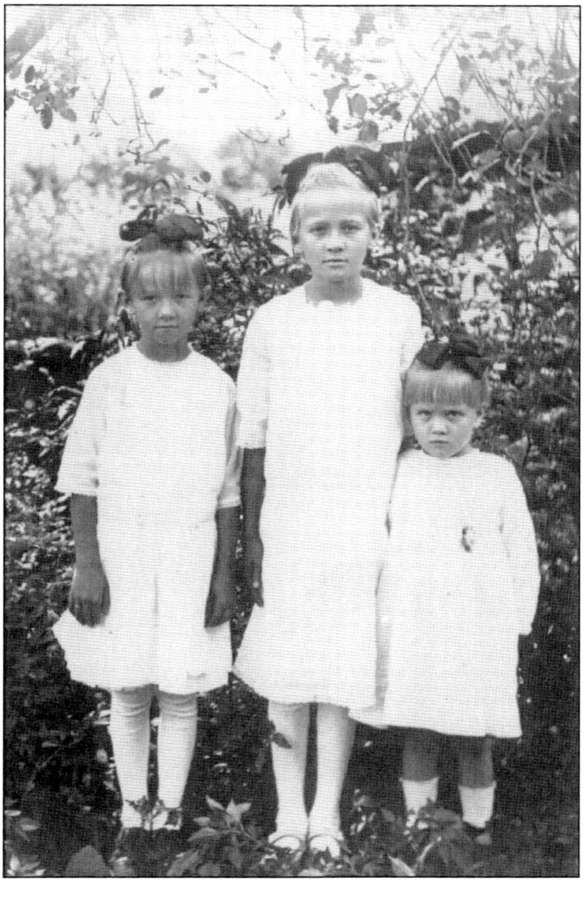

Lillian (left), Edna (center), and Beatrice McCarter are pictured in 1910. Mothers often made their children's clothing, as there were few stores where clothes could be purchased. (Courtesy of Carolyn Large Whaley.)

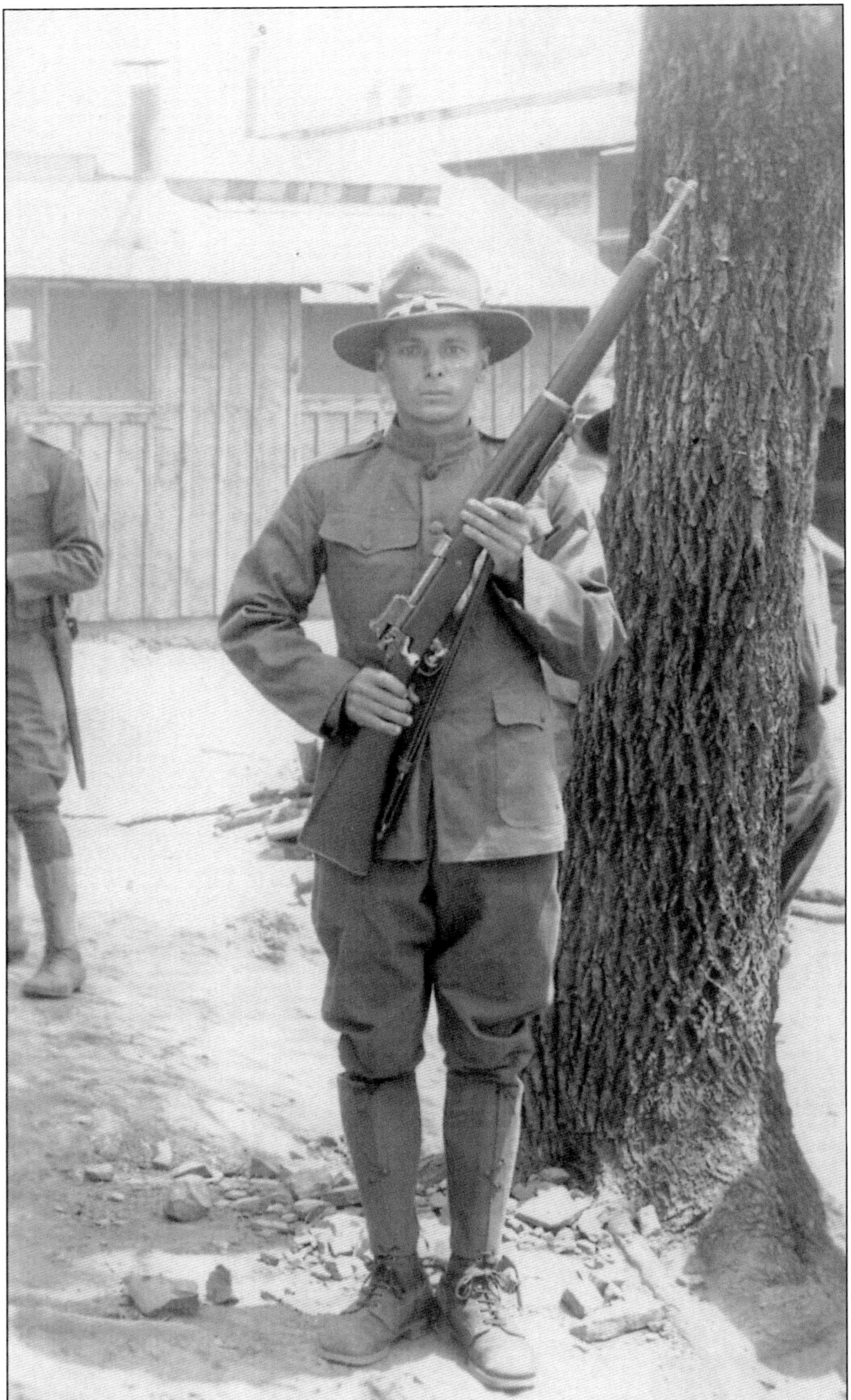

Horace McCarter is pictured at Camp Pike during World War I. More than 600 Sevier County men answered the call of duty during the Great War. McCarter was one of the fortunate servicemen who survived. (Courtesy of Carolyn Large Whaley.)

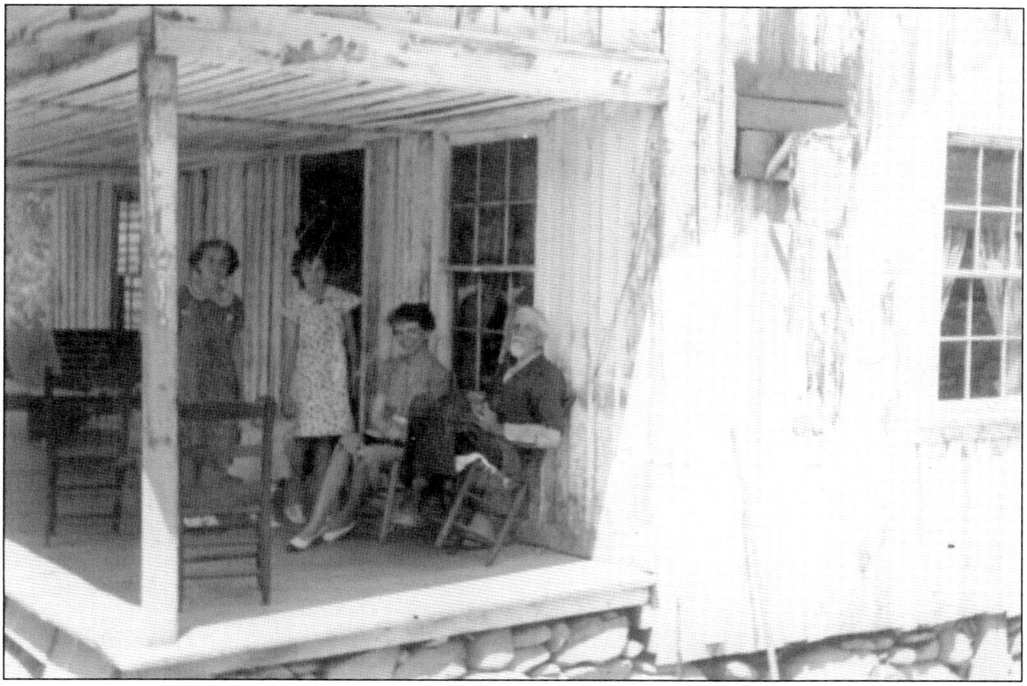

This is the home of Carl and Vernie McCarter. Pictured from left to right are Mildred McCarter, Mae Spurgeon, an unidentified woman, and James "Uncle Bud" McCarter. (Courtesy of Carolyn Large Whaley.)

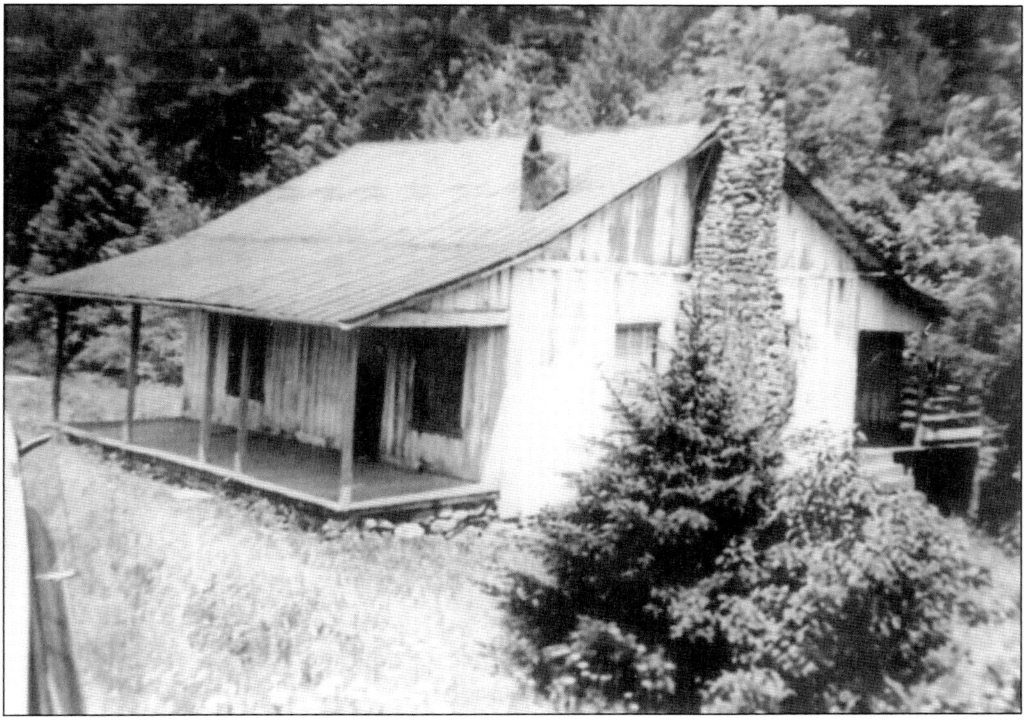

The home of Carl and Vernie McCarter stood near Webb's Creek. The family, like most in the region were farmers and subsisted mostly on produce they grew. (Courtesy of Glen Cardwell.)

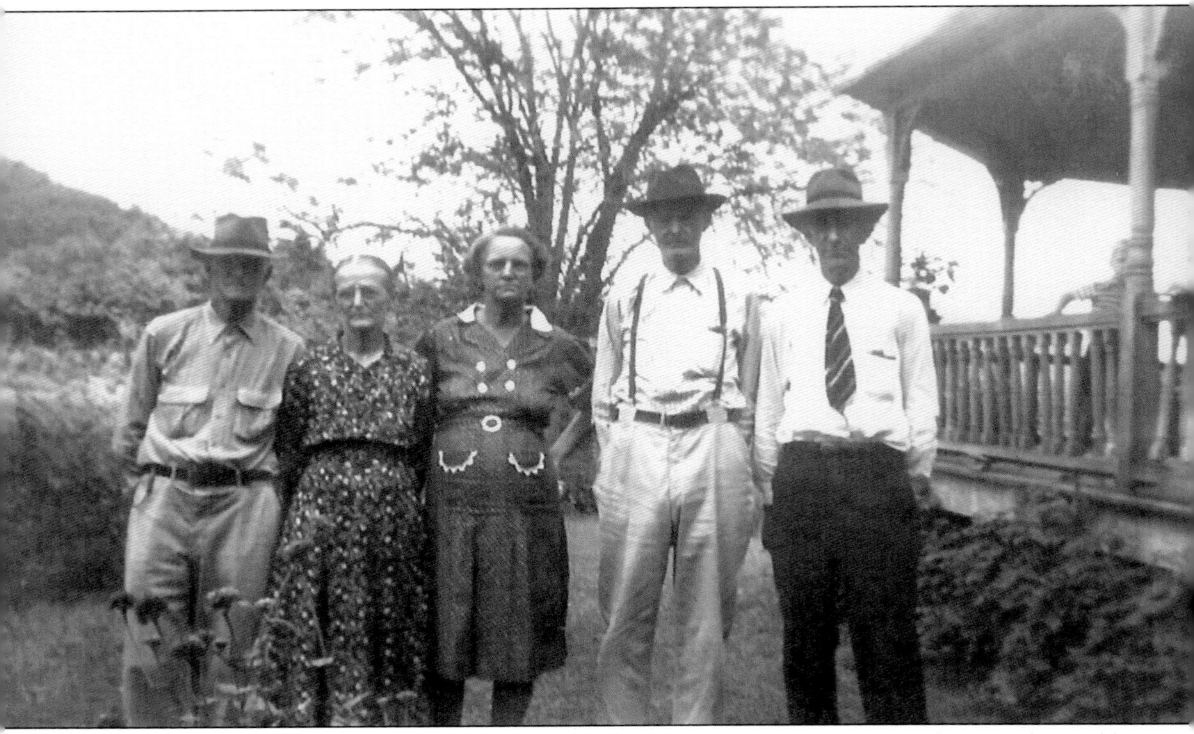

John Dennis is pictured with relatives at a family gathering. From left to right are John, Tilda Shepherd, Jane Huff, Robert Dennis, and George Henry. (Courtesy of Jackie Underwood.)

Beulah Dennis McCarter holds her nephew Jack McMahan at the Dennis family home. During the Great Depression, workers would ask to work at the Dennis farm in exchange for a bushel of corn. (Courtesy of Jackie Underwood.)

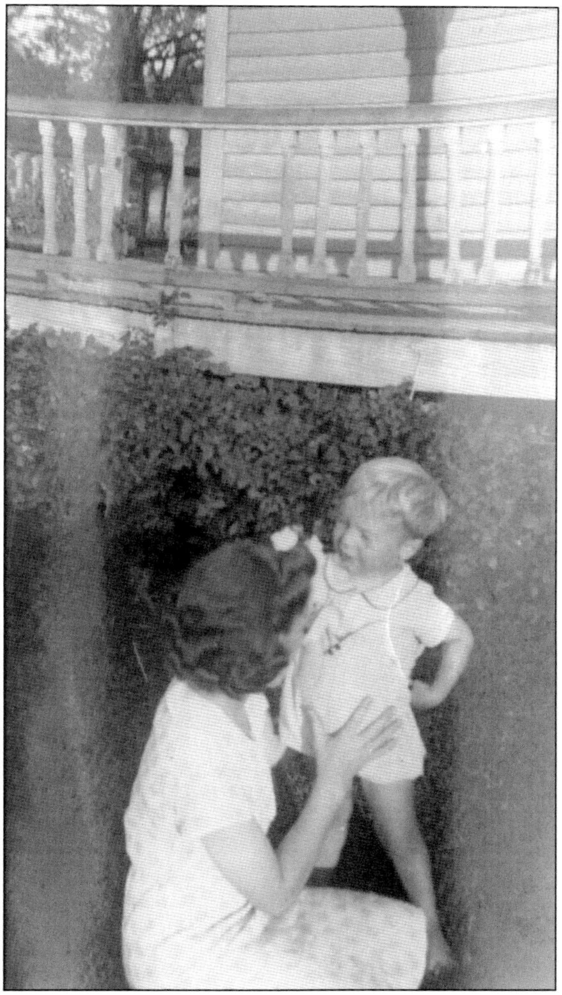

Pictured from left to right are sisters Archie Ray Dennis, Sarah Mae Dennis Large, Dora Dennis Proffitt, and Beulah Dennis McCarter, who lived in Pearl Valley. The sparsely populated area lies between Foxfire Mountain and Pittman Center. (Courtesy of Jackie Underwood.)

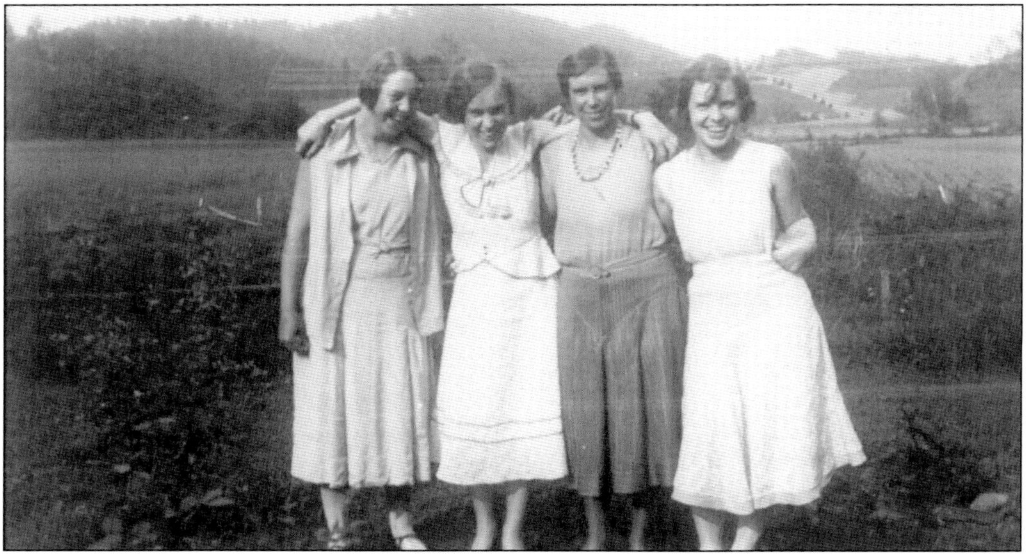

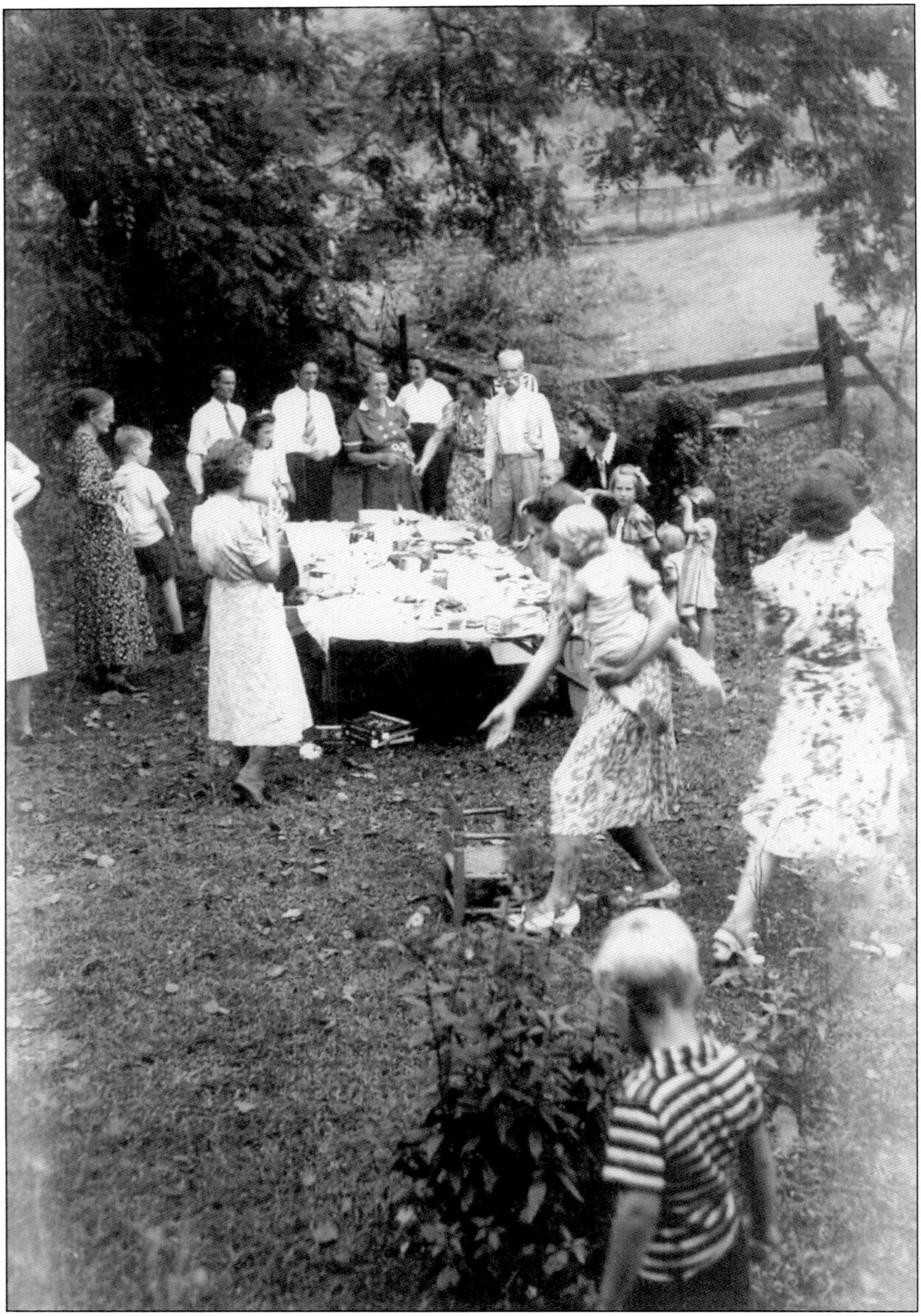

The McMahan and Dennis families are pictured at a family reunion in the 1940s. Archie Ray McMahan stands in the foreground with her son Tommy, and four-year-old Jack McMahan also stands in the foreground. (Courtesy Jackie Underwood.)

Ora and Roy McMahan are pictured at their family home in Richardson's Cove in the 1940s. Like many residents of Pearl Valley, the McMahans made their living farming. (Courtesy Jackie Underwood.)

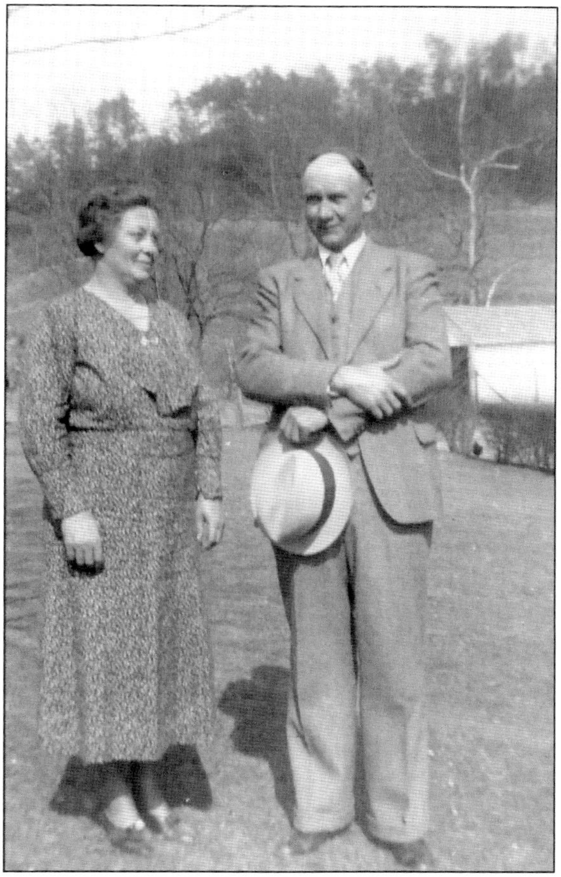

The Dennis family was among the earliest families in the region. Pictured from left to right are Elvira Dennis, Amber Dennis Webb, John Dennis, Gar Dennis, Anna Dennis, Vistoria Martin Dennis, and Ockie Dennis. (Courtesy of Jackie Underwood.)

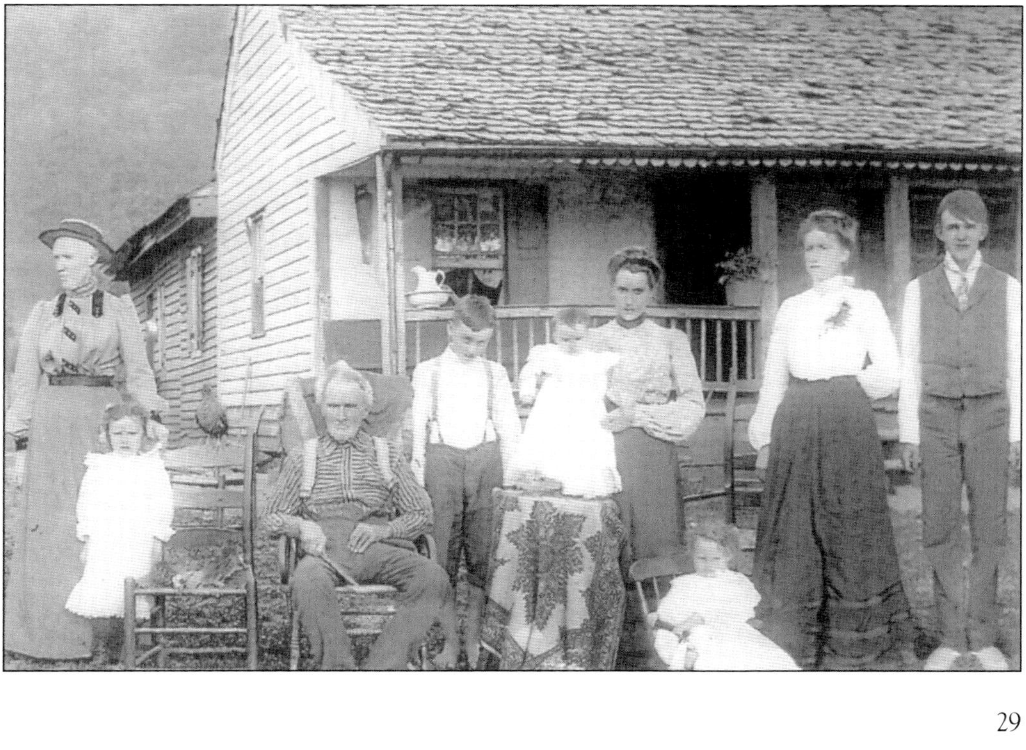

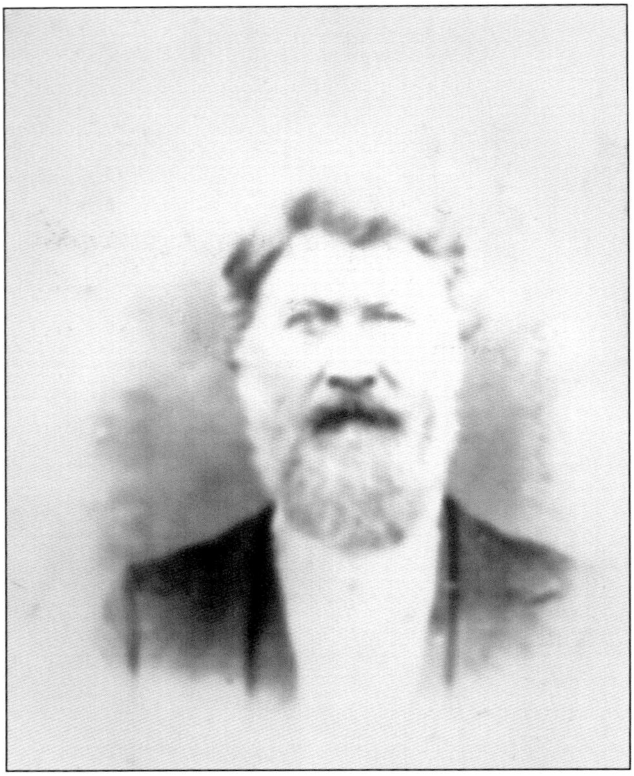

McNulty McMahan was born on June 18, 1826. He was one of the first settlers of eastern Sevier County. McNulty died on October 5, 1921. (Courtesy of Jackie Underwood.)

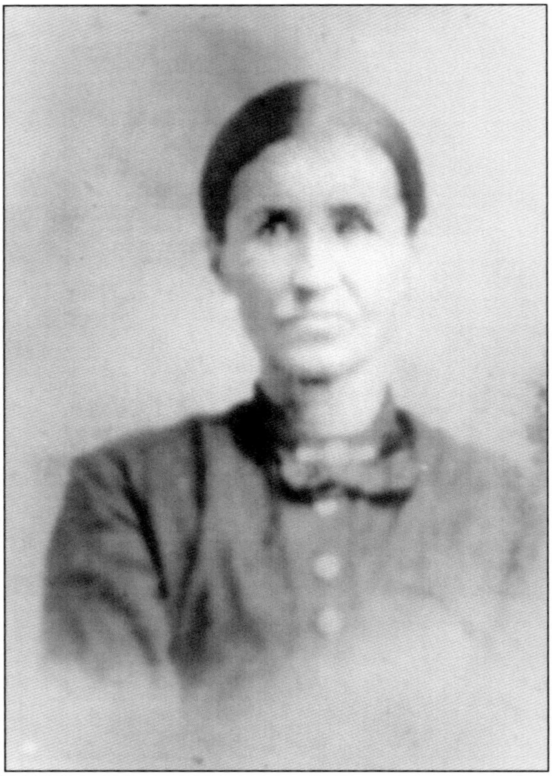

Leah Rhinehart was the wife of McNulty McMahan. She was born January 17, 1834. Leah bore 11 children. She died on February 5, 1918, and is buried next to her husband in Richardson's Cove. (Courtesy of Jackie Underwood.)

Thomas DeArnold McMahan was the most entrepreneurial of the McMahan family. Born in 1849, "TDW," as family and friends knew him, made a considerable income in livestock. He married Melinda Trotter, and the couple had eight children. He died in 1921. (Courtesy of Jackie Underwood.)

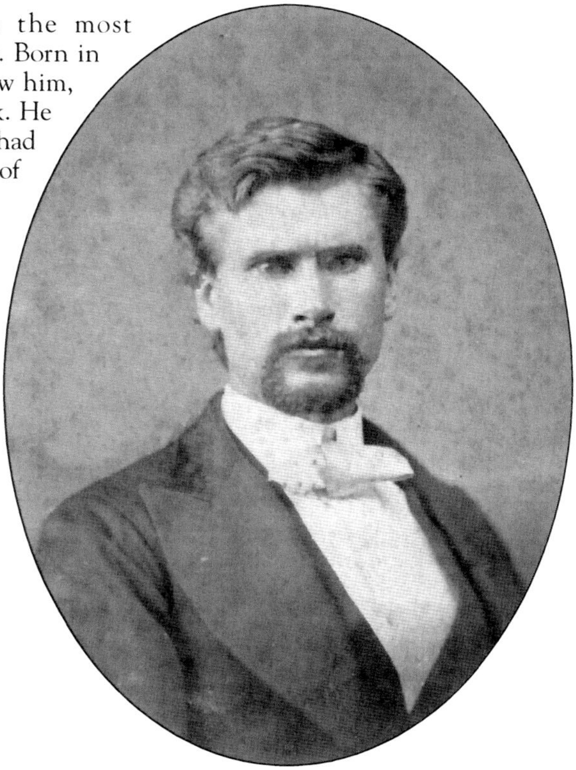

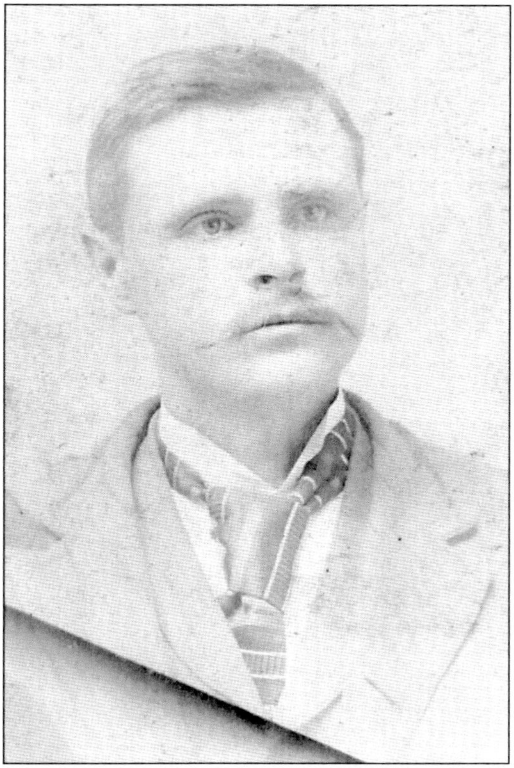

Noah McCarter lived in Richardson's Cove, where he farmed for a living. (Courtesy of Jackie Underwood.)

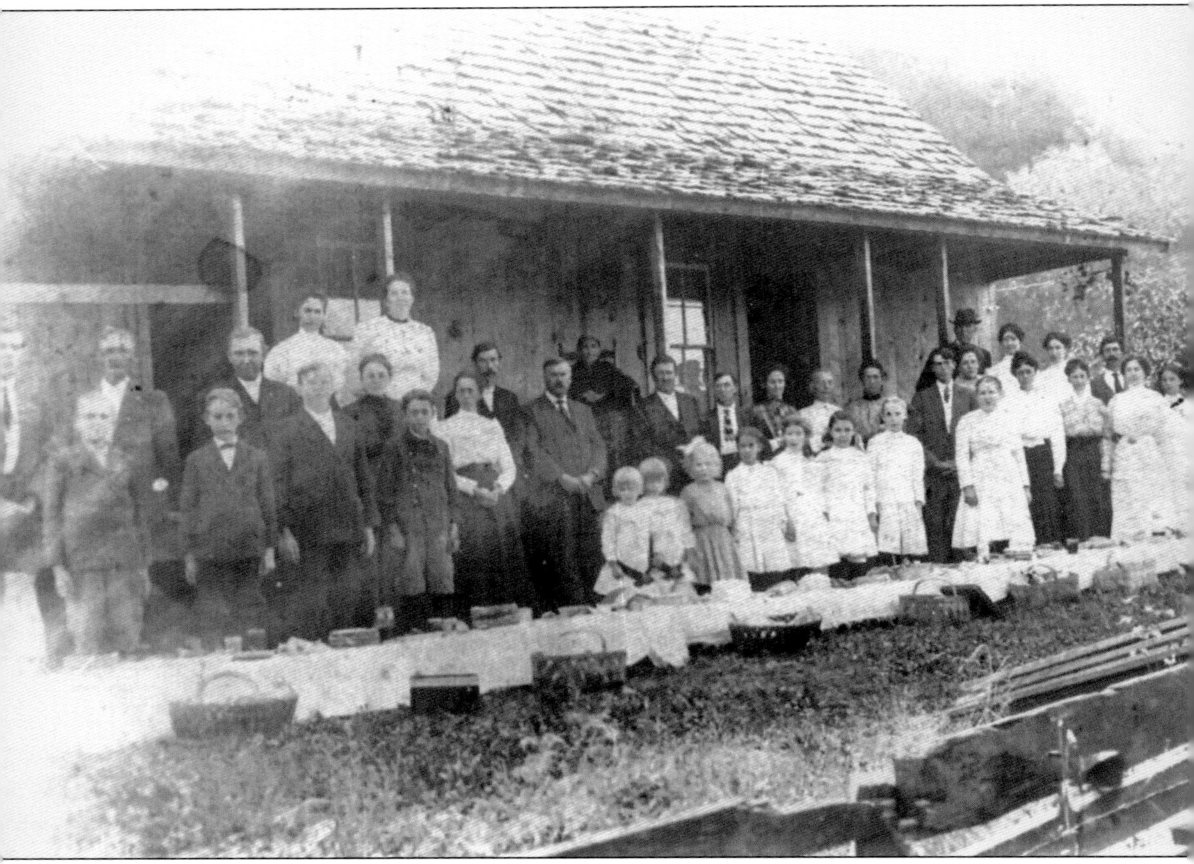

A McMahan family reunion is pictured in the early 1900s. The reunion was held at the McMahan family farm. (Courtesy of Jackie Underwood.)

Six-month-old Jack McMahan, son of Fred and Archie Ray McMahan, sits in his stroller at the home of Roy and Ora McMahan. The McMahan family was among the first to settle in the Richardson's Cove area. The family lived on land granted to them by then governor James K. Polk. (Courtesy of Jackie Underwood.)

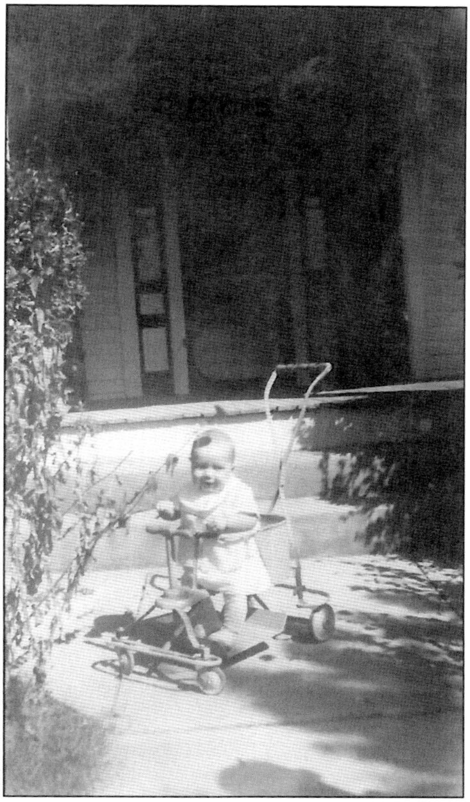

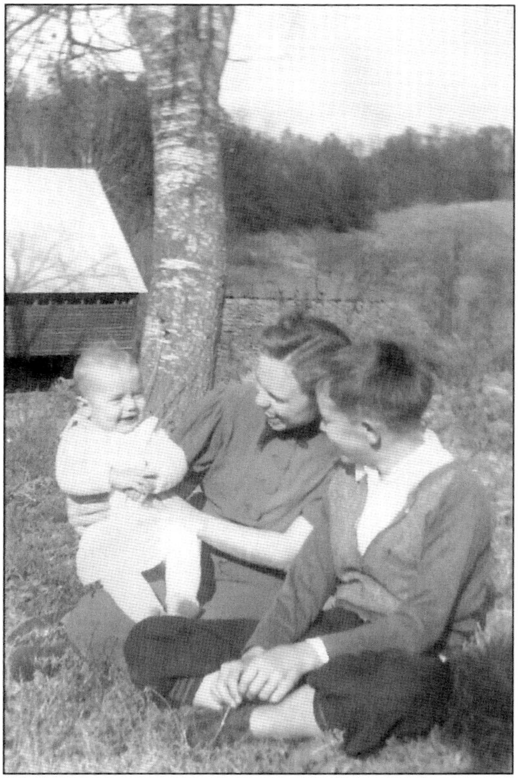

Beulah Dennis McCarter holds her nephew Jack in this photo dated in the 1940s at her sister Archie Ray McMahan's home in Richardson's Cove. (Courtesy Jackie Underwood.)

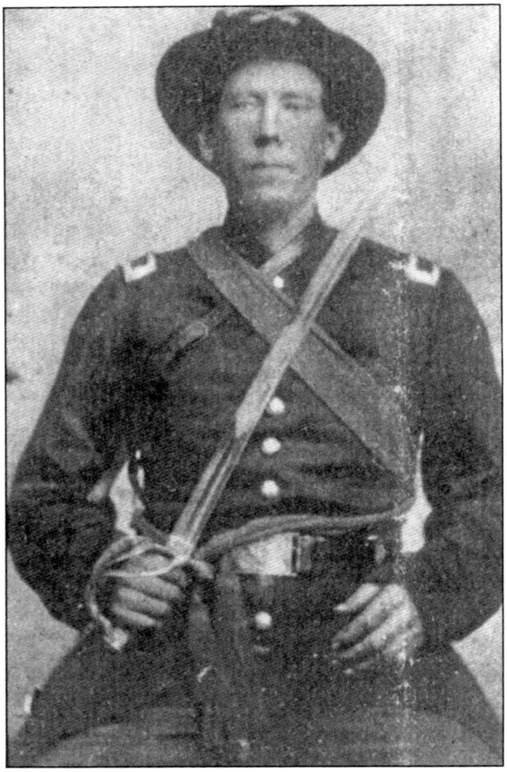

During the Civil War, the county was evenly divided. Many young men preferred to don the Confederate gray, while others, such as Sanders McMahan, chose to side with the North. (Courtesy of Carroll McMahan.)

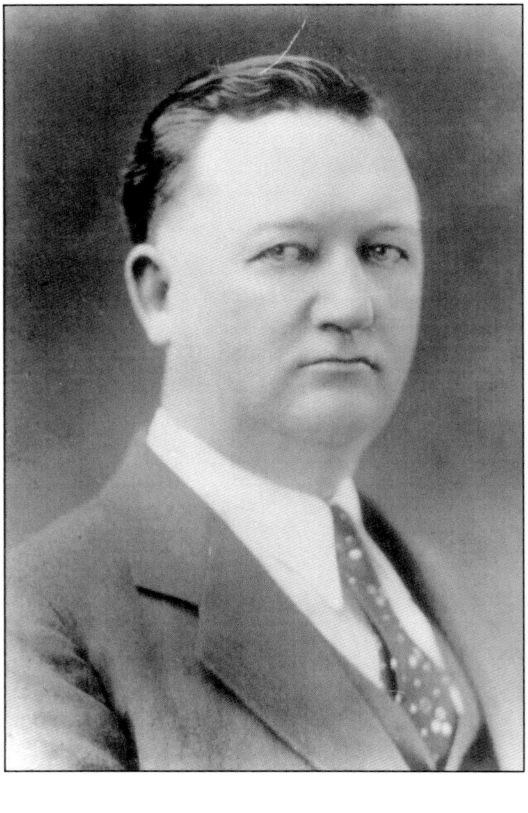

Rev. John Wesley May was pastor of the Pittman Methodist Circuit. He arrived in eastern Sevier County in 1919. Many ministers traveled by mule from church to church to preach. For this reason, many churches held services just once a month. (Courtesy of Glen Cardwell.)

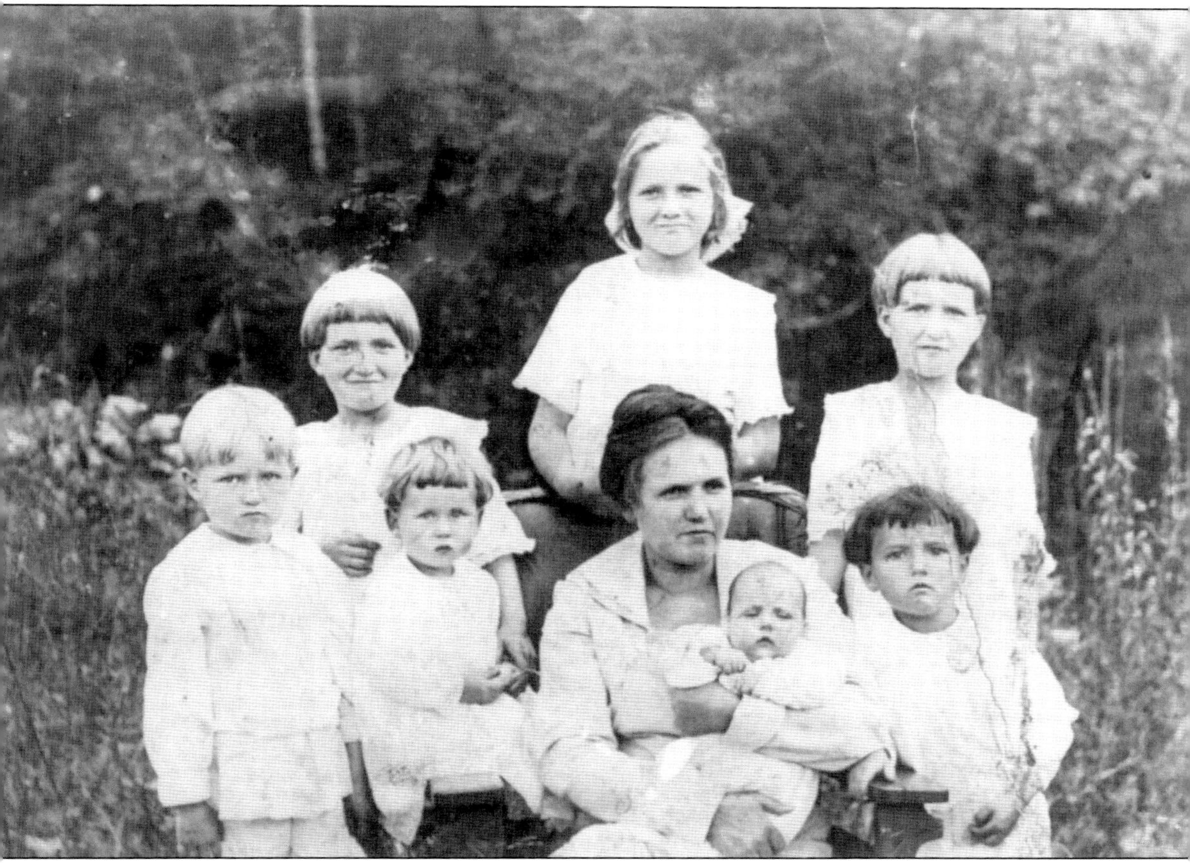

The May family is pictured in the early 1920s at its home in Pittman Center. This photograph includes, from left to right, (first row) John Wesley May Jr., William Eugene, Ninna Jane (holding Martha Cornelia), and James; (second row) Evelyn Pauline, Virginia, and Carolyn. (Courtesy of Glen Cardwell.)

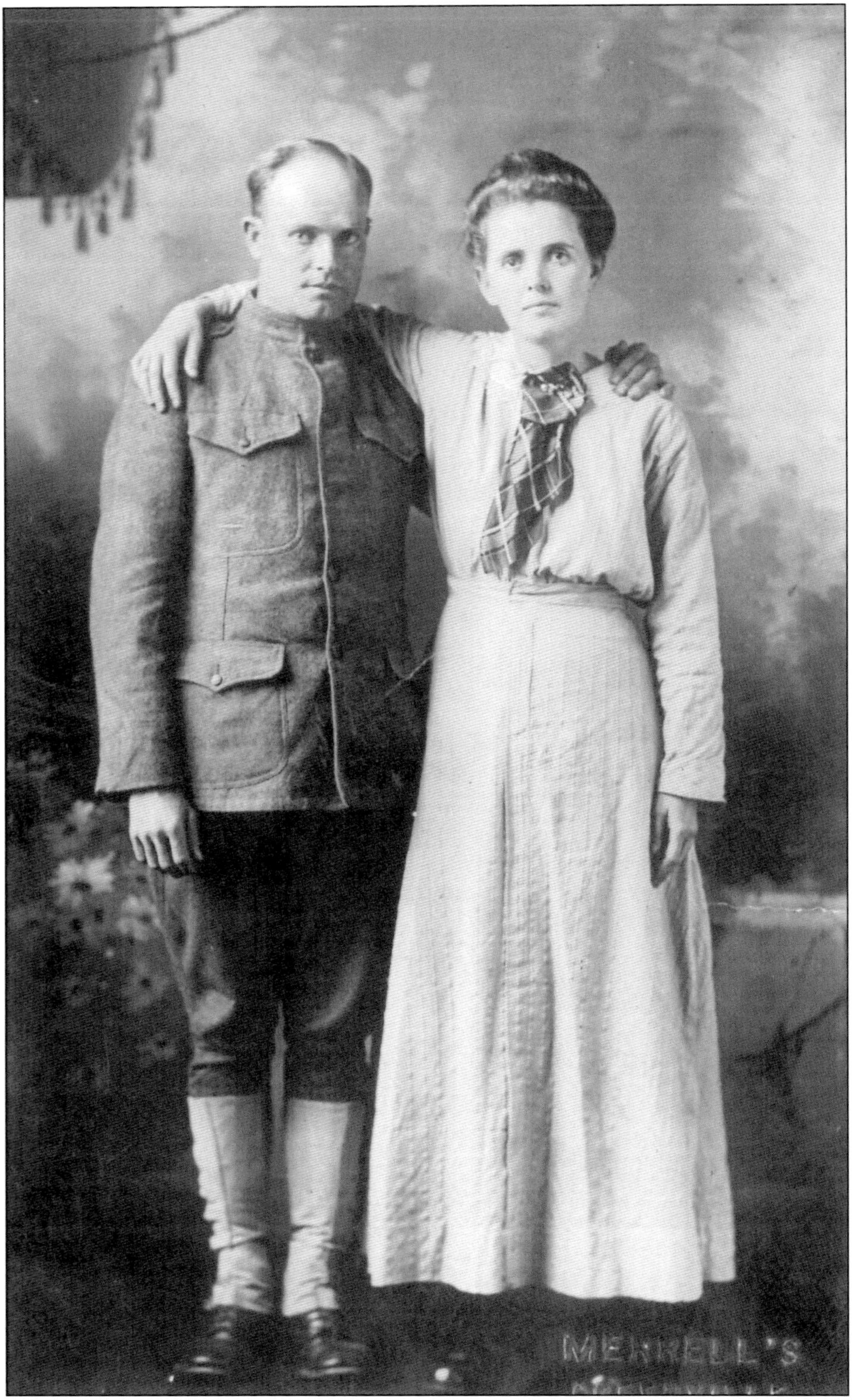

Jim and Winnie Reagan are seen here around 1918. Jim was a veteran of World War I. His son Neil served in World War II. (Courtesy of Carolyn Large Whaley.)

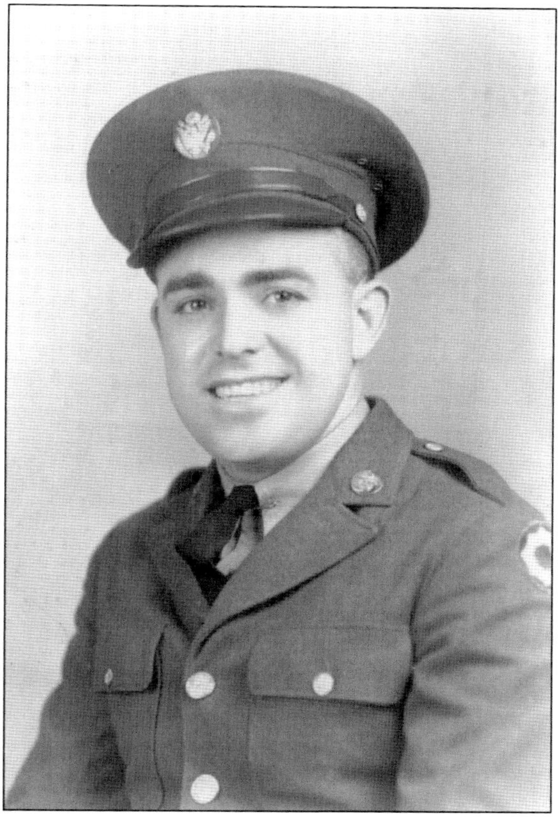

Neil Reagan was the son of Jim and Winnie. Like his father, he served in the military in time of war. Tragically, Neil was not as fortunate as his father. In 1944, he was killed in France during World War II. Below, Lawrence Ramsey (left) and Paul Grooms are pictured at Kooser Camp in 1937. (Both, courtesy of Carolyn Large Whaley.)

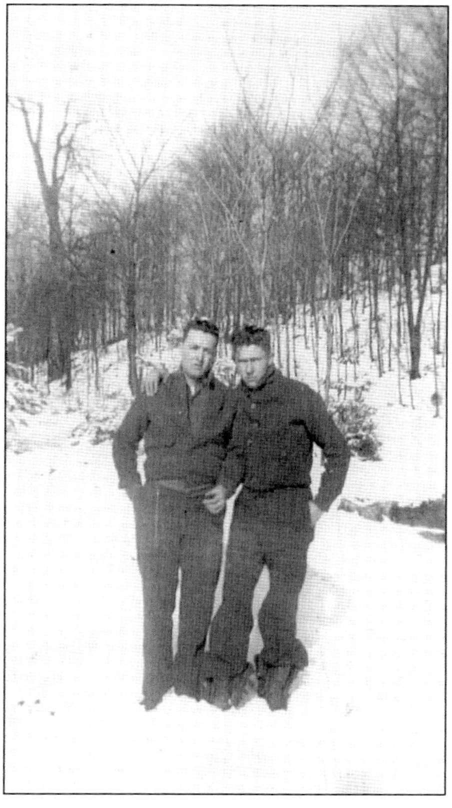

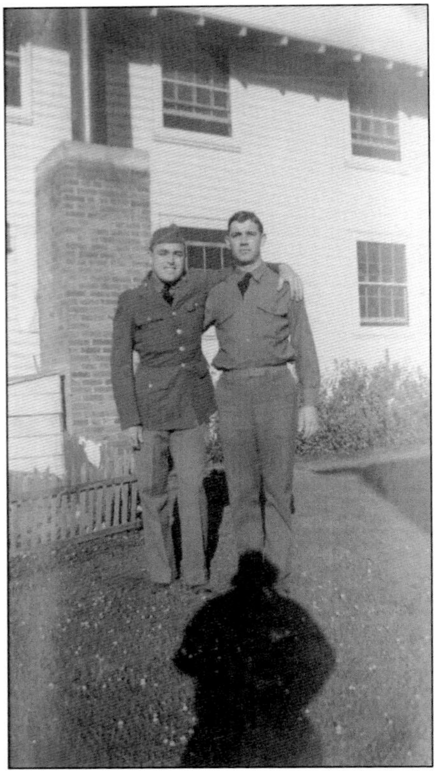

Neil Reagan (left) is pictured with an unidentified friend at boot camp. (Courtesy of Carolyn Large Whaley.)

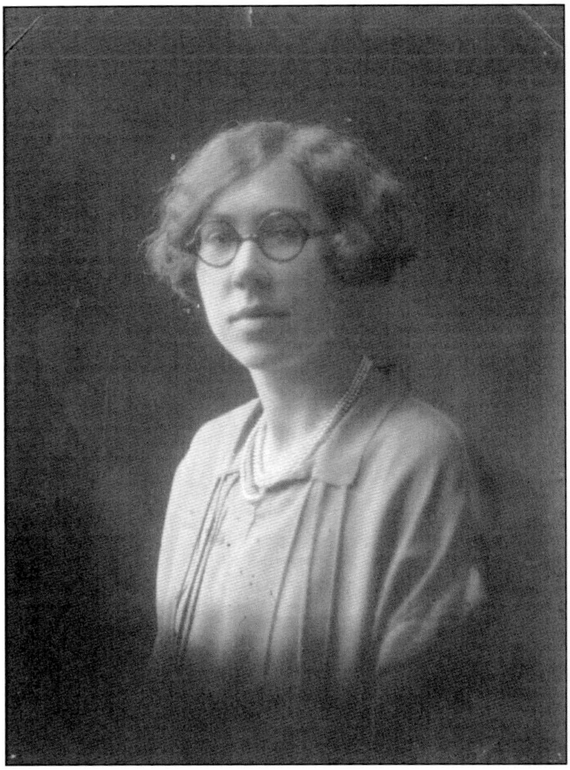

Originally from New York, Anne Handlon came to eastern Sevier County to teach school at Webb's Creek School shortly after the Pittman Center community was created. (Courtesy of Glen Cardwell.)

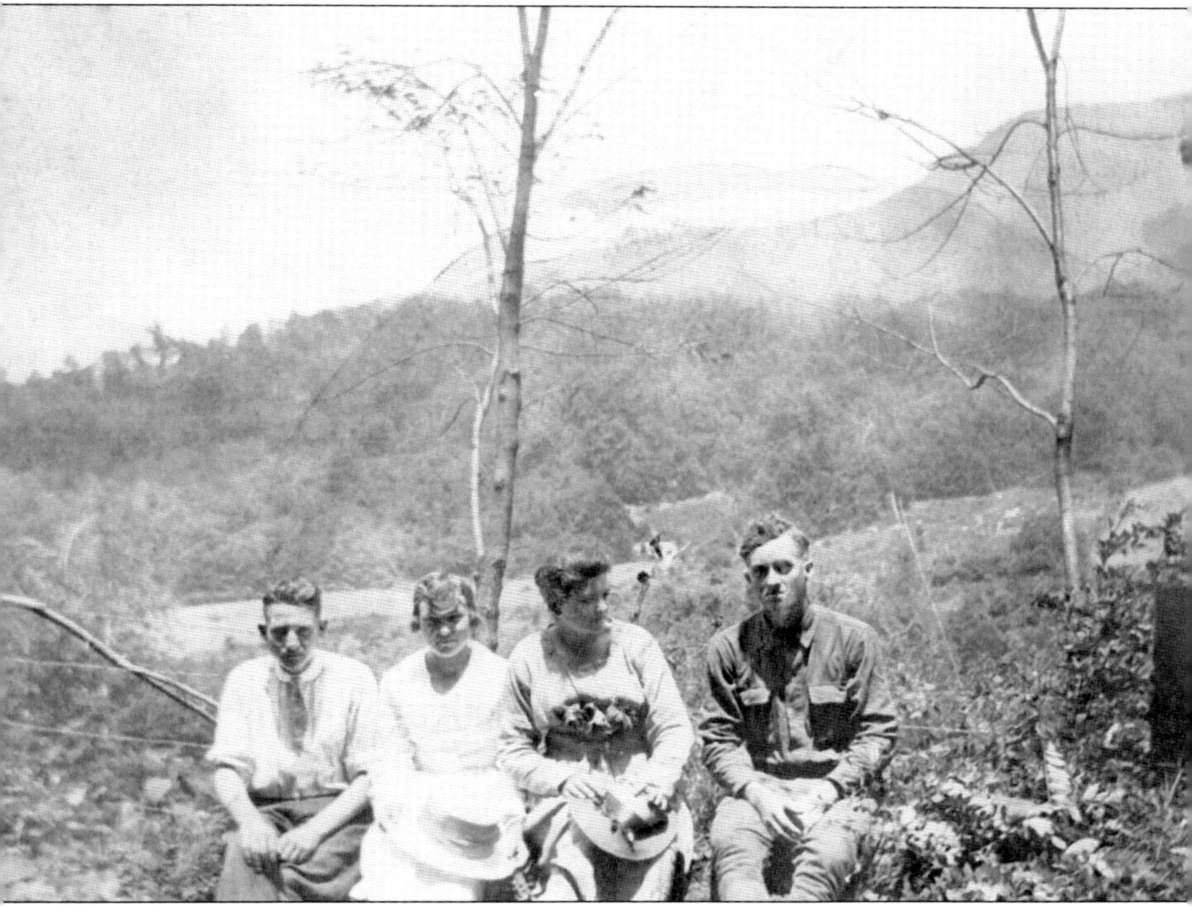

Jimmy Raefield (left) is pictured with three unidentified friends on August 18, 1919, shortly after construction of Pittman Community Center began. (Courtesy of Glen Cardwell.)

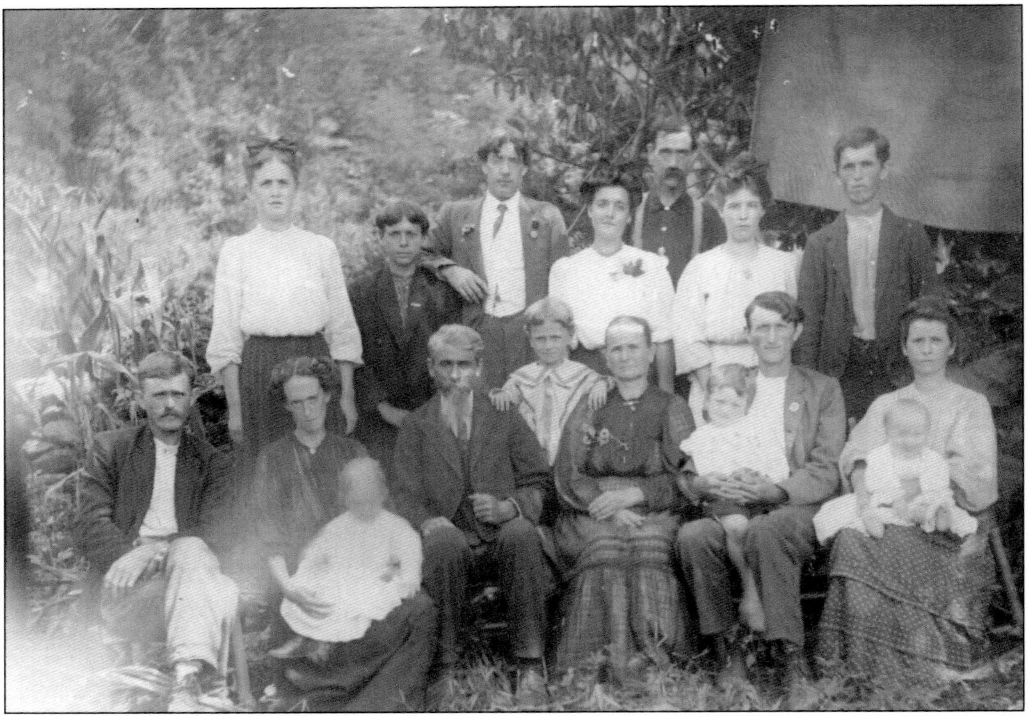

James "Uncle Bud" McCarter and Josephine Shults McCarter are surrounded by their family. From left to right are (first row) Preston; Flora, who is holding Roy; James; Carl; Josephine; George; and Polly Roberts, who is holding Fred and Vernie; (second row) Winnie McCarter; Horace; Claude and Emily McCarter Ramsey; an unidentified man in suspenders; Laura; and Steve McCarter. (Courtesy of Carolyn Large Whaley.)

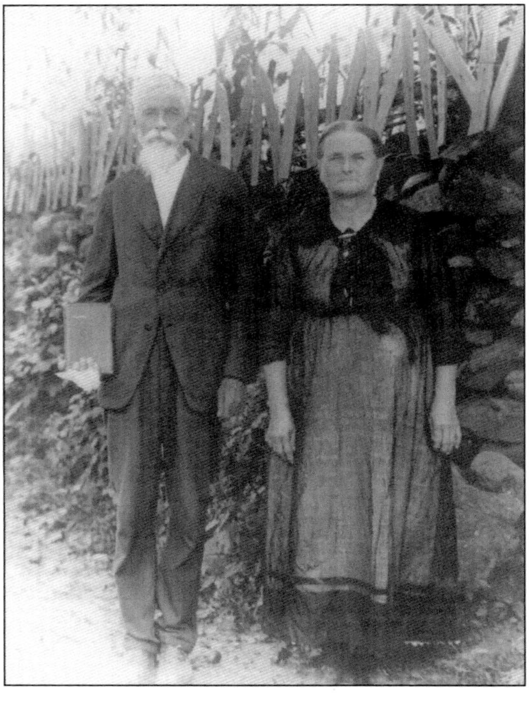

James and Josephine McCarter are pictured in the early 1930s. Like most of the residents of Webb's Creek, the McCarters had little and survived on the meager crops they produced. The creation of the Pittman Community Center was intended to bring prosperity to the tiny East Tennessee area. Only 10 years after the establishment of the school, the nation was plunged into the Great Depression. For many in the area, the Depression went unnoticed, as they were accustomed to living in poverty. (Courtesy of Carolyn Large Whaley.)

Ance and Vira Ramsey operated a small farm in the area. The couple is pictured in the 1930s. (Courtesy of Carolyn Large Whaley.)

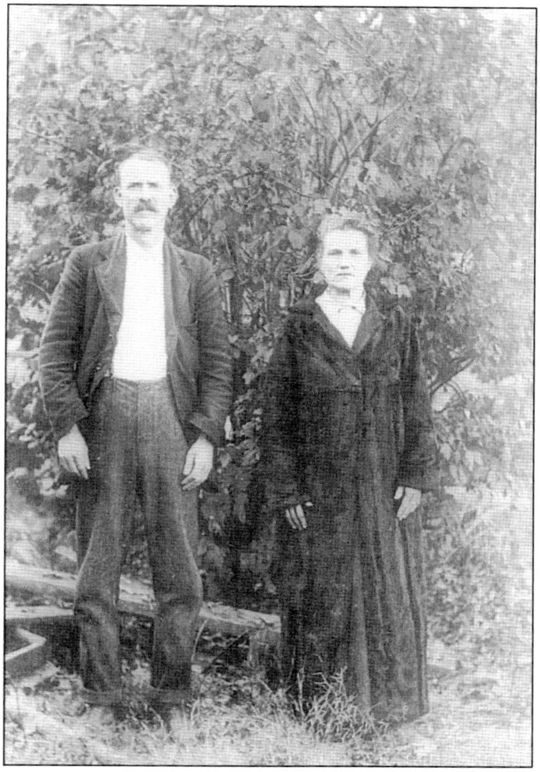

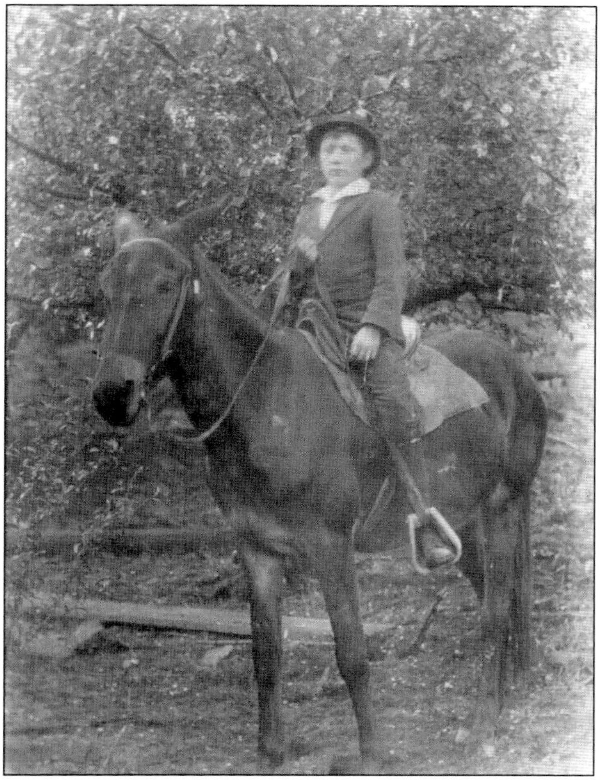

Perry Ramsey was the son of Ance and Vira Ramsey. The family farmed in Pittman Center, where they grew tobacco and corn. (Courtesy of Carolyn Large Whaley.)

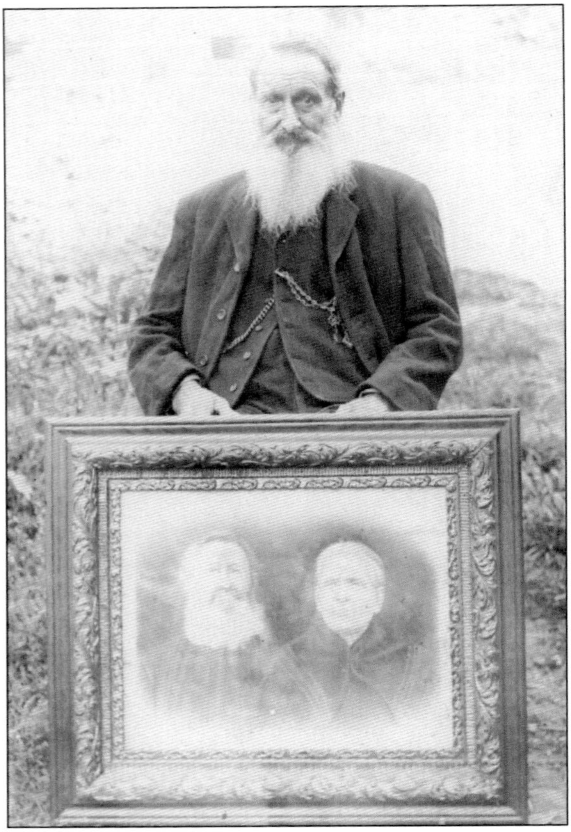

Preston Shultz displays a portrait of himself and his wife, Martha, in 1910. Preston died in 1919. (Courtesy of Glen Cardwell.)

Tyson and Ellen Shultz McCarter are shown around 1900. They were born in 1878 and 1880, respectively. (Courtesy of Carolyn Large Whaley.)

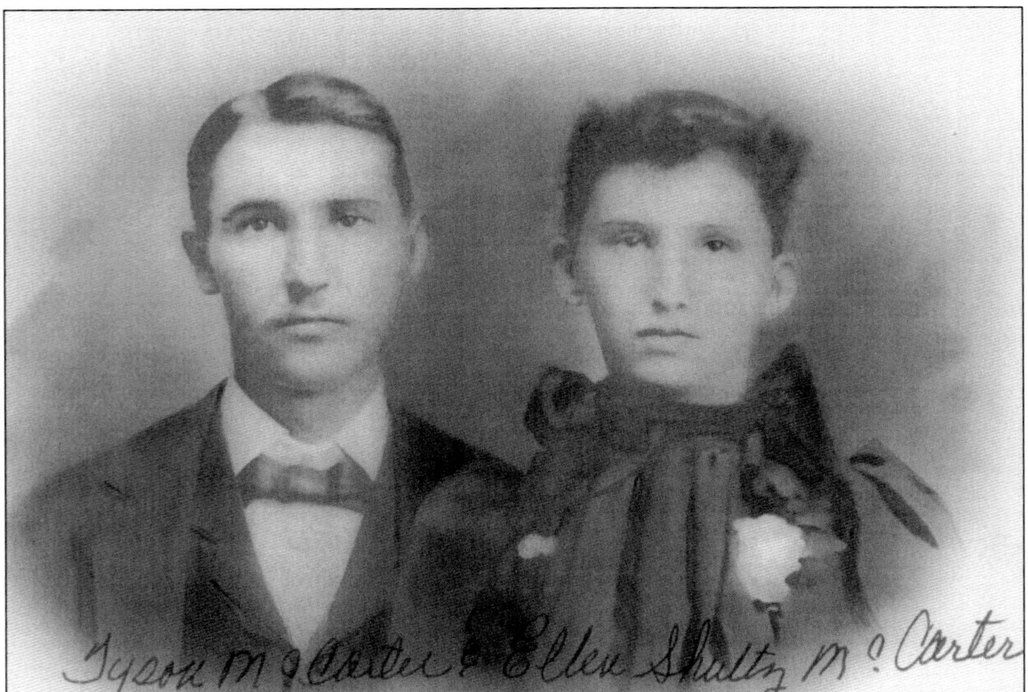

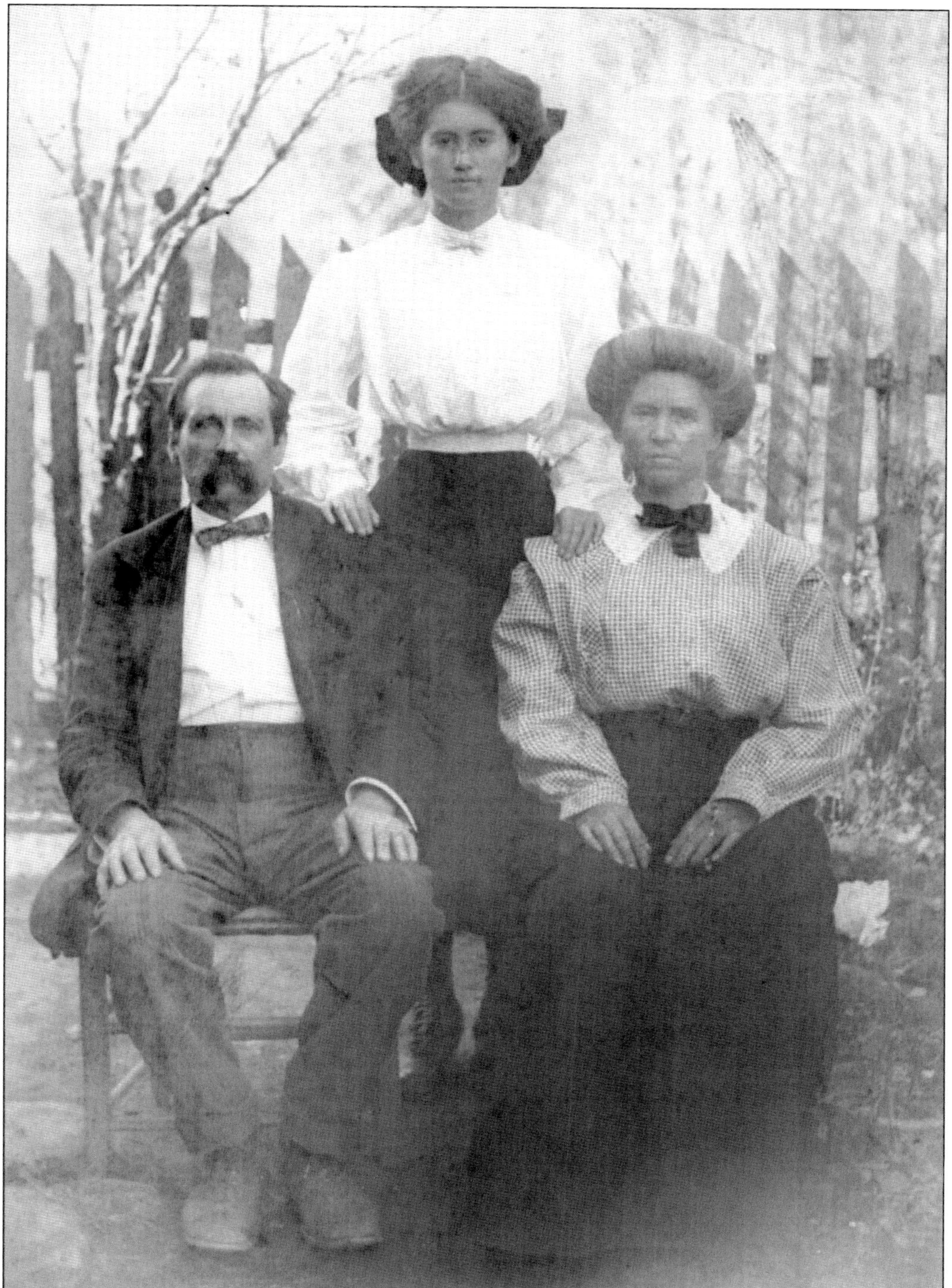

Phil Shultz and his daughter Hettie and his wife, Arbezina, are depicted in 1890. The Shultz family was among the first to settle in the area of the Pittman Community Center. (Courtesy of Carolyn Large Whaley.)

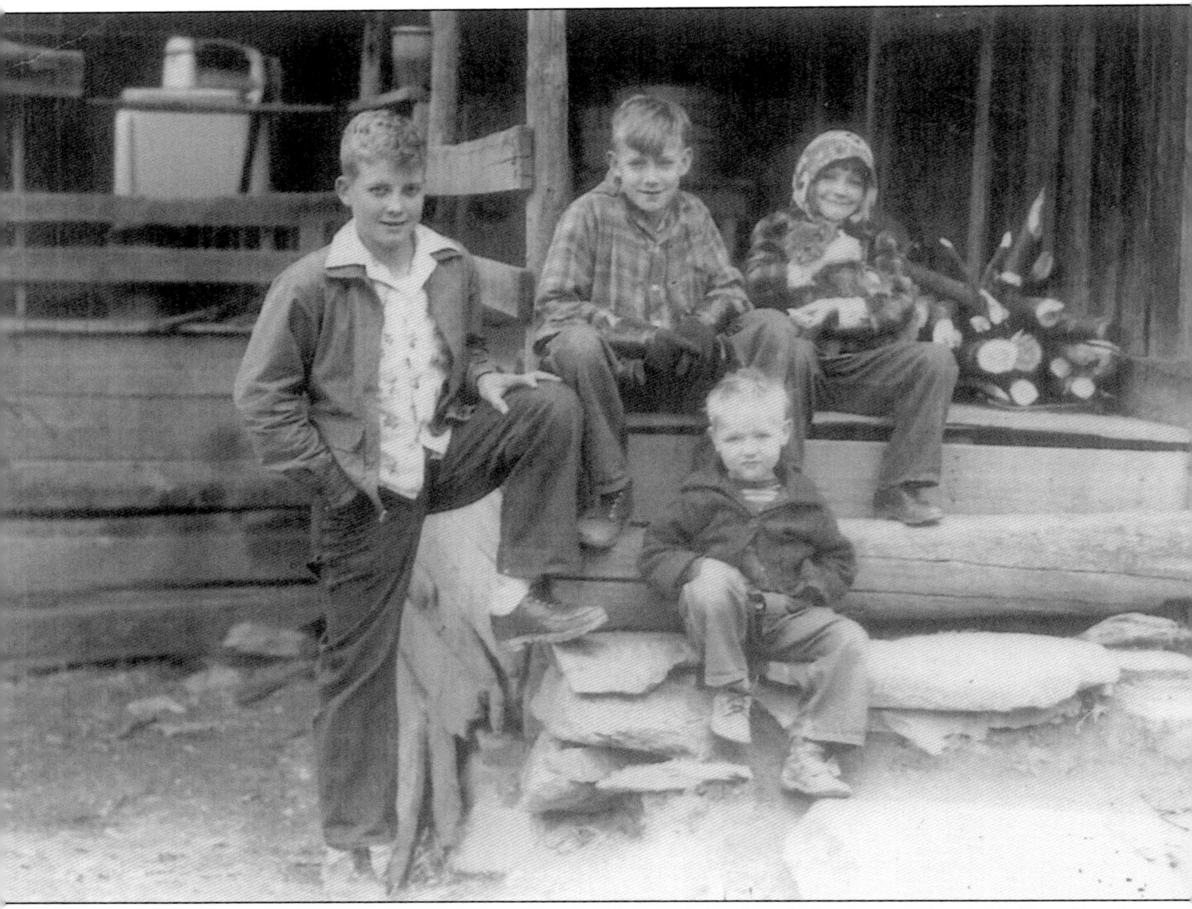

Ethel and Virgil Whaley's kids are pictured in front of the family home on King's Hollow Road. They are, from left to right, Wendell, 13; Lowell, 10; Linda, 7; and Jerry, 4. (Courtesy of Carolyn Large Whaley.)

John Myers is pictured during the Great Depression. Most of the inhabitants in the area of Pittman Community Center had little, and most were used to living frugally. Many never noticed the Great Depression, as they were accustomed to difficult times. (Courtesy of Carolyn Large Whaley.)

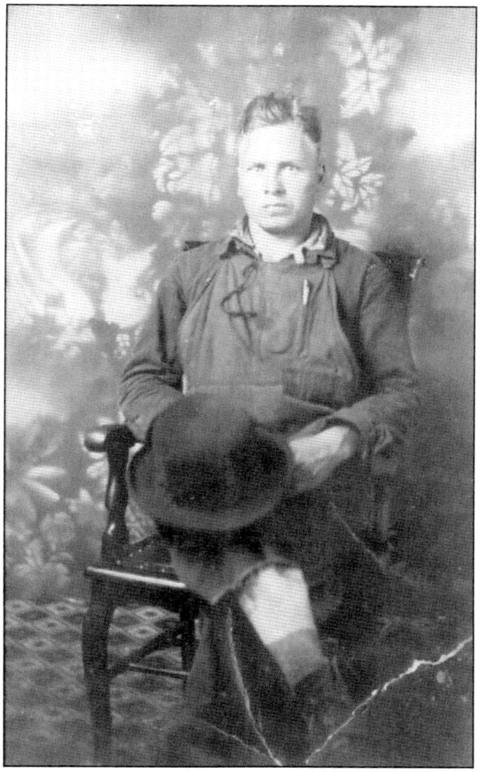

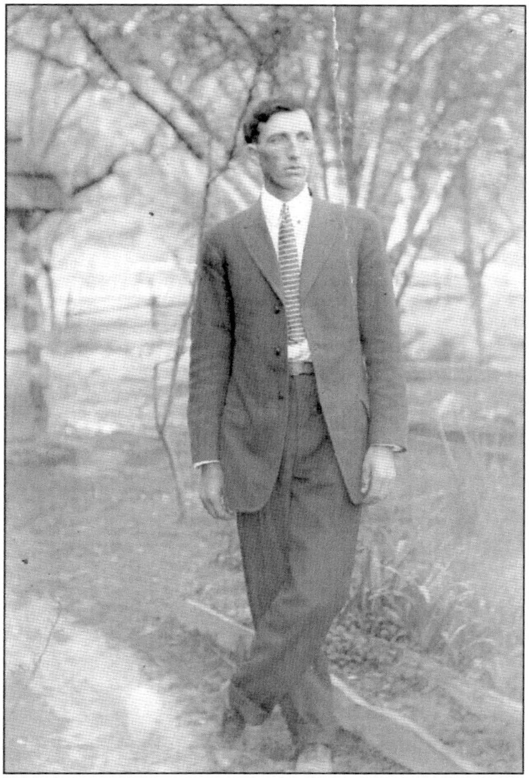

Arthur Baxter is pictured in Jones Cove in the 1930s. The Baxter family owned a grocery store. Many area farmers supplied the store with produce, eggs, and other farm-made products. (Courtesy of Jackie Underwood.)

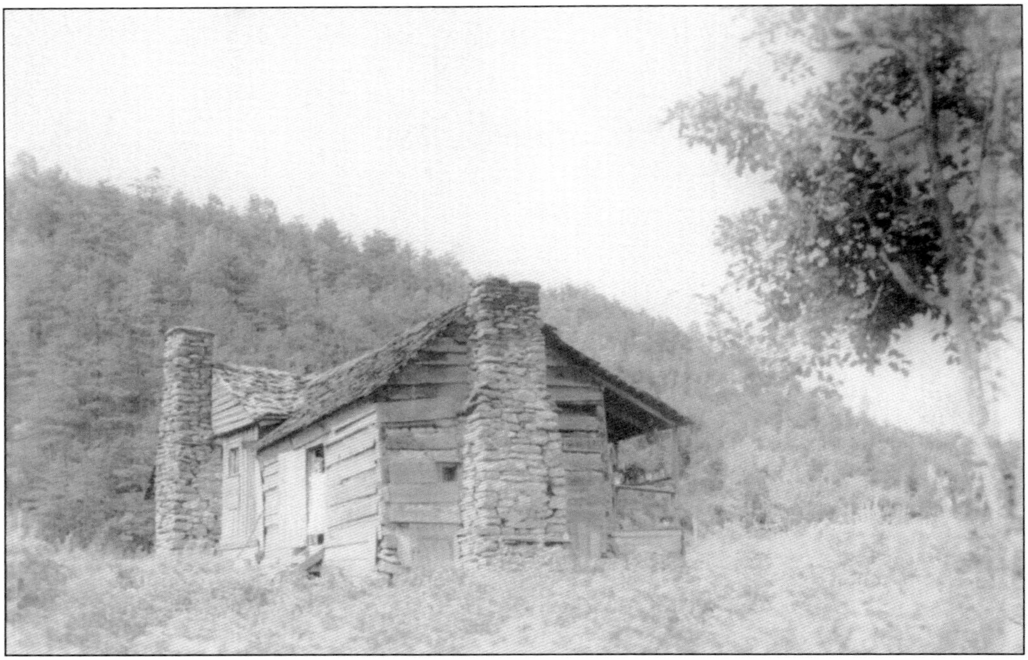

This cabin is representative of the poverty that was common among the mountain people when the Methodist Episcopal Church decided to build the Pittman Community Center school, which is the present-day town of Pittman Center. Most of these old cabins had no running water or electricity. (Courtesy of Carolyn Large Whaley.)

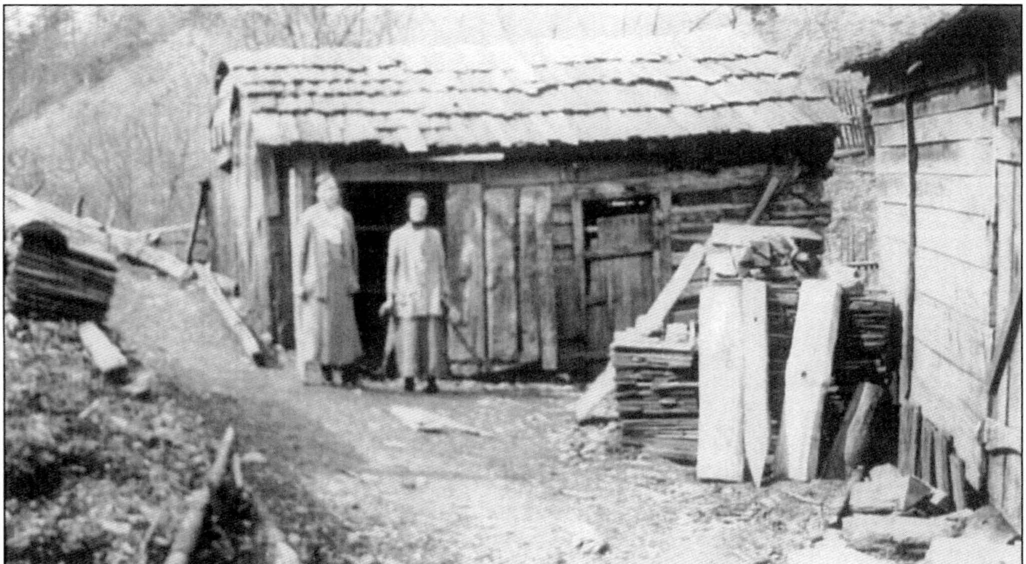

This 1920s photograph depicts a mountain family's storage building where tools were kept. The structure was referred to as a crib. During these early days, the homes had no running water, no electricity, and no indoor plumbing. (Courtesy of Glen Cardwell.)

Two

Work and Leisure

Until the 1930s, there were few options for entertainment in eastern Sevier County. There were no theaters or other venues for diversions. Up until the late 1930s, there was no electricity or running water in area homes, so there were no televisions, phonographs, or radios. The local high school's athletic program consisted of one sport—basketball, which provided area locals an option for entertainment.

Life in eastern Sevier County meant long hours working on the farm, which left little time for recreation and leisure. Swimming in area swimming holes offered a respite from the sometimes sweltering summer heat. Another method for beating the heat was caving. Guided by the faint light of a lantern or a torch, locals would explore area caves. These caves have average year-round temperatures of 58–60 degrees, which provided summertime relief.

Fishing and hunting provided not only a form of recreation but also a food source. Music was a popular form of recreation. Many in the area became self-taught banjo players, guitarists, violinists or fiddlers, and singers. They were inspired by the music of their ancestors, the Irish, Germans, and Scots who settled the area. Singing was taught in local schools, where pupils learned traditional songs as well as gospel tunes. Storytelling was another popular form of entertainment at family gatherings and church socials.

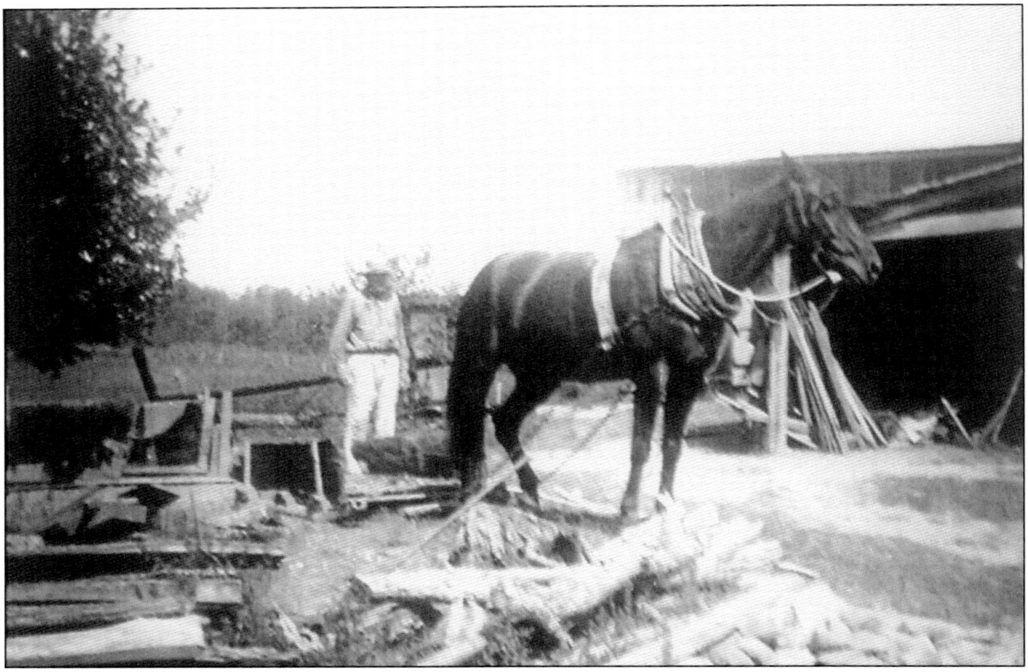

Like most of the people of eastern Sevier County, John Dennis worked as a farmer in Richardson's Cove. Here, he is pictured with his workhorse Mac, whom he used to till the soil. (Courtesy of Jackie Underwood.)

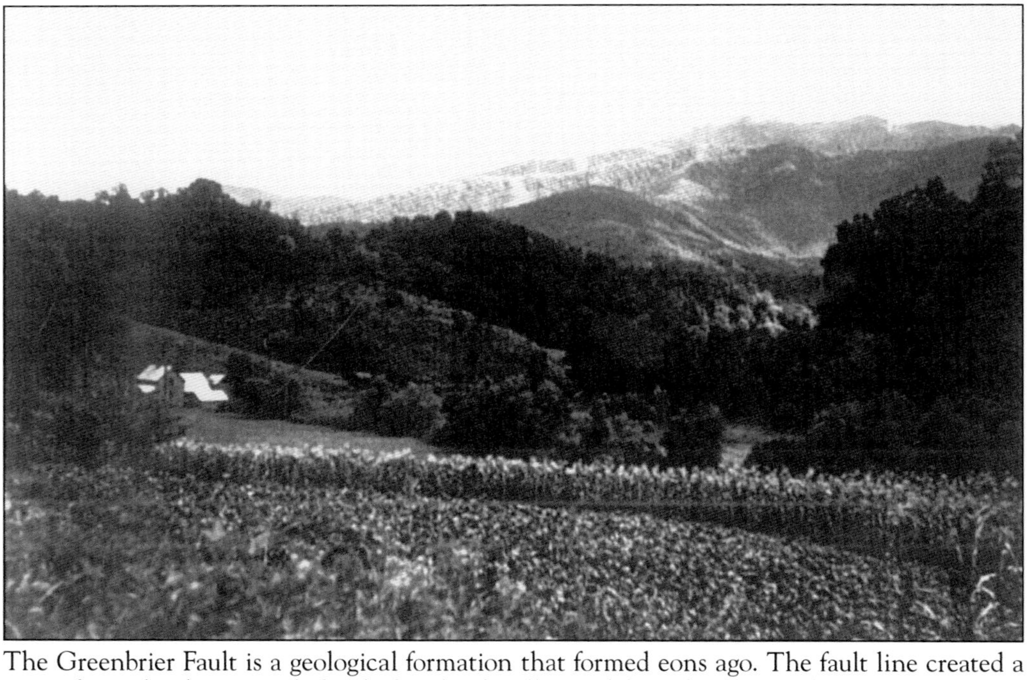

The Greenbrier Fault is a geological formation that formed eons ago. The fault line created a magnificent landscape with fertile farmland well suited for cultivation. This photograph was taken in 1930 by Albert "Dutch" Roth. (Courtesy of Glen Cardwell.)

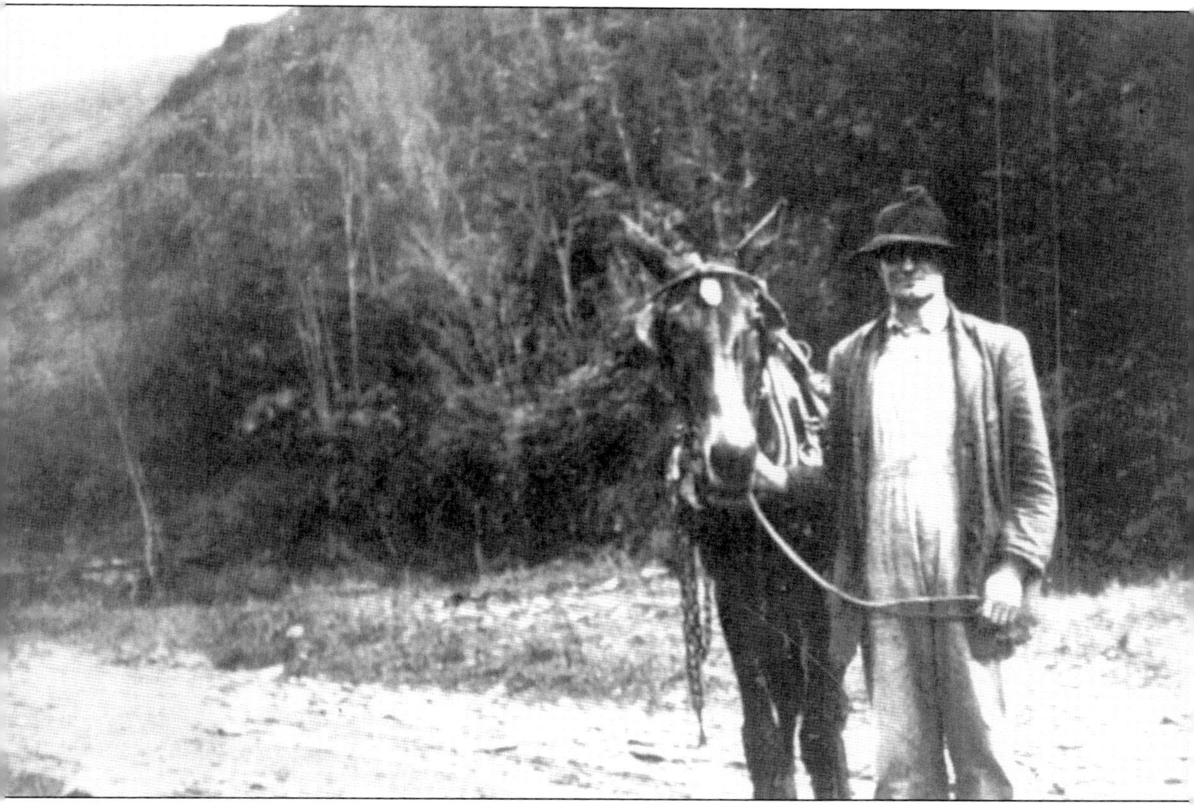

John Dennis poses with his workhorse at the family farm near Pearl Valley. In the pre-mechanized days, farming was extremely tedious, with farmers working long hours and harvesting smaller crop yields. (Courtesy of Jackie Underwood.)

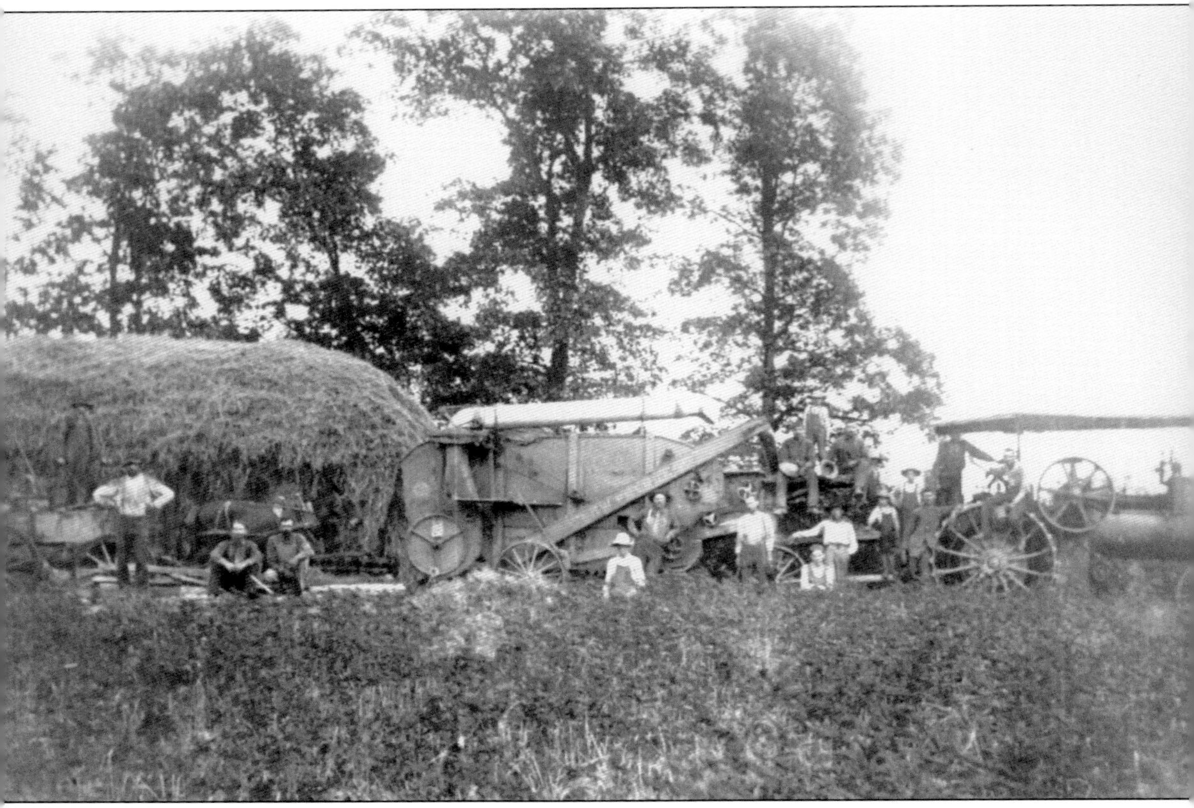

A steam-powered thrasher is used on the McMahan farm. Prior to the mass production of gas-powered combustible engines, steam was the primary means of locomotion for many farming machines. (Courtesy of Jackie Underwood.)

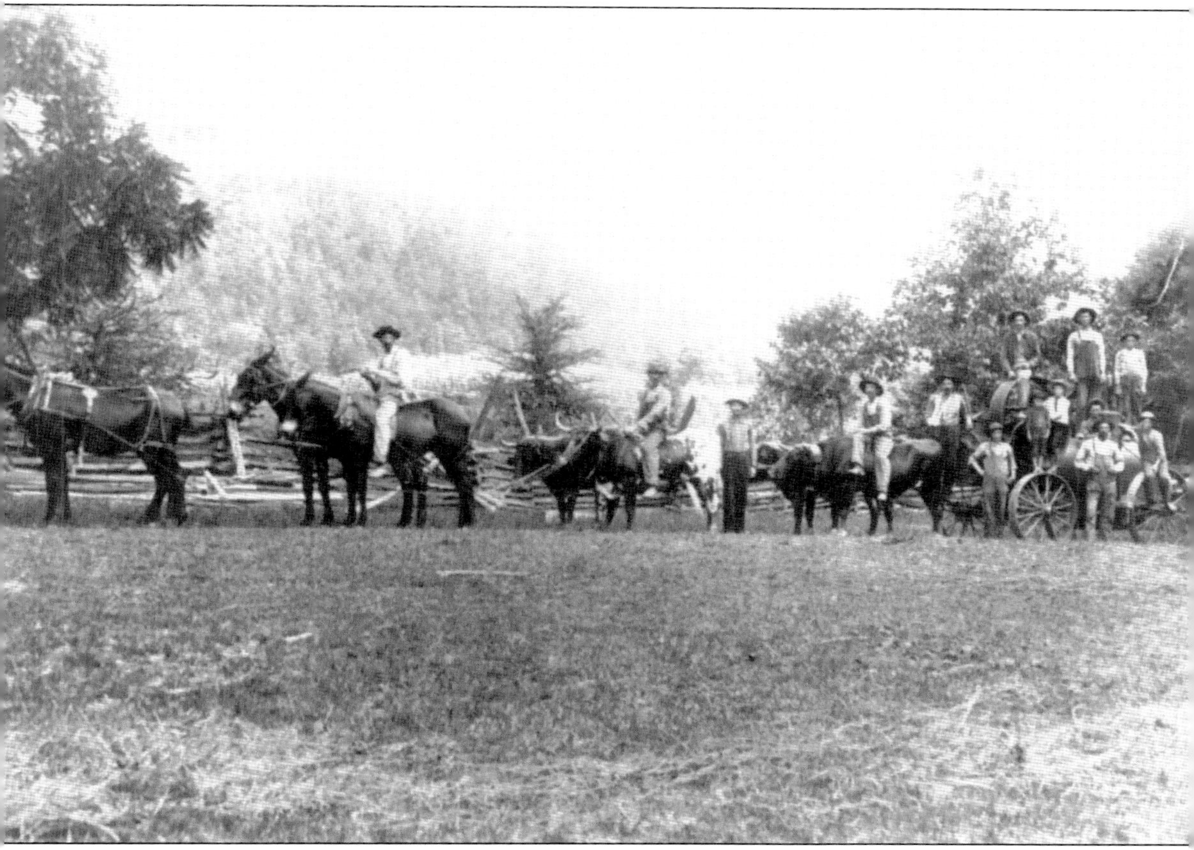

The thrasher is moved by mules and oxen. Many farmers had no tractors to move such heavy machinery. (Courtesy of Jackie Underwood.)

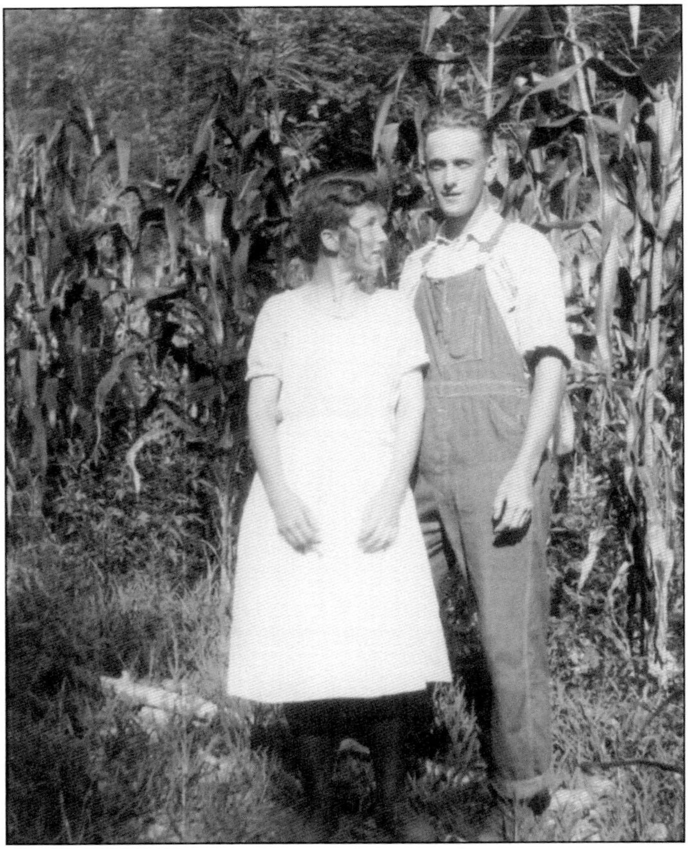

Carl McCarter poses with an unidentified young woman near a cornfield. Corn was a major staple in the diet of the people of the region and a major cash crop for those who took their crops to market in neighboring Sevierville. (Courtesy of Carolyn Large Whaley.)

Carl McCarter and Bryson Branan (third and fourth from left) are pictured with two unidentified people in the 1920s. (Courtesy of Carolyn Large Whaley.)

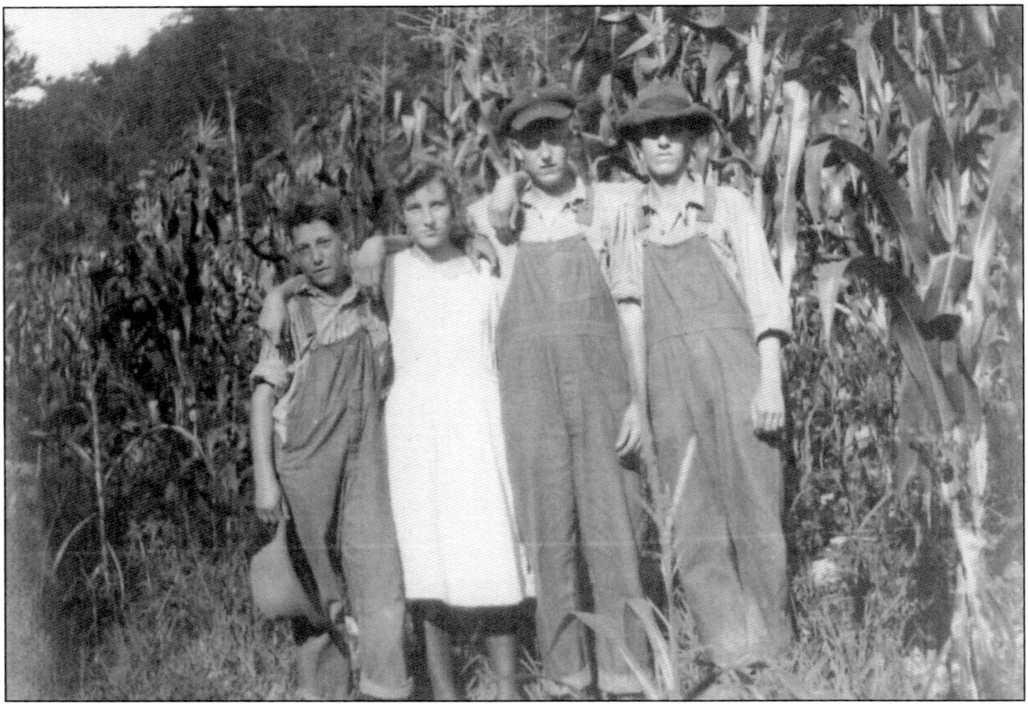

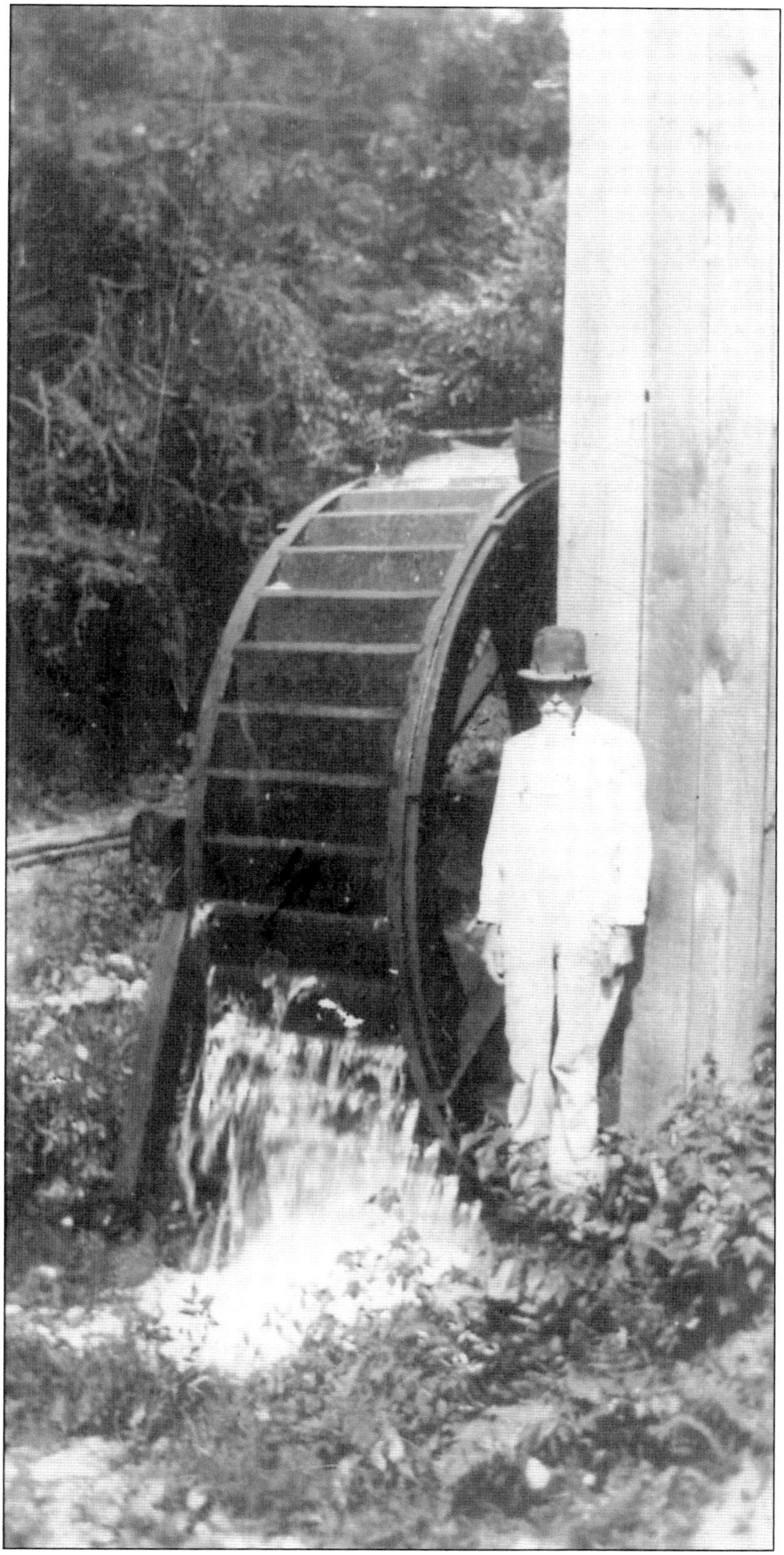

James McCarter stands next to a waterwheel at a gristmill in the 1940s. Before World War II, numerous gristmills served the community. Local farmers would bring corn to the mill to have it ground into cornmeal with a large grinding stone that was powered by the waterwheel. (Courtesy of Glen Cardwell.)

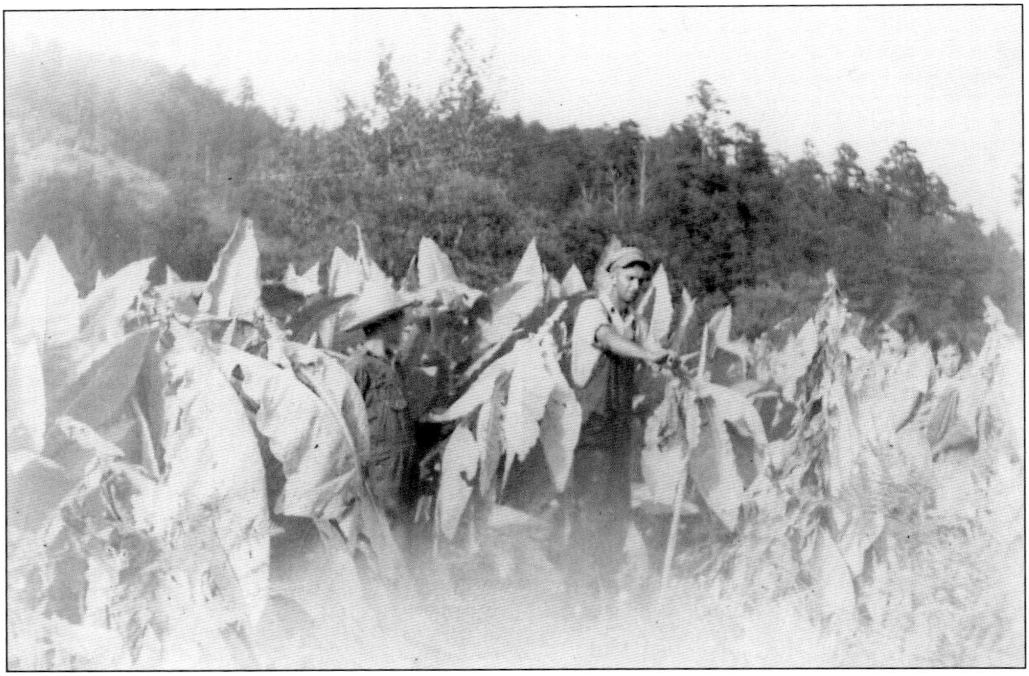

Carl McCarter and his son Lester harvest tobacco on their family farm. During the 1930s, when this photograph was taken, tobacco was a major cash crop in eastern Sevier County. Most farmers had to wait until after they sold the harvest to buy shoes for their children. (Courtesy of Glen Cardwell.)

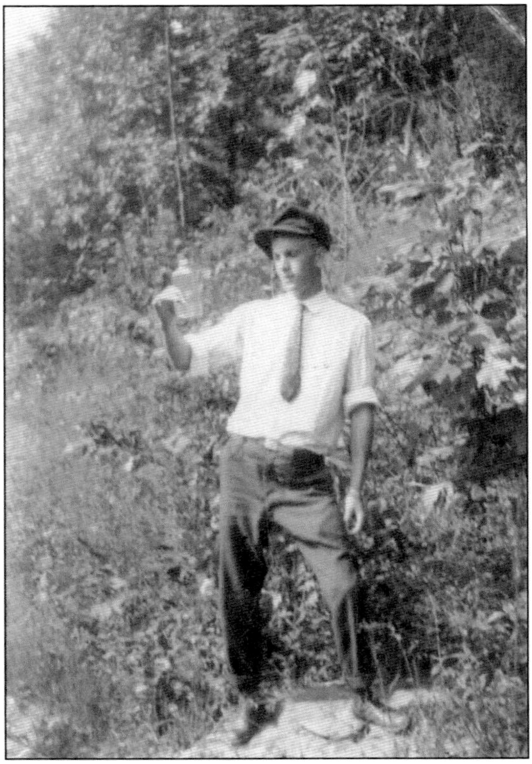

Carl McCarter inspects a mason jar filled with moonshine. Numerous local farmers made the elixir, and many of them used the drink for medicinal purposes. McCarter was said to have never drunk moonshine. (Courtesy of Carolyn Large Whaley.)

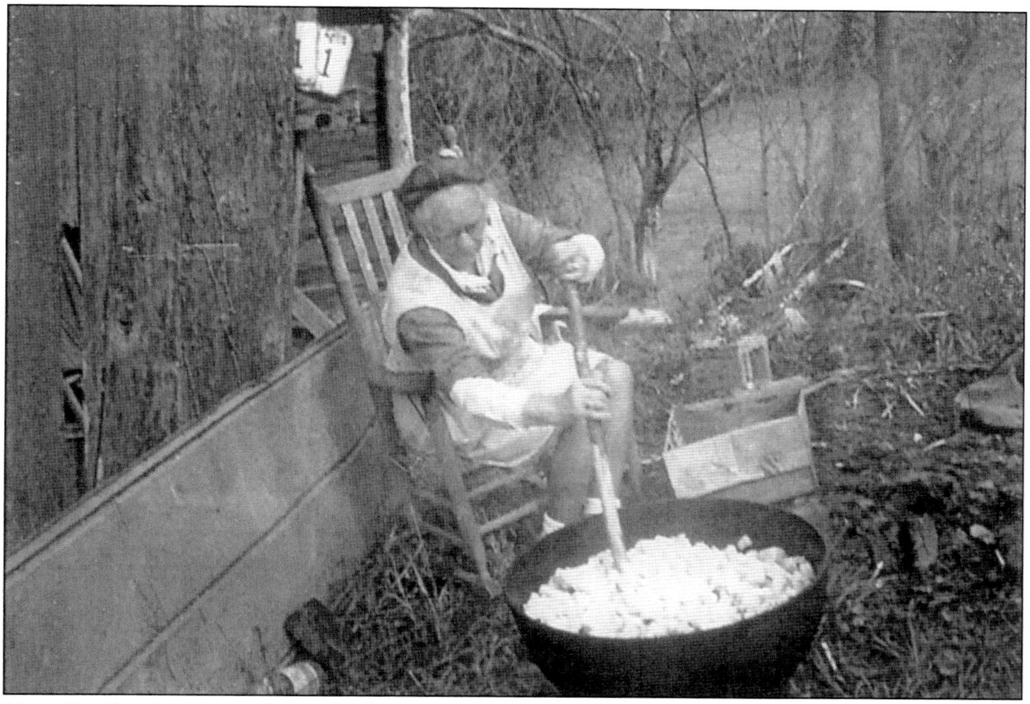

Dora Proffitt is seen rendering lard. Rendering lard was the method used to make lard from animal fat. The lard was used in cooking. Prior to the advent of the car and the construction of paved roads, the people of Richardson's Cove were somewhat isolated from the more urban Sevierville and had to be self-reliant in making lard, soap, clothes, and other necessities. (Courtesy of Jackie Underwood.)

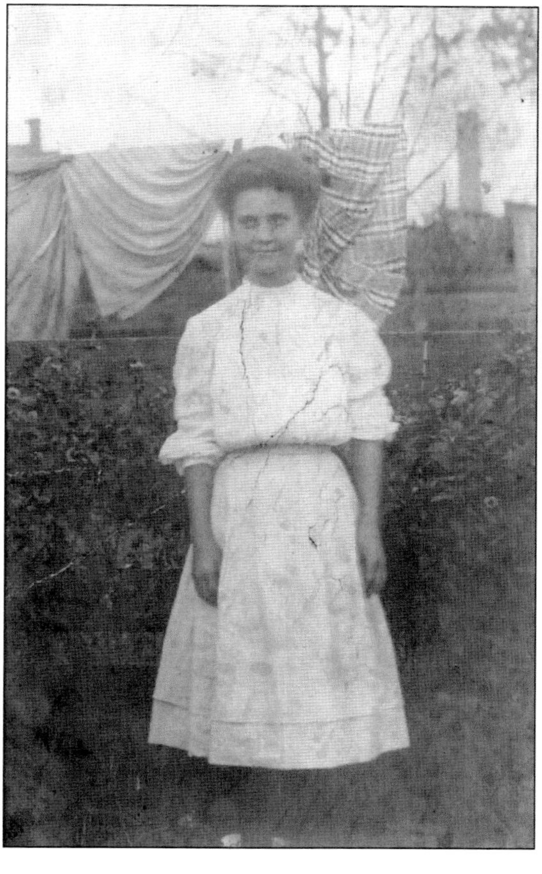

Luella Wright hangs clothes on her clothesline in the 1920s. The Tennessee Valley Authority introduced electric power to the region in the 1930s. Before electricity was made available, women went to nearby creeks to wash their clothes by hand before hanging them on a line. (Courtesy of Carolyn Large Whaley.)

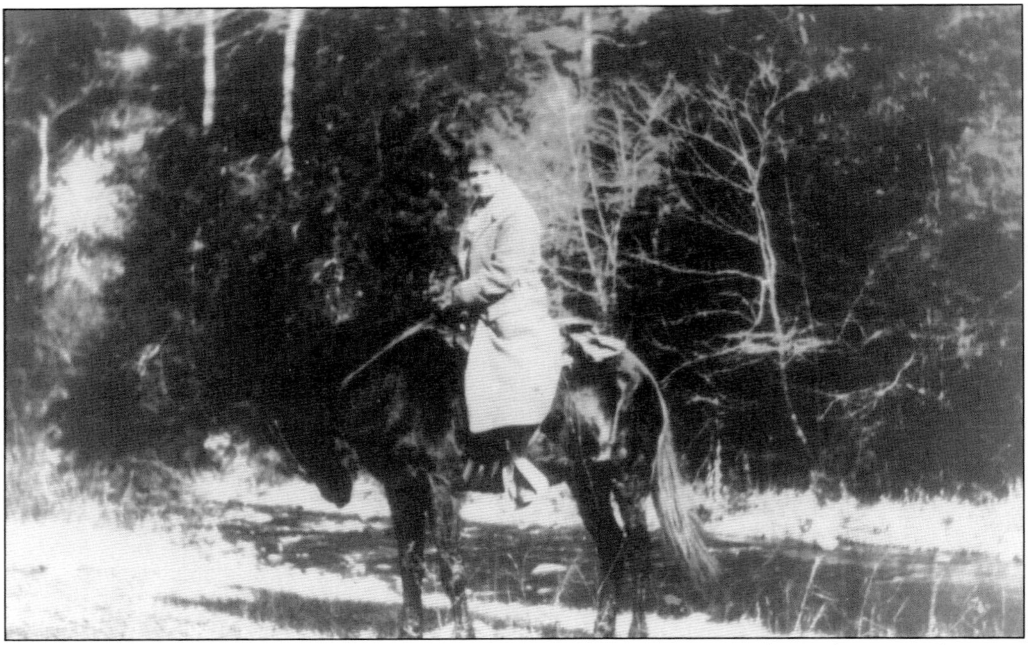

Mable Jackson, a nurse in Pittman Center, rides her horse in 1924. In the early years of eastern Sevier County, doctors and nurses made house calls on horseback to remote areas that were inaccessible by car. (Courtesy of Carolyn Large Whaley.)

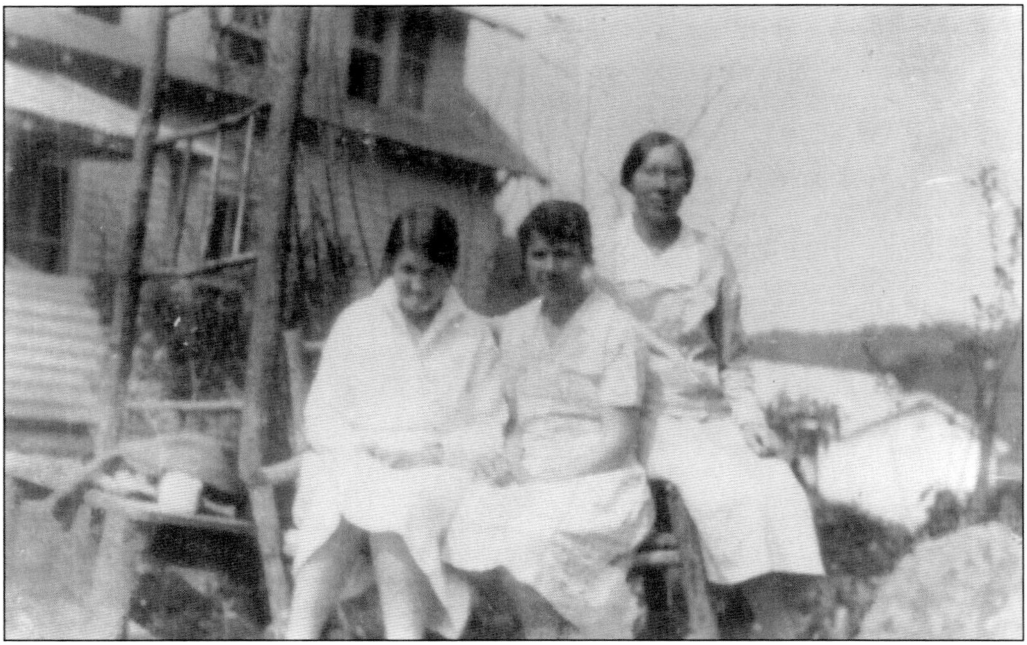

The nursing staff from the Pittman Center Clinic was photographed in 1929. They are Helen Blaksley (left), Docia Cate (center), and Anne Handlon. Among the many duties of the nurses was inoculating local residents who previously had no access to improved health care. (Courtesy of Glen Cardwell.)

Here is an early photograph of the Baldwin Clinic, which sat atop a hill overlooking the picturesque scenery of the Smoky Mountains. The clinic served mostly for first aid, treating minor injuries, and vaccinations. Some minor surgeries such as appendectomies were performed on the premises. More serious medical matters were taken to Sevierville, which was 20 miles away. (Courtesy of Glen Cardwell.)

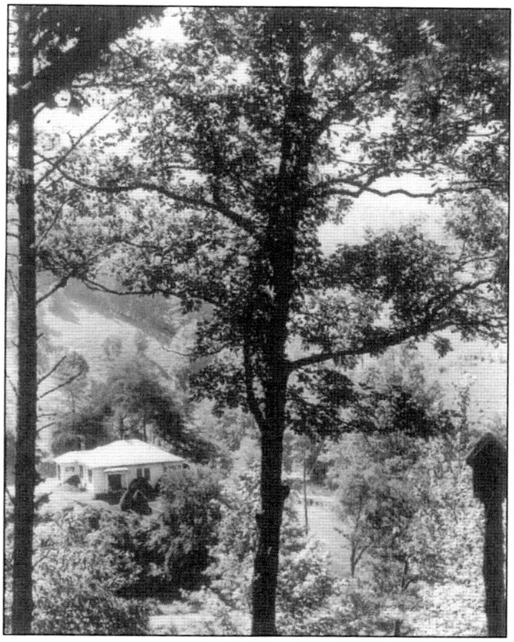

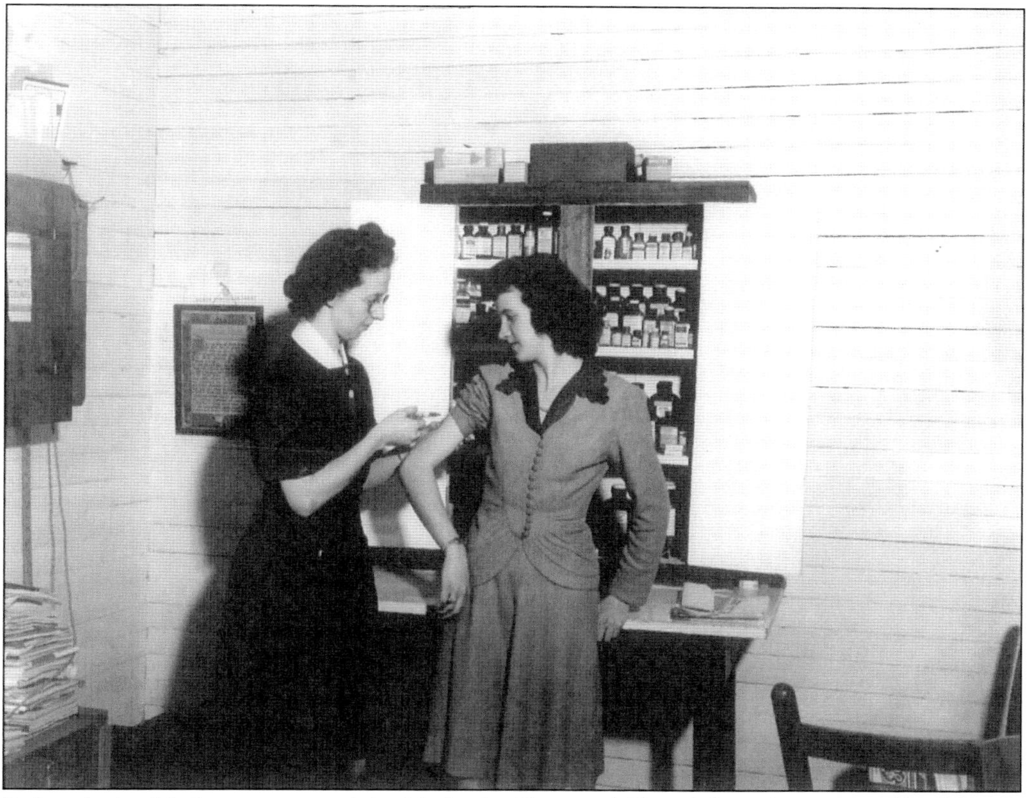

Before the health department and the Methodist Episcopal Church brought improved health care to the region, common illnesses that most Americans are routinely inoculated against proved fatal to area residents. Typhoid and influenza outbreaks frequently took the lives of those afflicted in Sevier County. (Courtesy of Carolyn Large Whaley.)

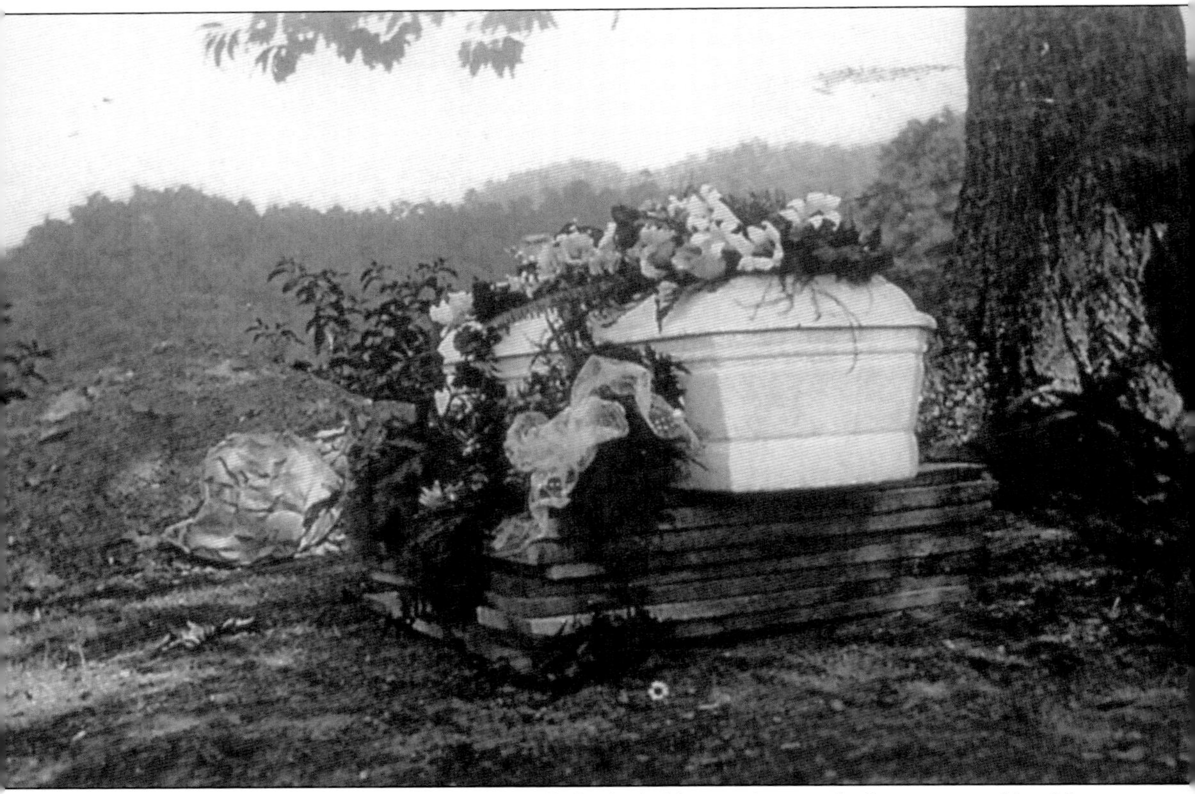

Childhood diseases resulted in an unusually high child mortality rate before improved health care was introduced to eastern Sevier County. Freddie Ray Proffitt was a four-year-old girl who died of an accidental overdose. The child climbed upon a countertop and took four pink Cascara pills, which were commonly used for upset stomachs. The dose proved fatal to the child. (Courtesy of Jackie Underwood.)

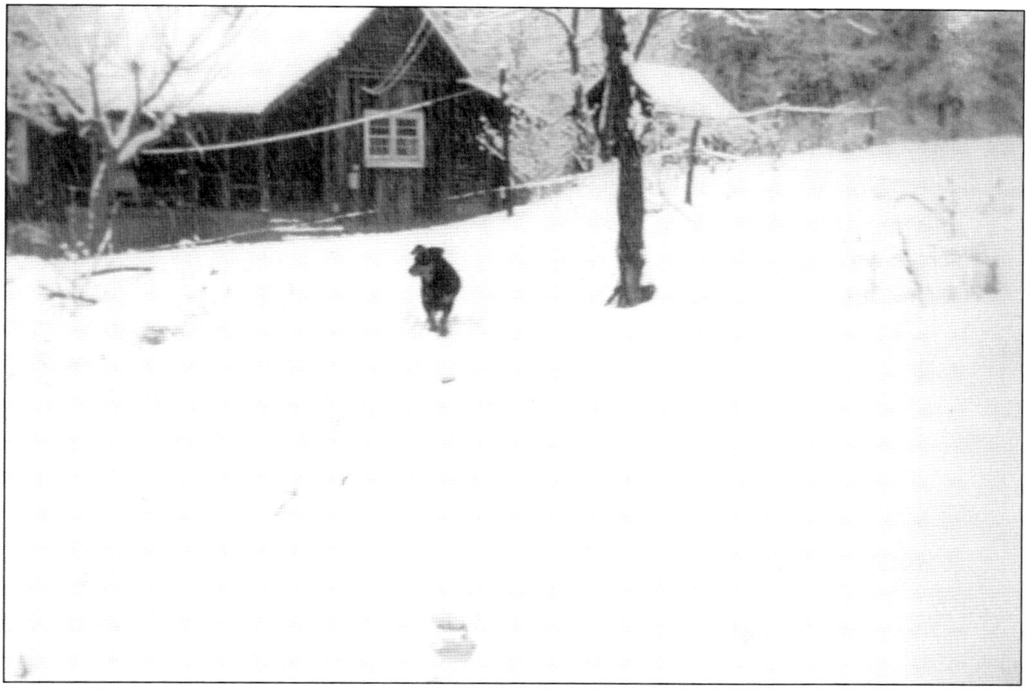

Snow falls deep at the higher elevations of eastern Sevier County. This photograph taken at the Whaley home depicts the family dog Tige trudging through deep snow. (Courtesy of Carolyn Large Whaley.)

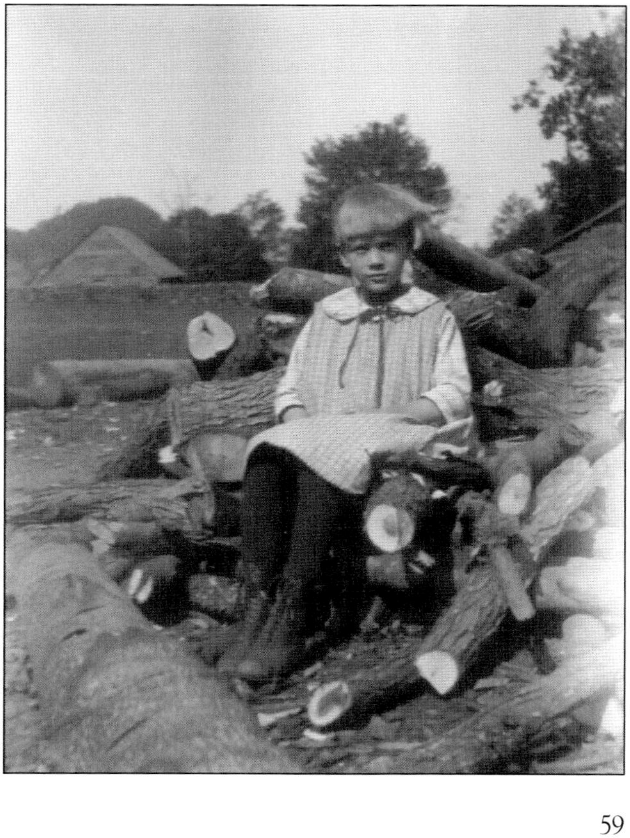

Firewood was the primary means of heating homes before the Tennessee Valley Authority introduced electricity to the area. Here, Beatrice McCarter sits atop a cord of wood in 1920. (Courtesy of Carolyn Large Whaley.)

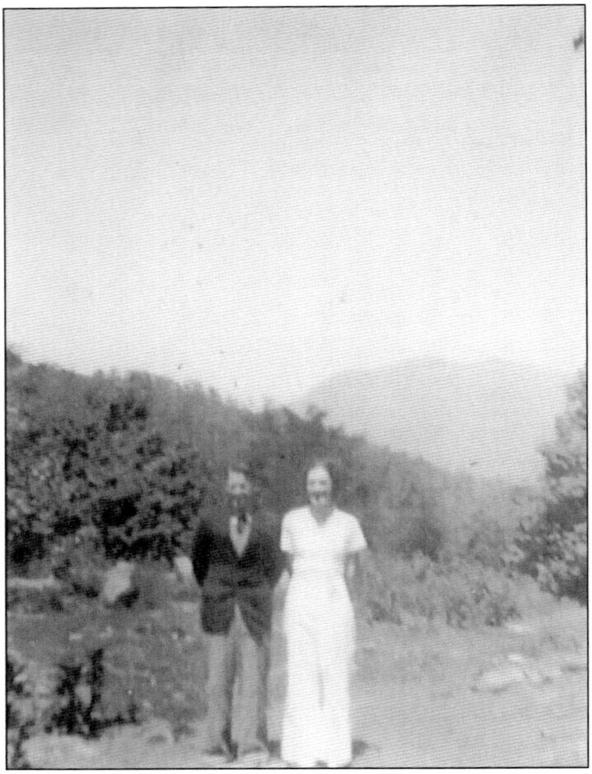

Virgil Whaley is pictured here on the day he proposed to the future Ethel King near Spasmodic Springs in Greenbrier in April 1935. The couple was married on July 6, 1935. In order to obtain a marriage certificate, a man had to travel to Sevierville to get a marriage license. The 20-mile journey could take as long as two days to complete on foot or horseback. (Courtesy of Carolyn Large Whaley.)

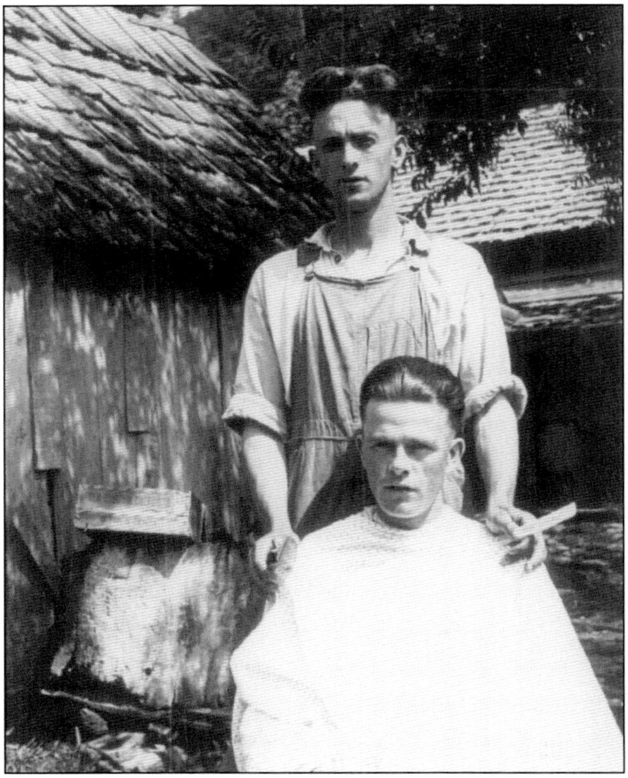

Since there were no barbers in town, haircuts were performed by neighbors or family members. One technique sometimes employed by the makeshift barbers was the bowl method. The barber would simply place a large bowl on the head of the person getting the haircut and then proceed to cut around the bowl. (Courtesy of Carolyn Large Whaley.)

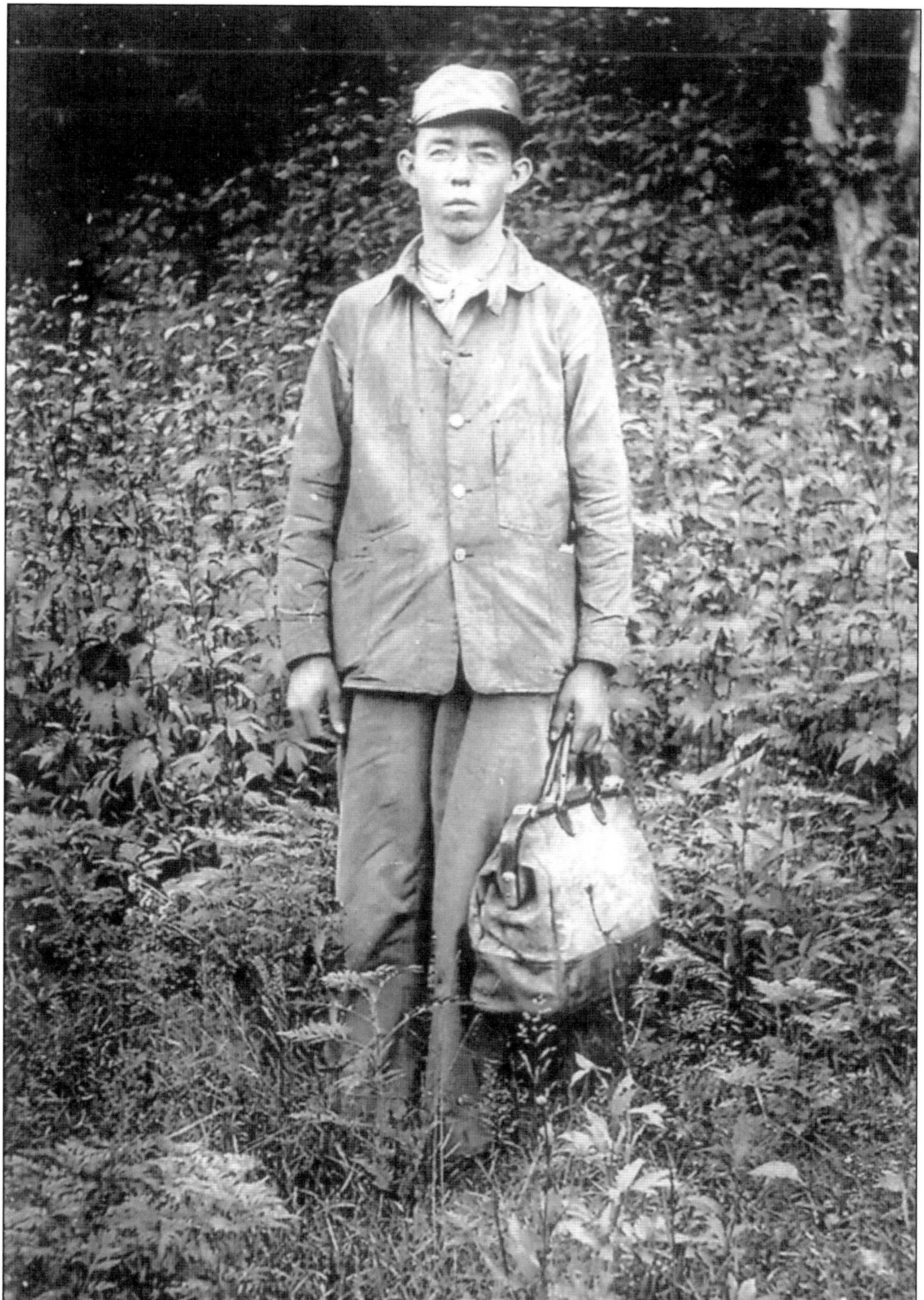

In the early 20th century, mail was delivered on foot in eastern Sevier County. Rural carriers such as John Dennis, pictured in the 1930s, had to carry mail over creeks and down trails to remote residences. (Courtesy of Jackie Underwood.)

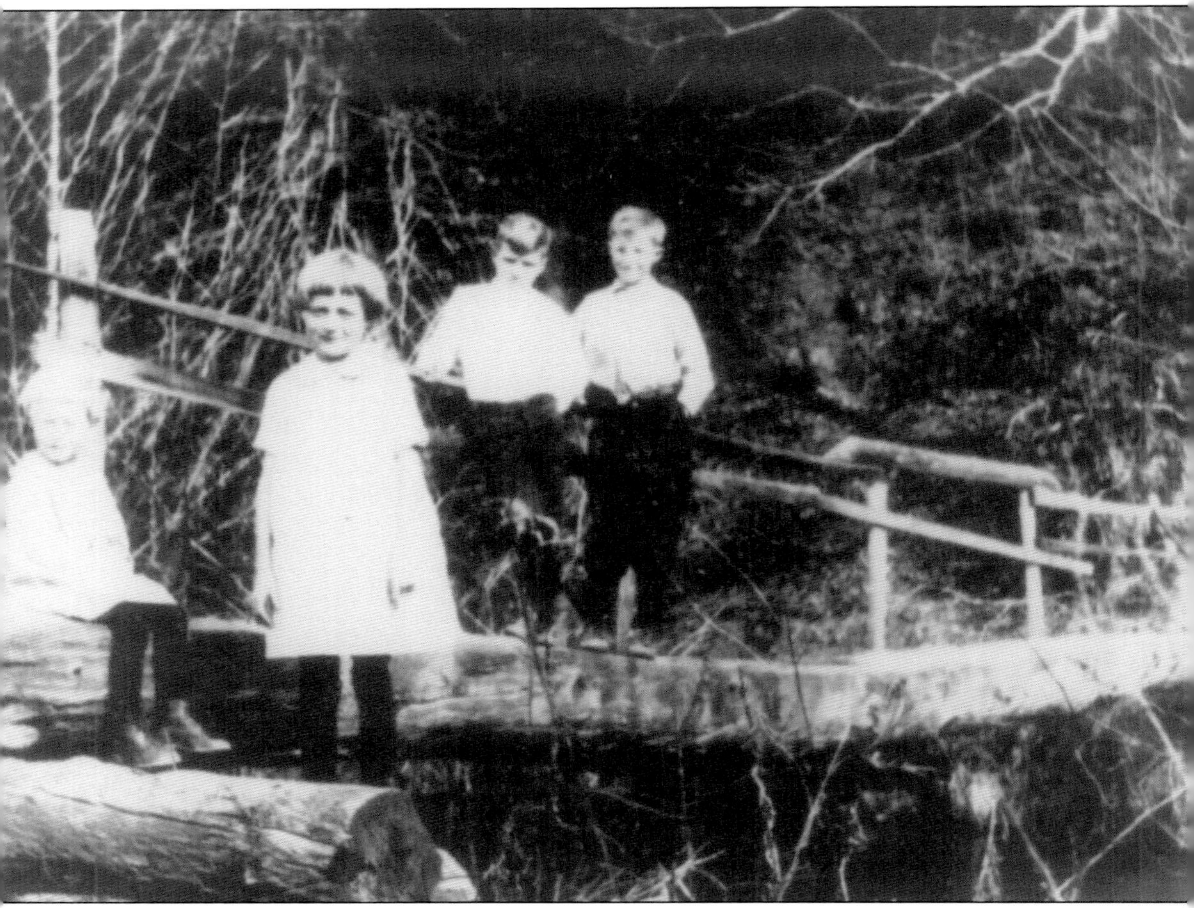

The children of Lum and Mary Reagan are pictured in 1924 on a footbridge made from a rough-hewn log. From left to right are Grace Reagan, Vida Reagan, Dale Jackson, and Max Reagan. (Courtesy of Carolyn Large Whaley.)

Mules were a common form of transportation in the days prior to the automobile and the construction of modern roads. Dewey Huskey is shown riding his mule in the 1930s. (Courtesy of Carolyn Large Whaley.)

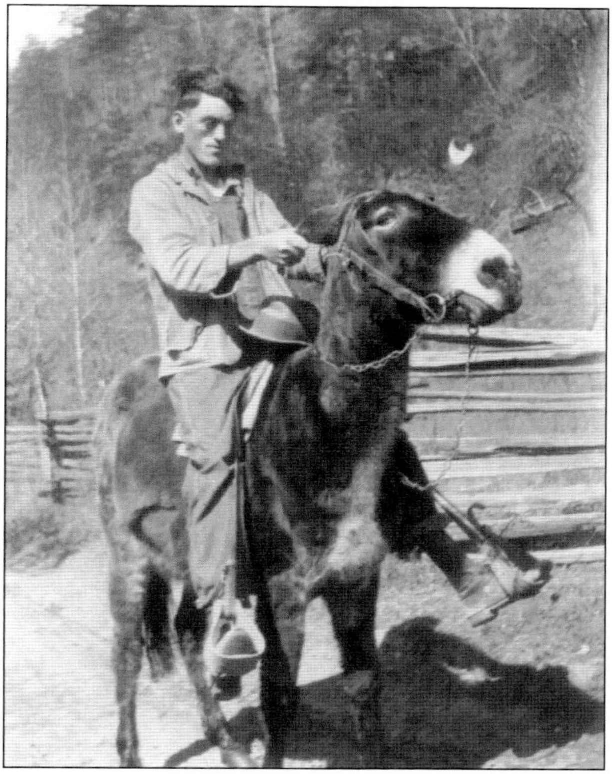

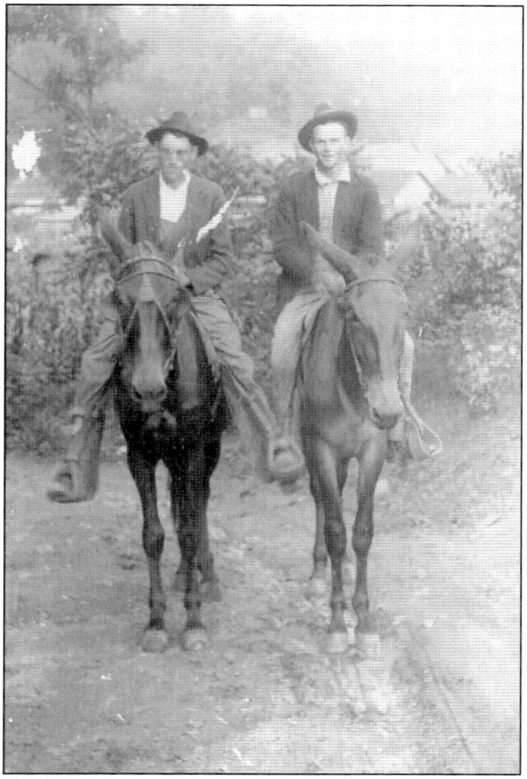

Dewey Huskey (left) and Homer Bradley ride mules in this undated photograph. Mules and horses were the primary means of transportation in the region. Few roads existed at the time. The Civilian Conservation Corps created many roads, which made accessing surrounding communities easier. (Courtesy of Carolyn Large Whaley.)

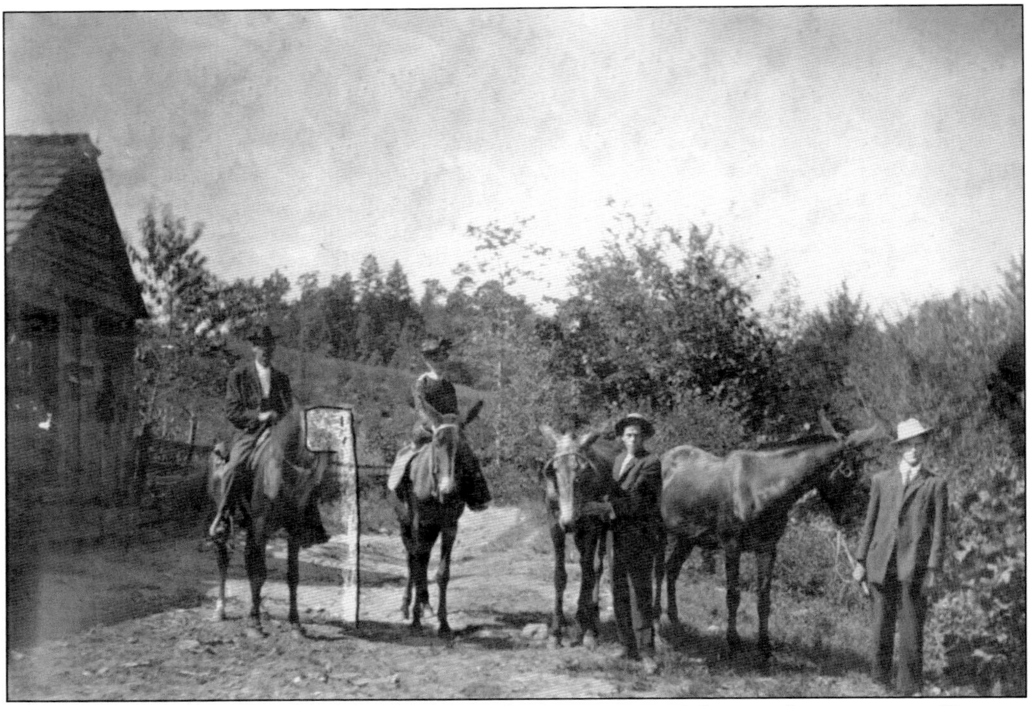

Horses were helpful in early Sevier County. There were several foot trails connecting Pittman Center to Sevierville, but many of the paths that did exist were prone to flooding. (Courtesy of Carolyn Large Whaley.)

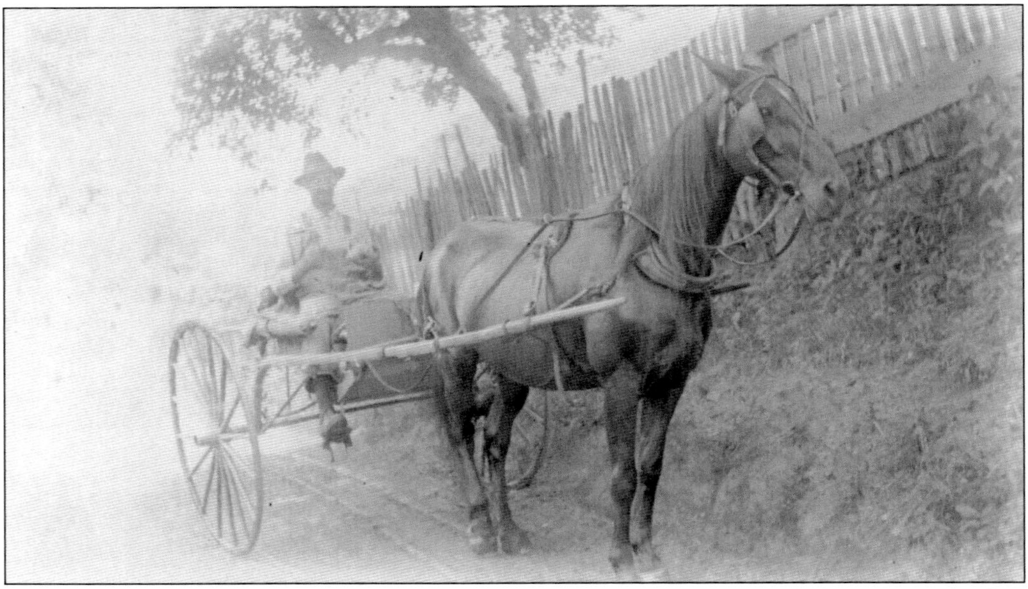

Horse-drawn carriages were commonly seen around Pittman Center until the 1950s. The first time the residents of Pittman Center saw a car was in the 1920s. According to Carolyn Whaley, whose grandparents lived in the area at the time, locals who first saw the car were convinced it was the end of time. (Courtesy of Glen Cardwell.)

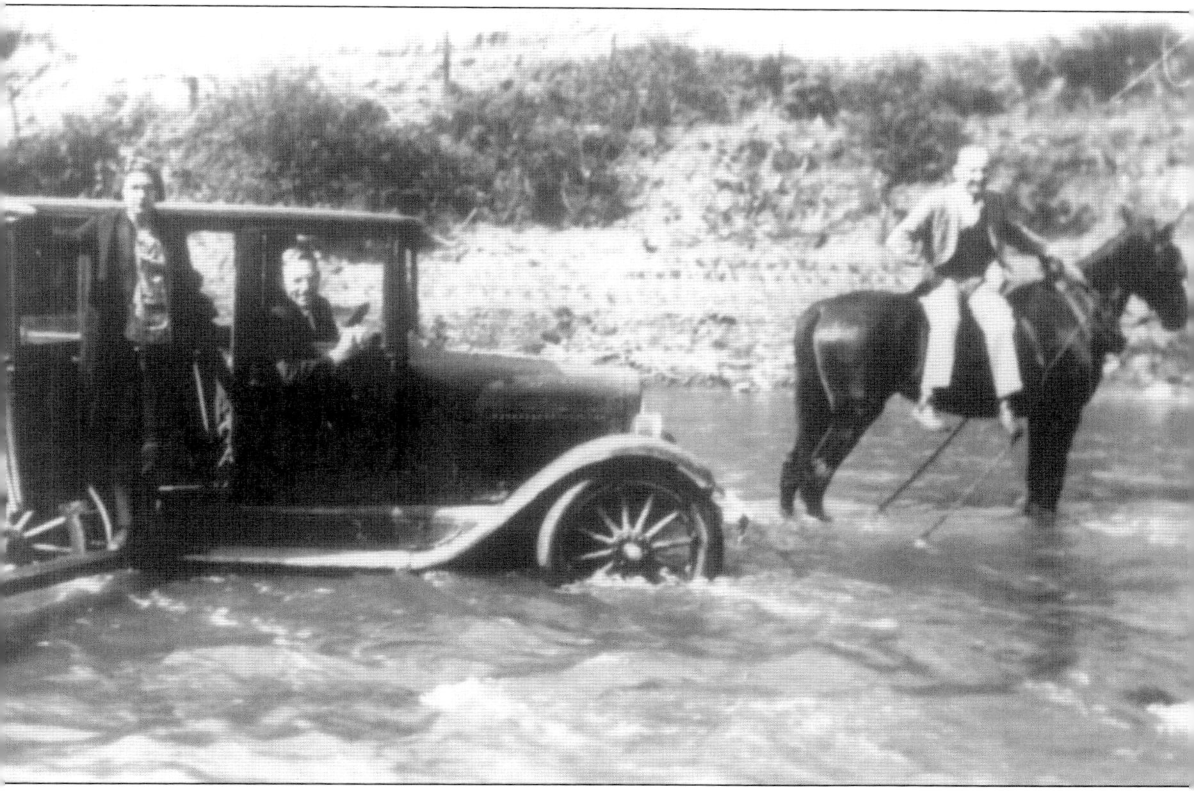

With no paved roads and flooding occurring on occasion, roads frequently became a muddy quagmire. Often, horses were used to pull stranded motorists from the rising floodwaters. The passengers in the car are Dr. R.F. Thomas and his wife, Eva; they had just returned from New York. The couple had no trouble on their journey until they reached Pittman Center. The photograph is dated 1929. (Courtesy of Glen Cardwell.)

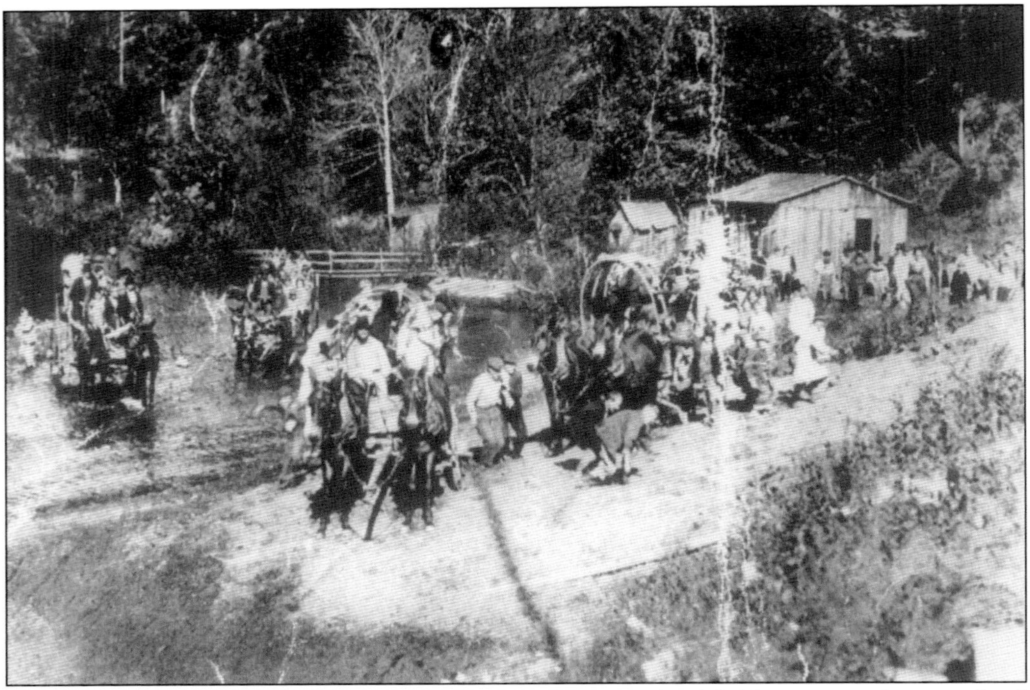

During the early days of the Pittman Community Center, schoolchildren were taken to school on covered wagons. The wagons were the precursor of the modern-day school buses. (Courtesy of Glen Cardwell.)

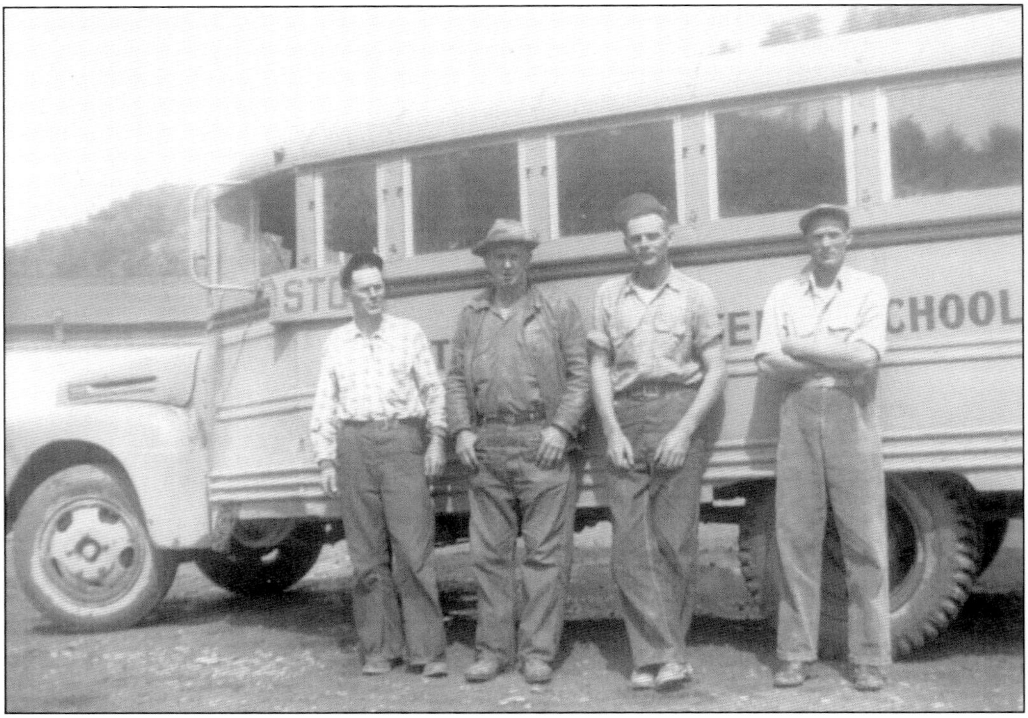

The first buses in eastern Sevier County began running in the 1940s. (Courtesy of Carolyn Large Whaley.)

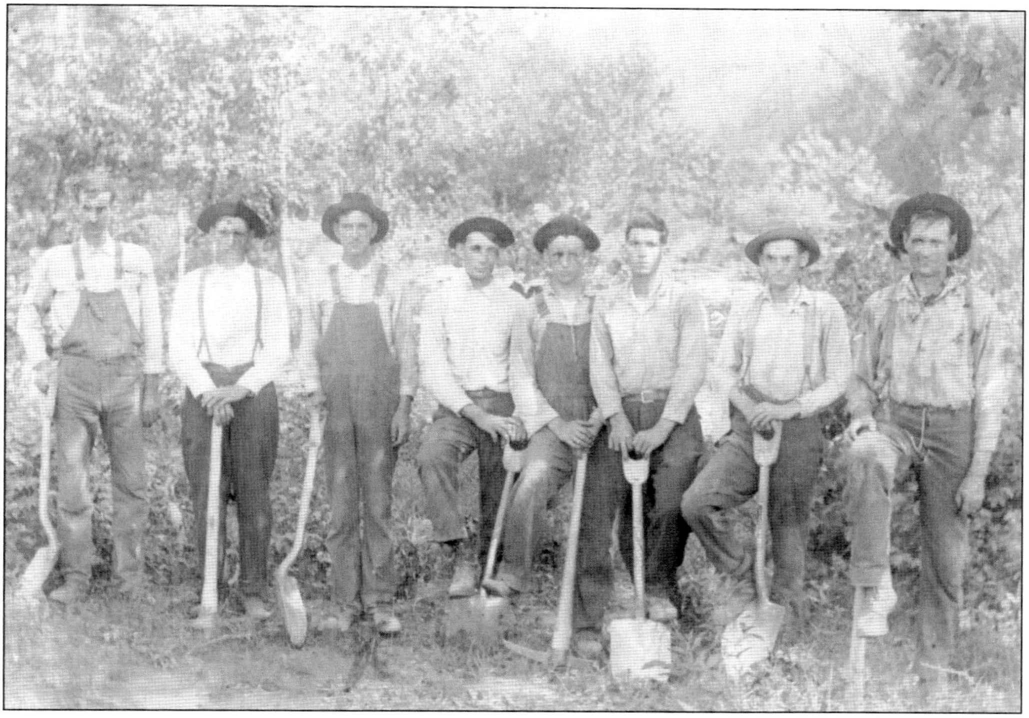

All men above the age of 16 were required by law to volunteer for six days a year on the road crew responsible for the maintenance of the roads in the area. If an able-bodied male did not wish to work on the road crew, he could pay someone $6 to take his place or pay the county $9. With few jobs in the area, many able-bodied young men were glad to stand in for others who did not want to serve on the crew. (Courtesy of Glen Cardwell.)

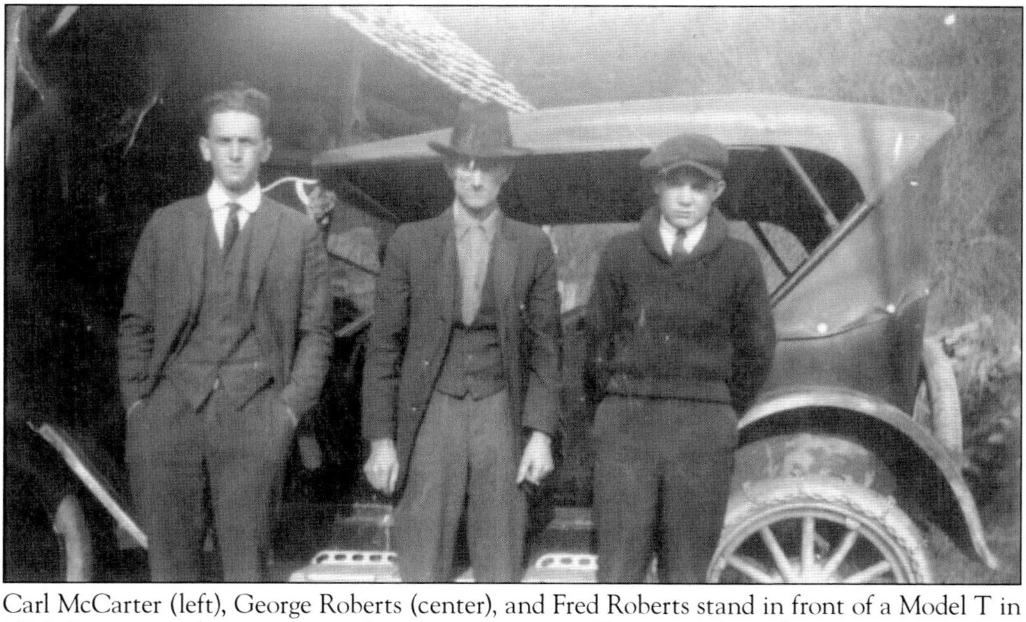

Carl McCarter (left), George Roberts (center), and Fred Roberts stand in front of a Model T in 1920. Cars were a luxury item in the area at that time. (Courtesy of Carolyn Large Whaley.)

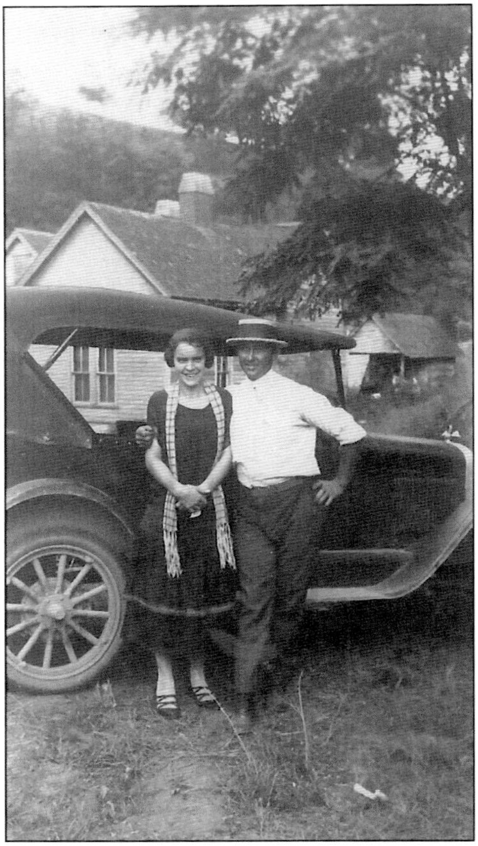

Rufus and Frances Mize are pictured standing next to a 1930s automobile. (Courtesy of Jackie Underwood.)

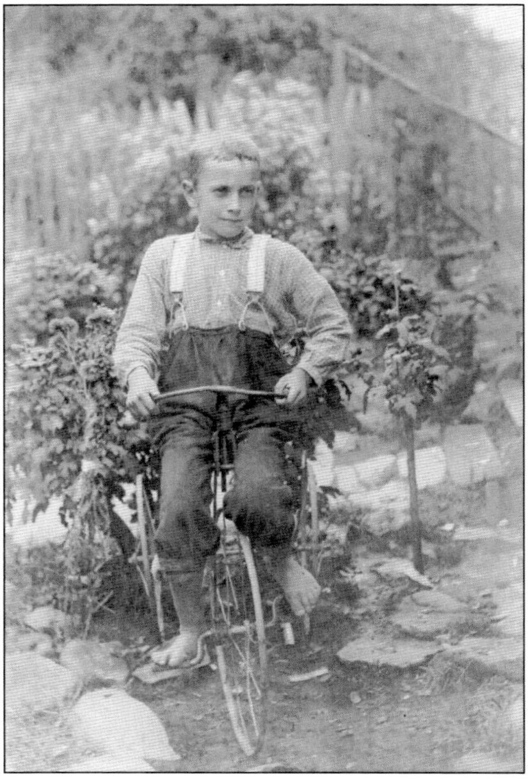

Carl McCarter is pictured in front of his home in 1912. Considered luxury items, bicycles were rare in Pittman Center. (Courtesy of Jackie Underwood.)

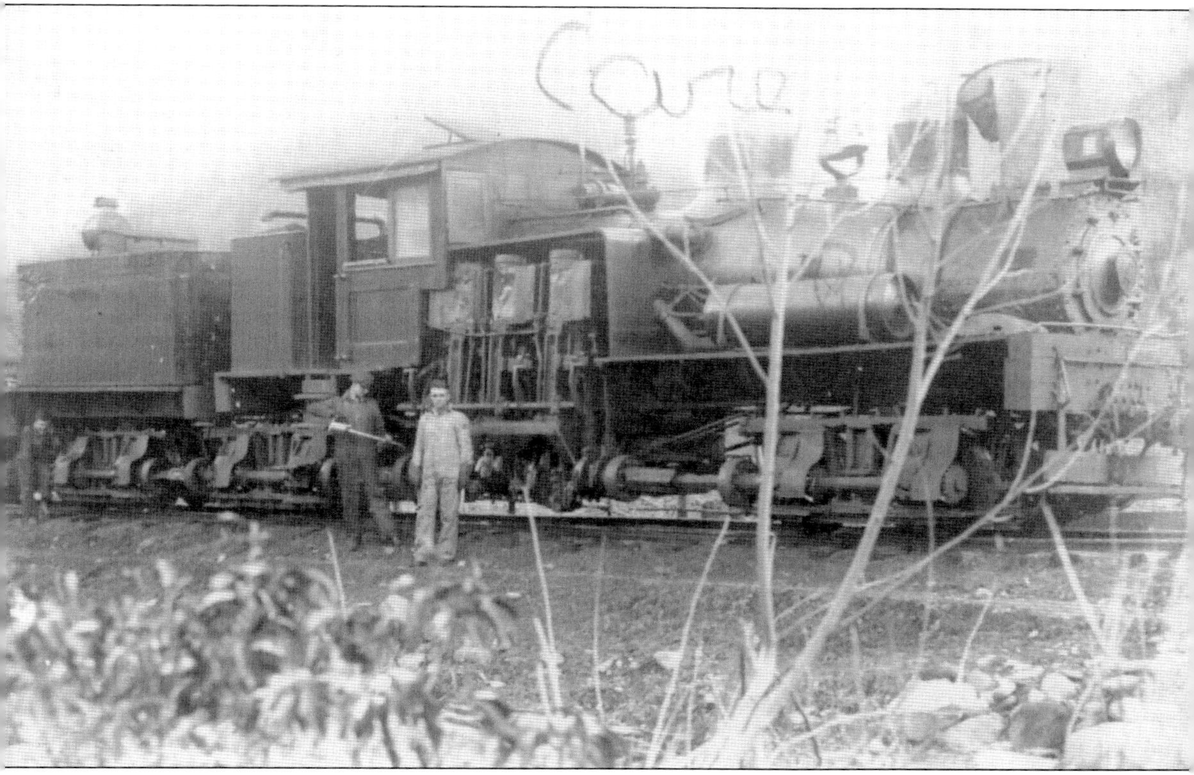

Sevierville has always served as the county seat of Sevier County. Communities in the east were isolated, and a trip from Pittman Center to Sevierville was approximately 10 miles and usually took an entire day by mule or by foot. Sevierville was the only community in the county with a train depot. (Courtesy of Carolyn Large Whaley.)

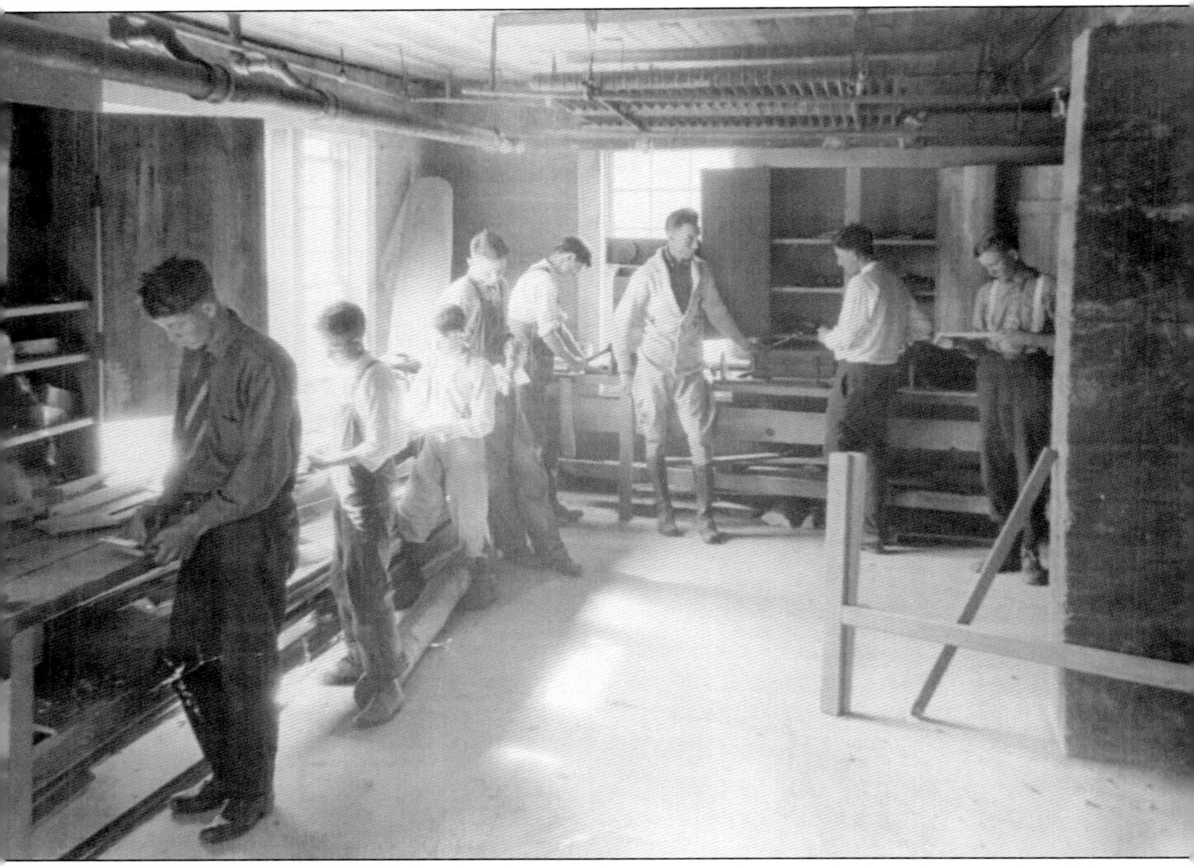

The shop class is pictured in 1922 at Pittman Community Center. Teacher J.J. Asher (third from right) is seen with students, from left to right, Wiley Martin, Earl Huskey, Clifford Price, Clarence Branam, Oliver Huskey, and two unidentified. (Courtesy of Carolyn Large Whaley.)

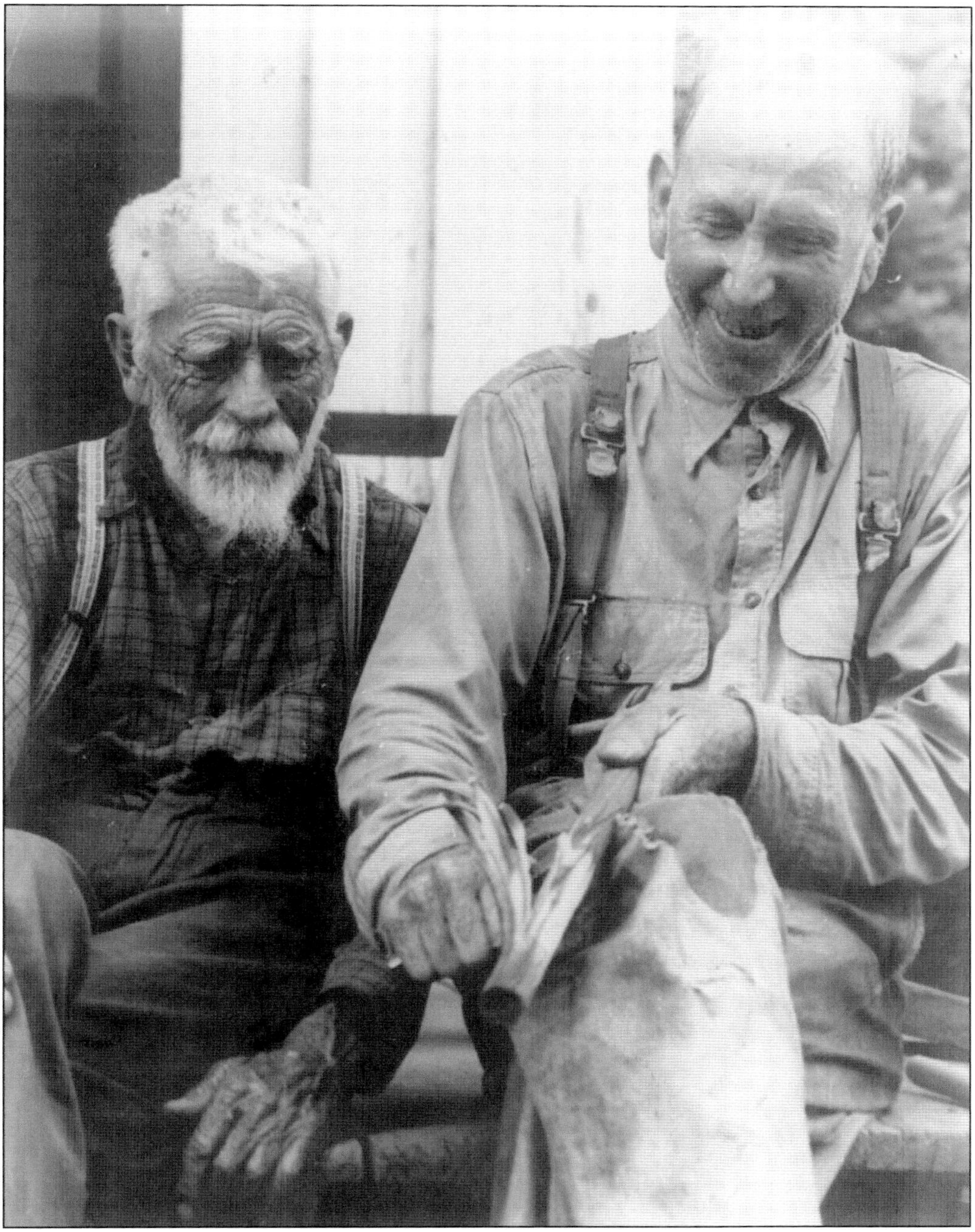

James McCarter (left) and Sammy Smith are pictured whittling. Life in the mountainous community was often tedious, and there were few activities to occupy spare time. Surrounded by an almost endless forest, men had a boundless source of wood for whittling and carving. Many mountain artisans carved wooden sculptures, which were sold through the local Goodwill Store that was established by the Methodist Church. (Courtesy of Carolyn Large Whaley.)

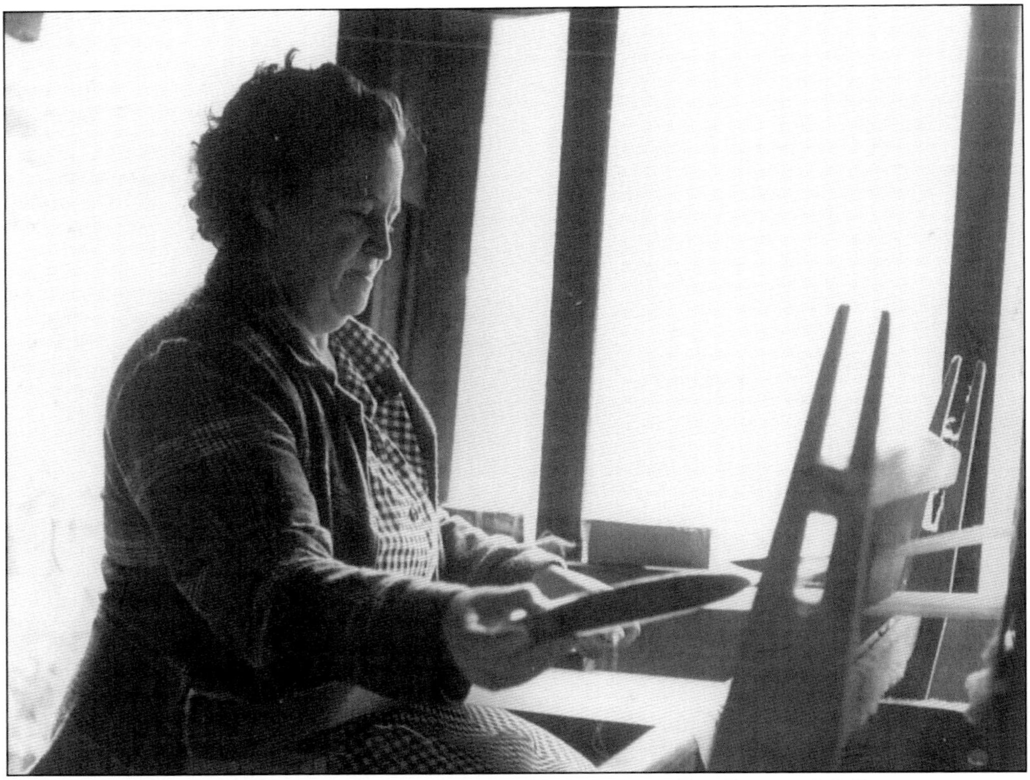

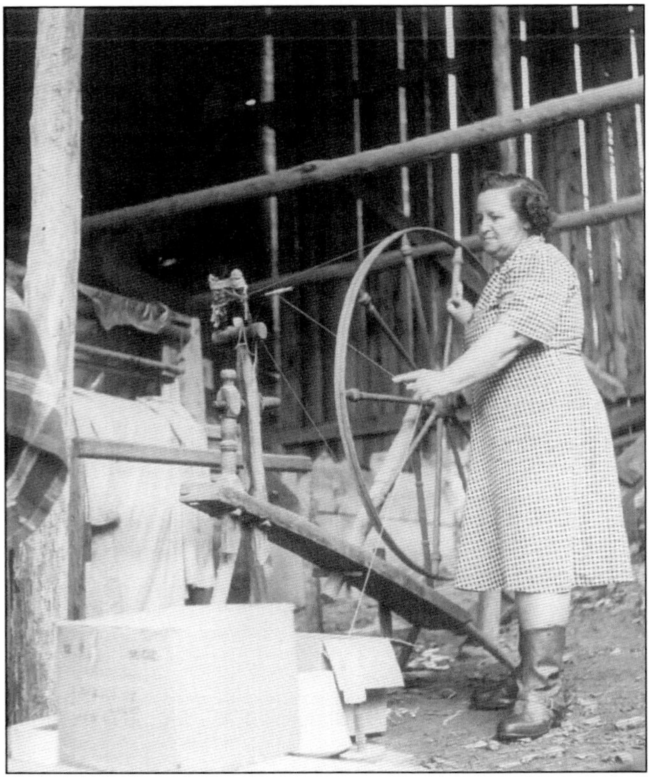

Eva Ramsey McCarter weaves on a loom in the 1950s. In the early days, most mothers made their own clothes for their children. By the 1950s, however, clothing was available at nearby stores in Sevierville, which was more accessible by then. Weavers still made towels and bed linens to be sold in stores. (Courtesy of Carolyn Large Whaley.)

Eva Ramsey McCarter works at a loom weaving cloth to make home linens. These products were a source of income for local craftsmen who sold their wares at retail outlets in neighboring Sevierville. (Courtesy of Carolyn Large Whaley.)

Tommy Roberts is pictured here playing with his toys. After reaching adulthood, he moved to Blount County, where he found better job opportunities. (Courtesy of Carolyn Large Whaley.)

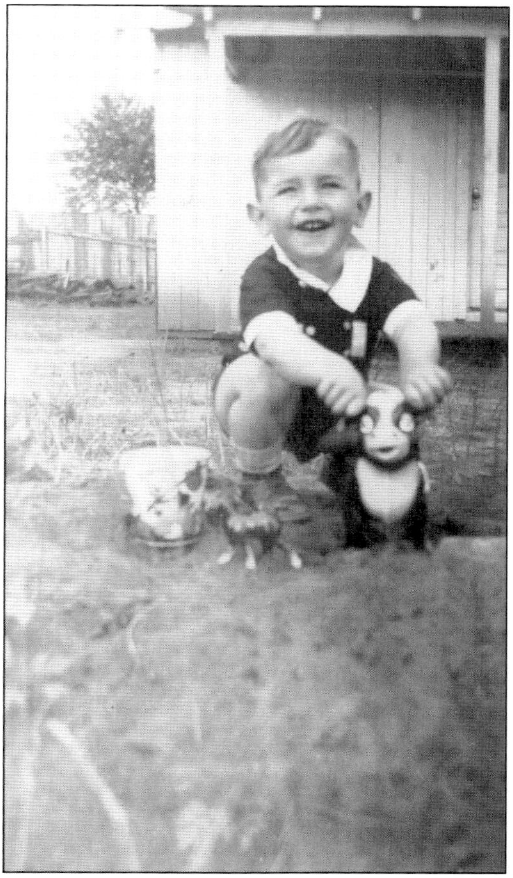

Mothers waited in line for the opening of the Goodwill Store in 1928. The store was located in Pittman Center and was stocked with donated items. Pictured, from left to right, are Lucy Parton, Magel Parton, Kate Free, Grace Free, Sally Loveday, Michell Ramsey, Tip McCarter, and Salley Bright. (Courtesy of Glen Cardwell.)

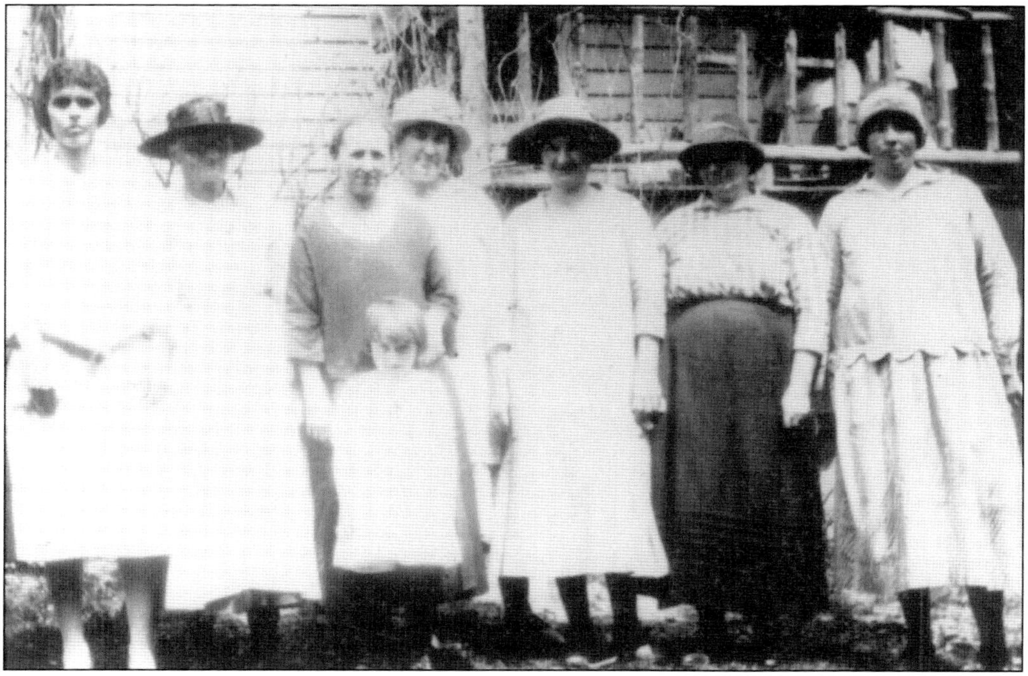

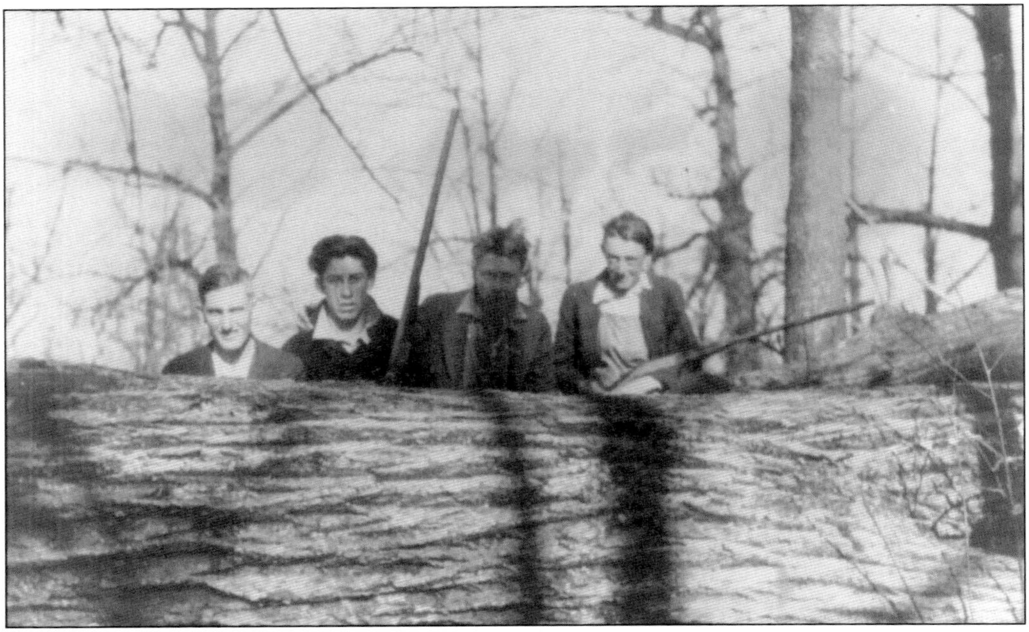

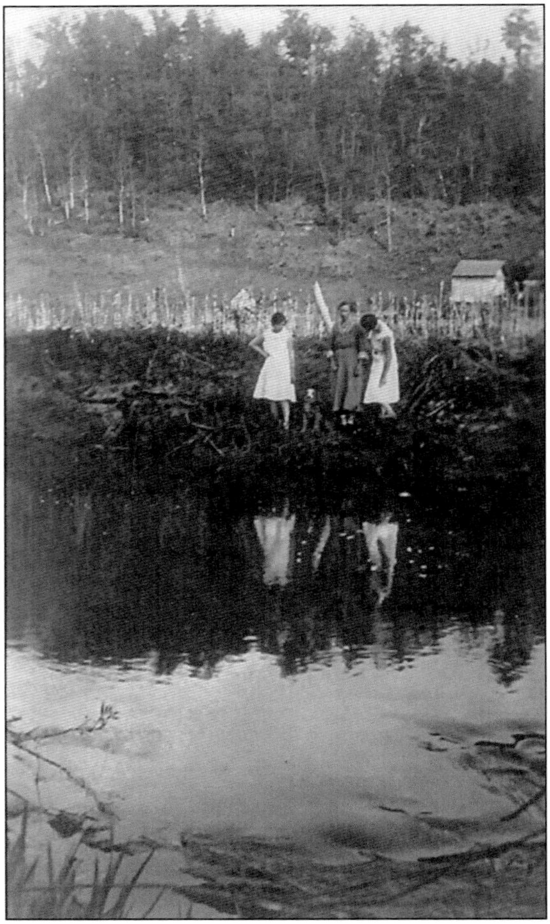

With shotguns in hand, four high school students enjoy an afternoon hike. They are, from left to right, Albert Johnson, Ray Lindsey, Roy Whaley, and Clifford Price. Many residents of the area hunted wild game in the years before the park opened. (Courtesy of Carolyn Large Whaley.)

Beulah Dennis Mary Quentine "Tiny" McMahan Dennis, Archie Ray Dennis, and Archie Ray Dennis McMahan stand near Dunn's Creek near the Lungford place. On hot summer days, local residents frequently went to Dunne's Creek to cool off with a refreshing swim. (Courtesy of Jackie Underwood.)

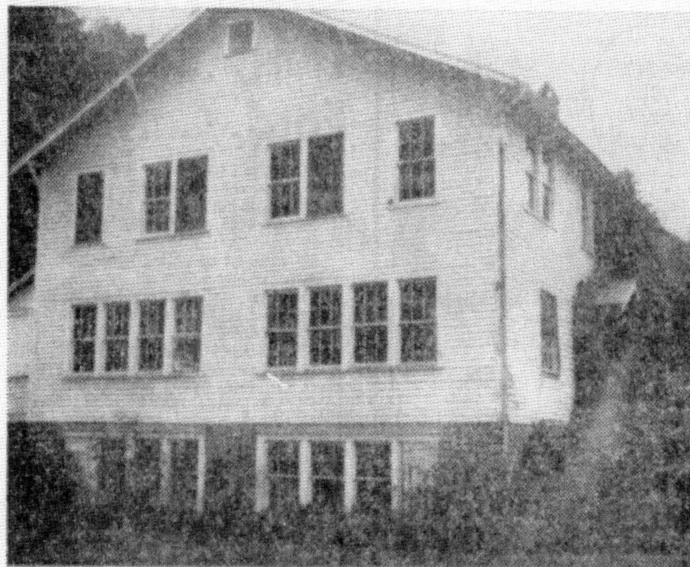

This Former Mission Building Is Pittman Center's City Hall

State's Latest City Faces Problem - Skinny Dippers

By WILLARD YARBROUGH
News-Sentinel Staff Writer

PITTMAN CENTER, Tenn. — This newest of Tennessee cities (population 365) is so peaceful and orderly that it couldn't qualify for the FBI's crime report.

However, a major problem arose this past summer, but there was no police department to deal with it. Residents complained of skinny-dippers in the Middle Prong of Little Pigeon River.

Recently, Mayor Conley Huskey and Aldermen Rex Howard and Mayford Price solved a minute matter. They had 15-mph speed zone signs erected near the elementary school, which is operated by the county, and 40-mph signs placed on Emert Cove Rd.

The 69-year-old mayor was reminded that "there isn't one sign anywhere telling visitors they've entered Pittman Center."

"Mountain shame on us," the mayor replied. "We'll take that up at the next City Council meeting."

The board won't be meeting at City Hall, but at the school. City Hall, a recent gift to Pittman Center from Global Ministries of United Methodist Church in New York City, is a three-story wooden building so long abandoned that kudzu vines are threatening to hide it from view.

"We'll put City Hall in order," Mayor Huskey said, "and have someone remove those vines. We plan to lease the first floor for shops and the top floor to residents. The middle floor is all we need for a seat of government."

PITTMAN CENTER'S First Lady once lived in such dorm buildings when

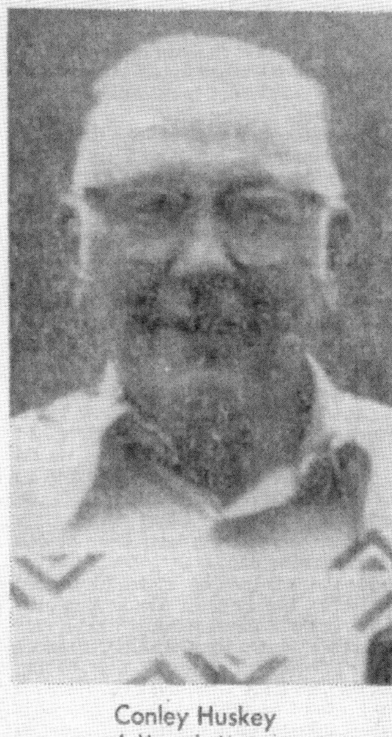

Conley Huskey
A Mayor's Mayor

arises, Gatlinburg's firefighters respond without obligation — something Gatlinburg City Council is restudying.

Can Pittman Center blacktop all its "road-streets?" No, the mayor replied, nor can Sevier County hardtop all its

Pittman Center has often been likened to the fictional Mayberry. In this old newspaper clipping, the mayor discusses the problem the city has had with skinny-dippers. (Courtesy of Carolyn Large Whaley.)

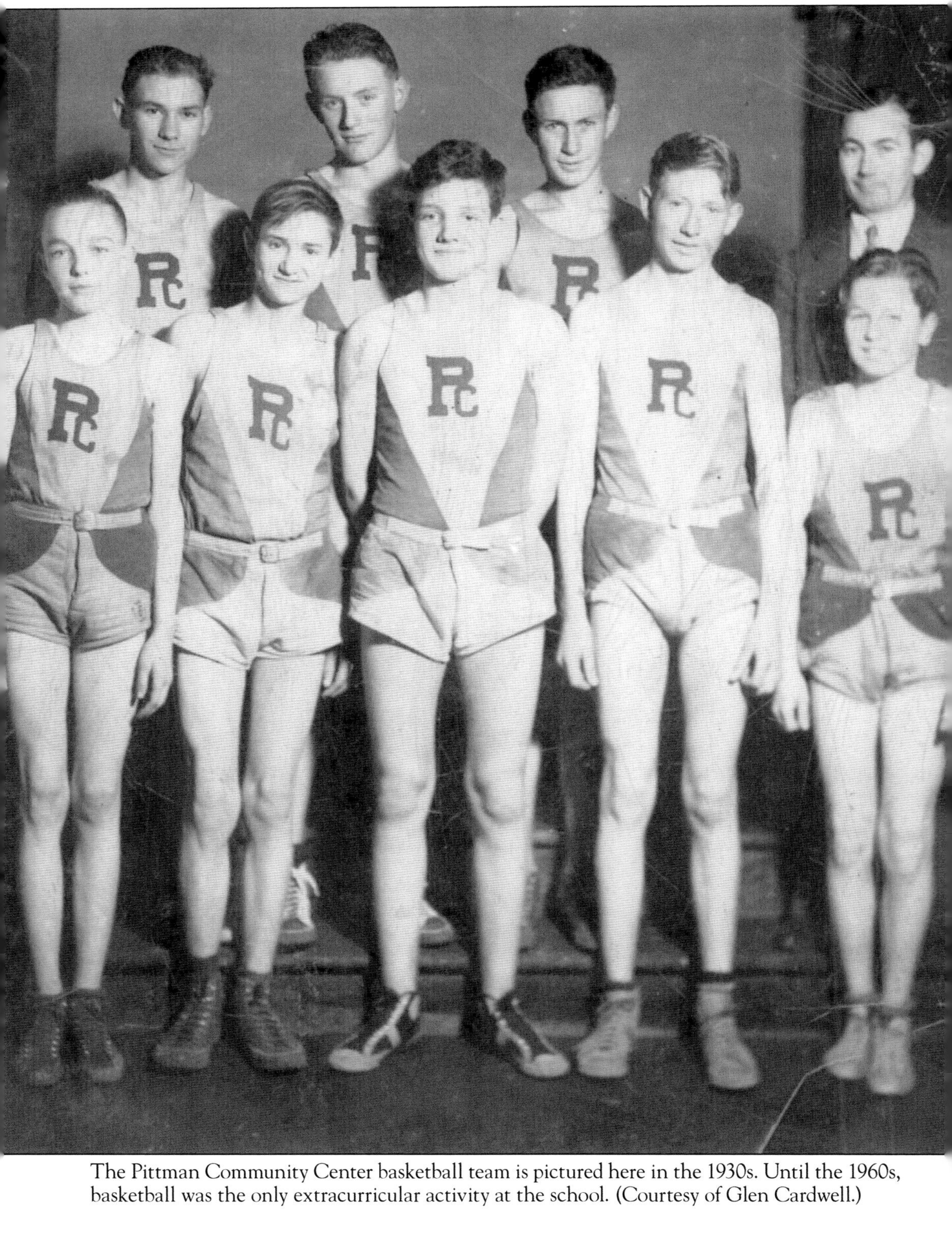

The Pittman Community Center basketball team is pictured here in the 1930s. Until the 1960s, basketball was the only extracurricular activity at the school. (Courtesy of Glen Cardwell.)

Raymond Huskey served as coach of the Pittman Community Center basketball team and taught the fifth grade. This photograph was taken in 1943. (Courtesy of Glen Cardwell.)

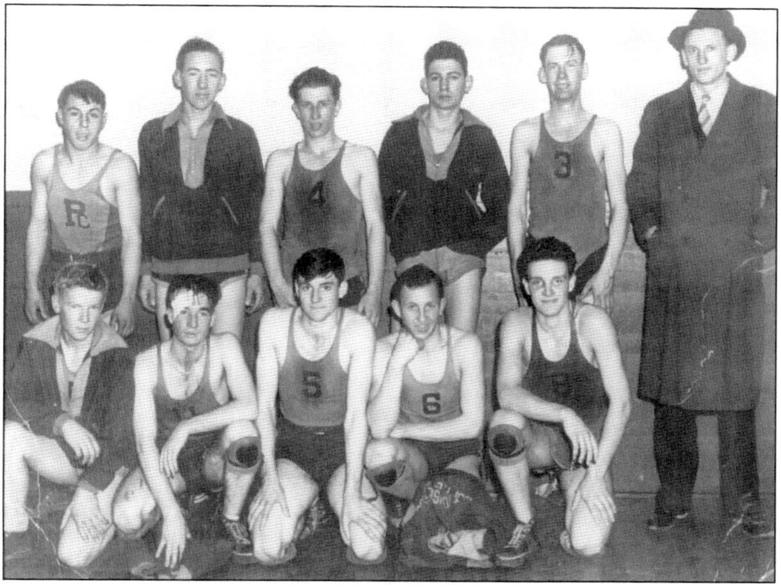

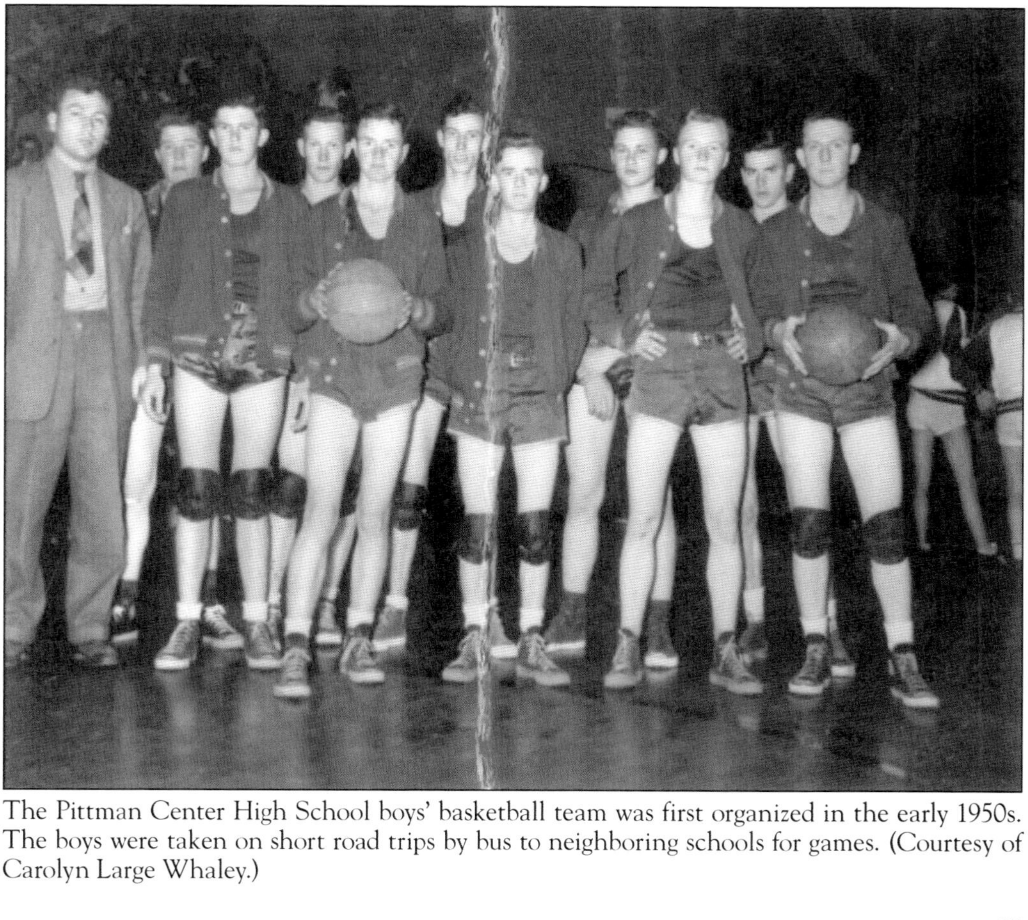

The Pittman Center High School boys' basketball team was first organized in the early 1950s. The boys were taken on short road trips by bus to neighboring schools for games. (Courtesy of Carolyn Large Whaley.)

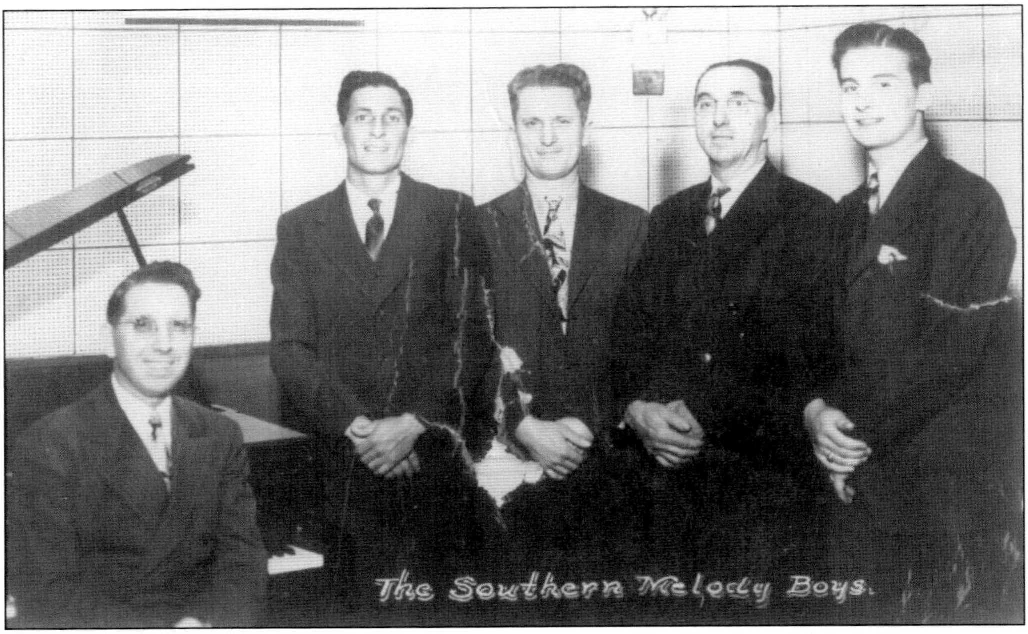

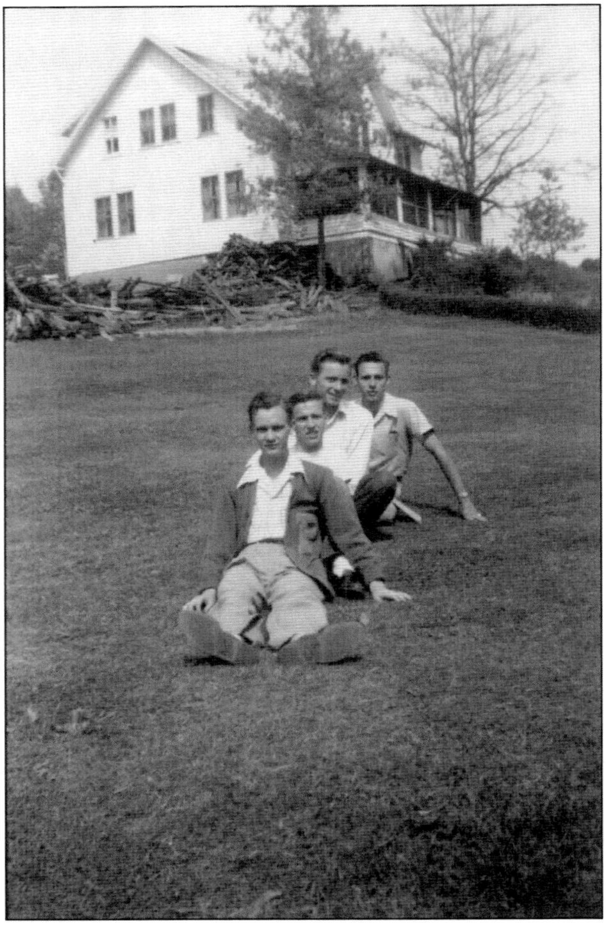

The Southern Melody Boys recorded several gospel albums and performed at different venues in East Tennessee as well as on radio shows. Here, Fred Roberts (standing second from left) of Pittman Center stands in the middle. (Courtesy of Carolyn Large Whaley.)

The male quartet of Pittman Community Center High School is pictured here in 1949. The young men are, from front to back, Carl Shults, Glen Cardwell, Jonathan Ogle, and Lon Cardwell. The girls' dormitory stands in the background. (Courtesy of Glen Cardwell.)

Lester McCarter strums a guitar in the early 1940s. With few recreational options available, music was an enjoyable pastime for many. (Courtesy of Glen Cardwell.)

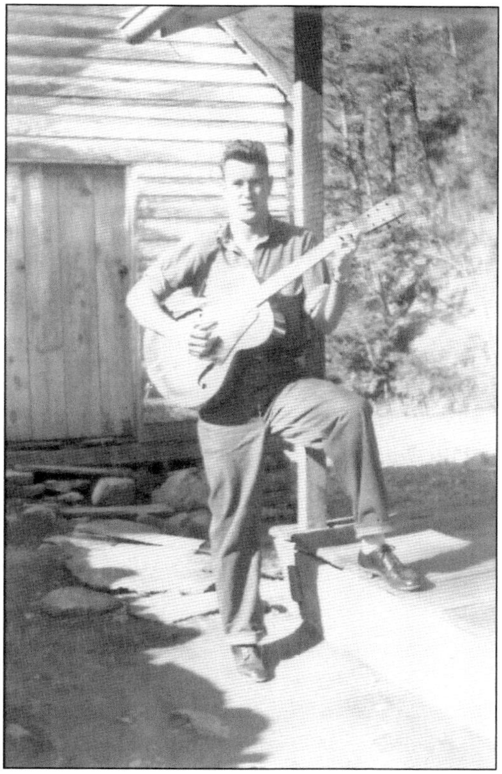

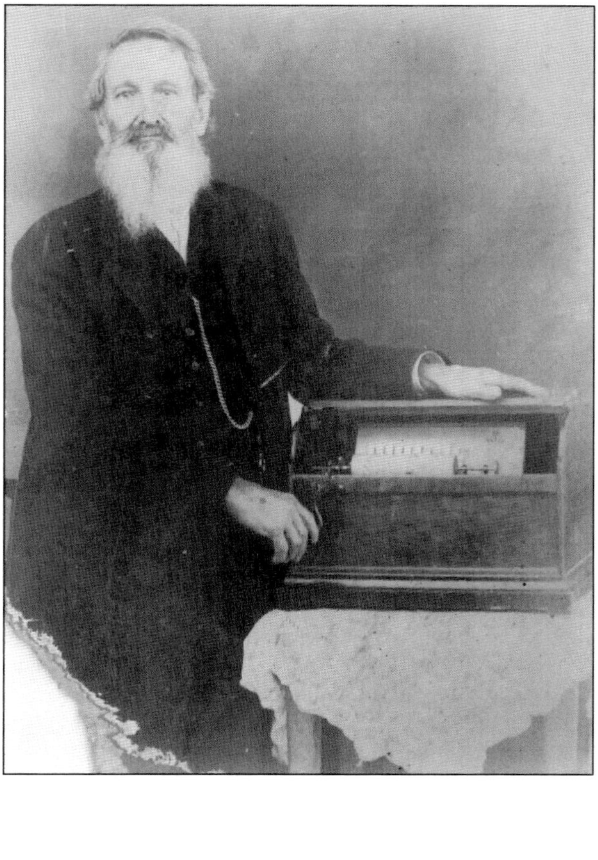

Pictured in 1910, Preston Shultz enjoys a phonograph record. Shults was among the few in the area who had electricity in his home at this time. Many locals considered the phonograph a luxury. (Courtesy of Carolyn Large Whaley.)

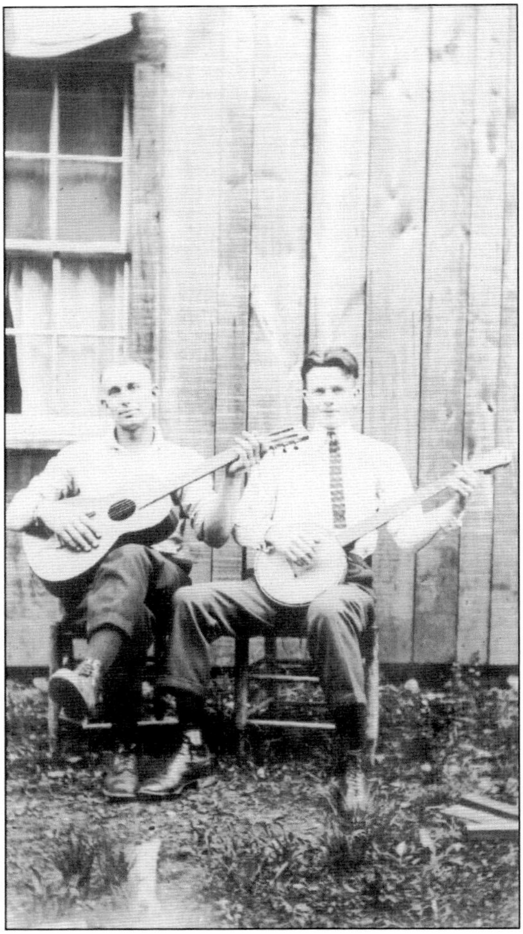

Unidentified banjo and guitar players are seen here in the early 1920s. Most players were self-taught. With few options for entertainment, storytelling and playing music were popular forms of amusement at community gatherings. (Courtesy of Carolyn Large Whaley.)

Mountain musicians Lawrence Proffitt (left), Ellis McCarter (center), and Ike McCarter celebrate the last day of school with an impromptu concert in 1921. (Courtesy of Carolyn Large Whaley.)

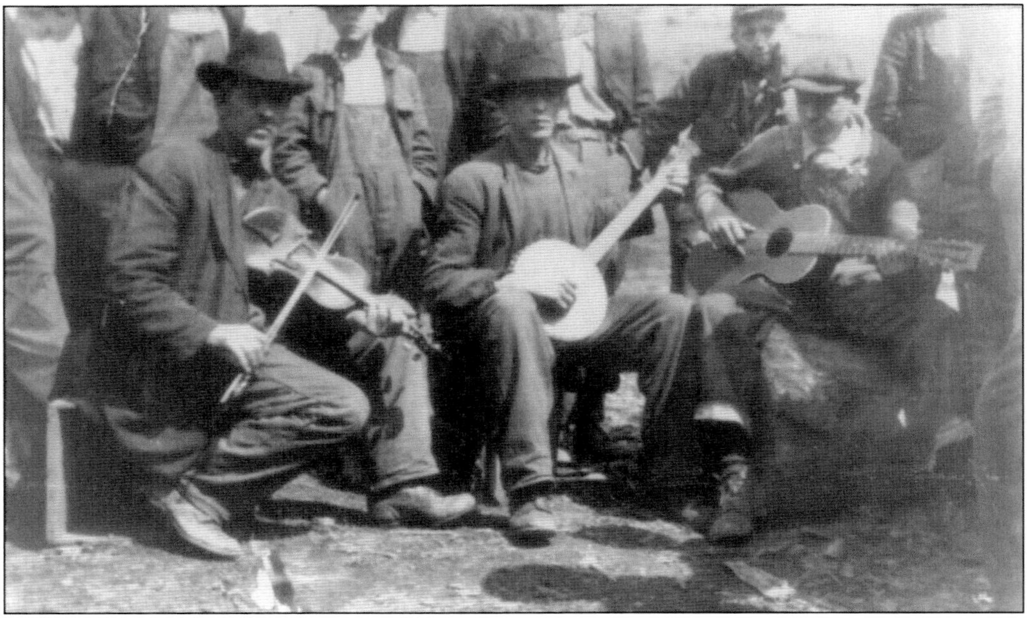

This photograph, taken in the mid-1930s, depicts an early version of the Girls' Club in Pittman Center. The club was a social gathering for young girls in the community. Pictured, from left to right, are Pauline Hoffman, Kitty Price, Lucille McCarter, and June Price. (Courtesy of Glen Cardwell.)

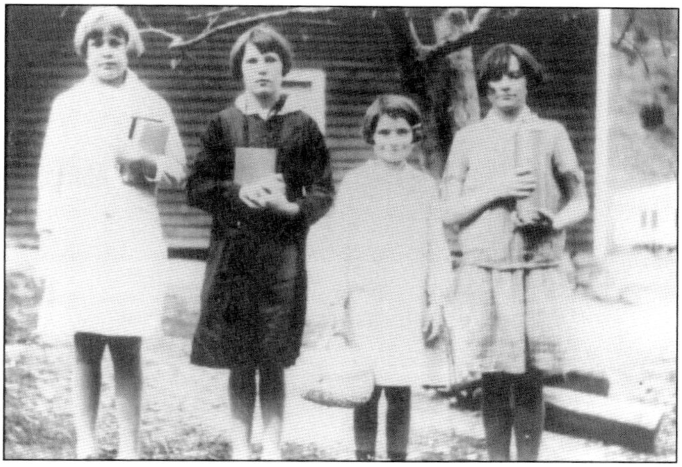

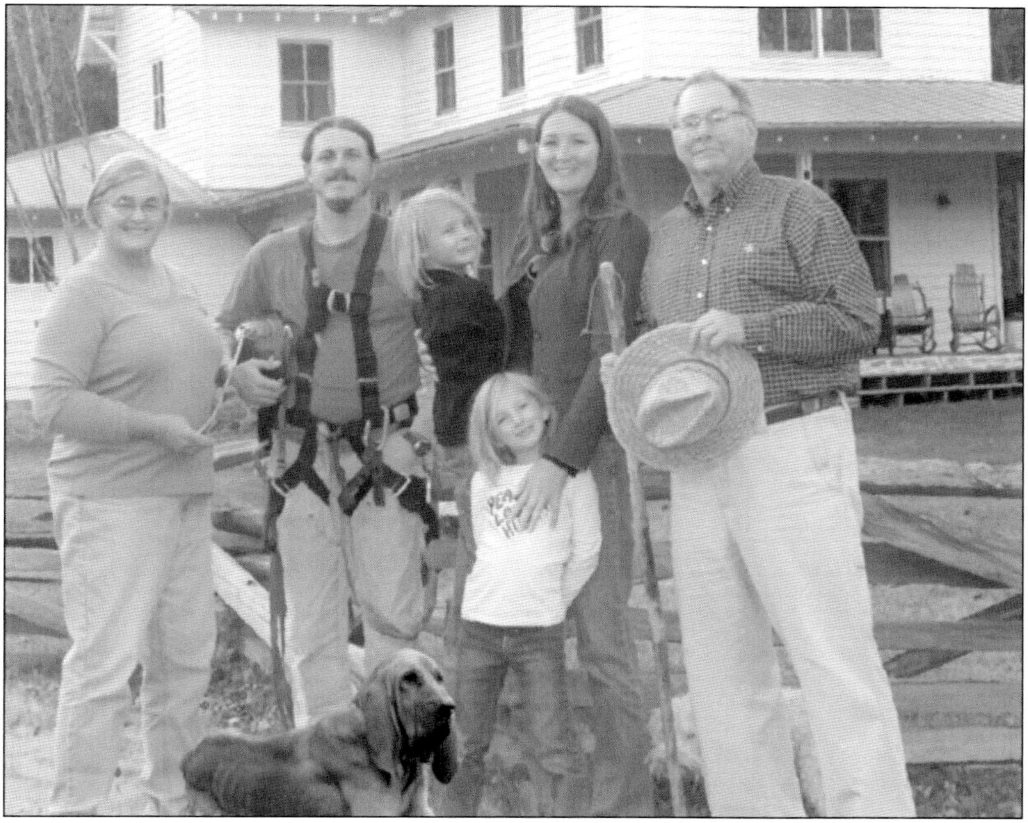

The Postlewaite family transformed Foxfire Mountain from a cattle farm into an adventure park. The Postlewaites raised prized Hereford breeder cattle on this farm for several years until 2009, when a serious drought caused hay and feed prices to escalate. It soon became unprofitable to raise expensive cattle. So, Marc and Marion Postlewaite decided that they had to sell the farm that they loved so much and move into an apartment in town. They then took a long-planned dream vacation to Alaska, where Marc rode a zip line and immediately told Marion to call the real estate broker to tell him to take the property off the market. Marc then began laying out plans to create a family-friendly adventure park. Pictured, from left to right, are Marion, Matthew, their dog Rufus, Liam, Cresson, Stephanie, and Marc. (Courtesy of Stephanie Postlewaite.)

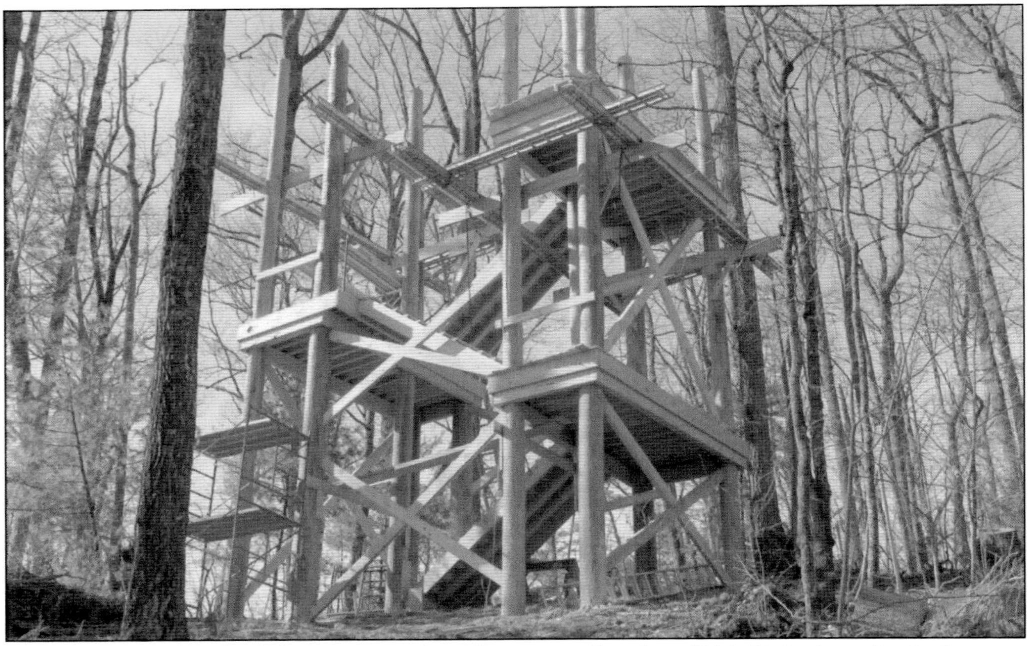

Construction of Goliath began in 2013 and was completed in 2014. Goliath is the highest zip line in the South, with heights reaching a dizzying 475 feet above the ground. The zip line is 170 feet higher than the torch of the Statue of Liberty. Helicopters were used to a run the lines from one mountain peak to the next. Riders on the mighty Goliath appear tiny as they cruise across the line at speeds of up to 40 miles per hour. The views from the line are magnificent and include the picturesque scenery of the Great Smoky Mountains National Park. (Courtesy of Stephanie Postlewaite.)

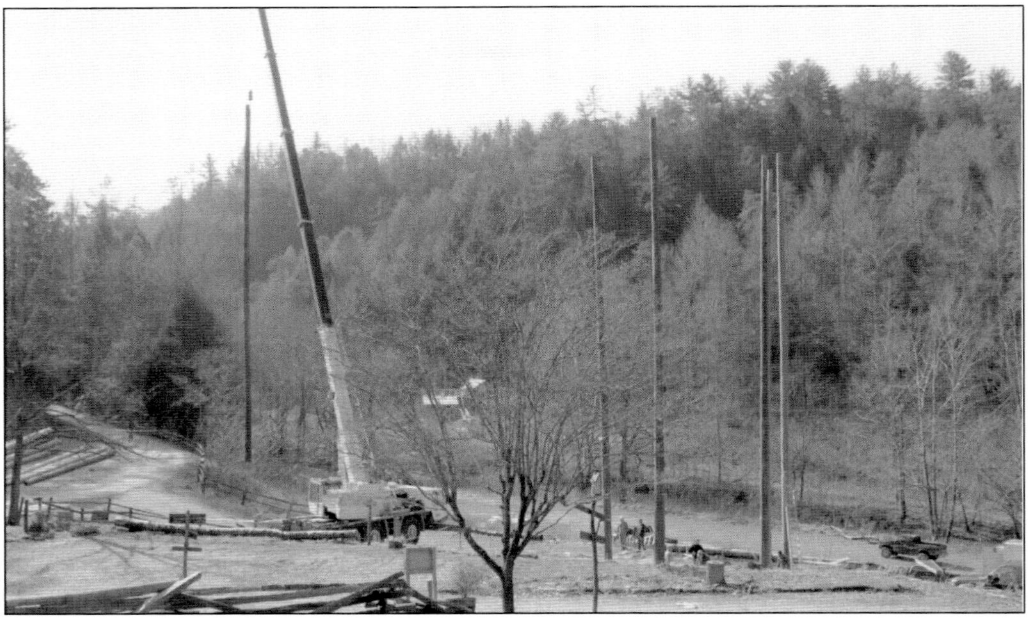

A crane was used to lift the massive center posts for the construction of the Gorilla, the highest rock climbing wall in Tennessee. The Gorilla hovers 60 feet above the ground and features five lanes that challenge all skill levels. (Courtesy of Stephanie Postlewaite.)

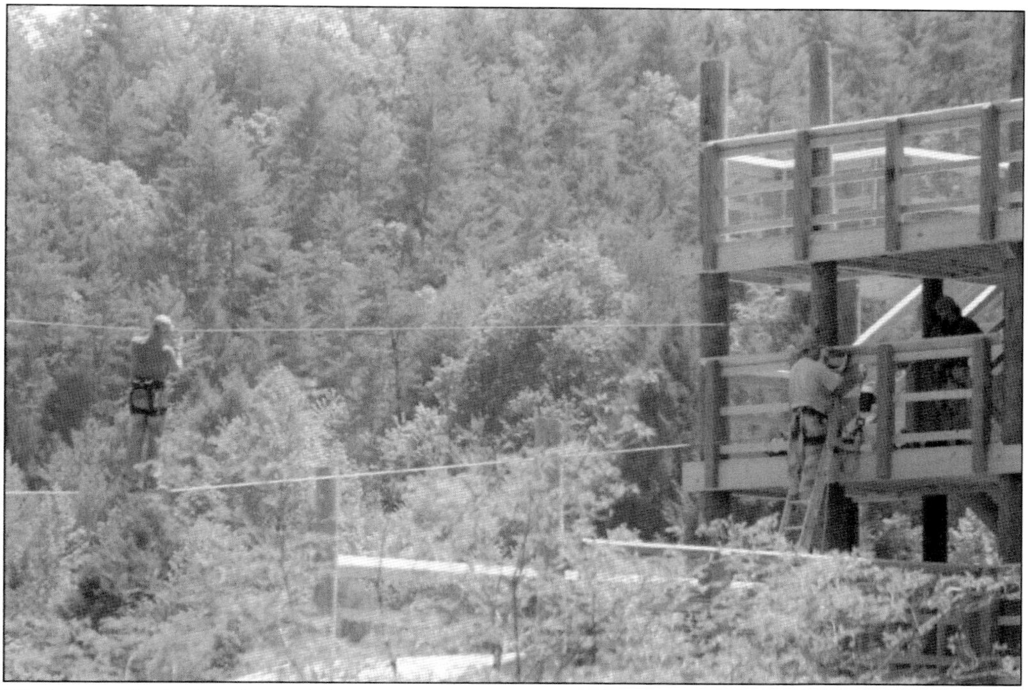

Workers walk the last line of the Goliath zip line course. The final line leads from a platform located in the hills surrounding Foxfire Mountain to the Gorilla, the highest rock climbing wall in Tennessee. The lines are subjected to rigorous daily checks. Such attention to detail has allowed Foxfire Mountain to maintain some of the highest safety standards in the industry. (Courtesy of Stephanie Postlewaite.)

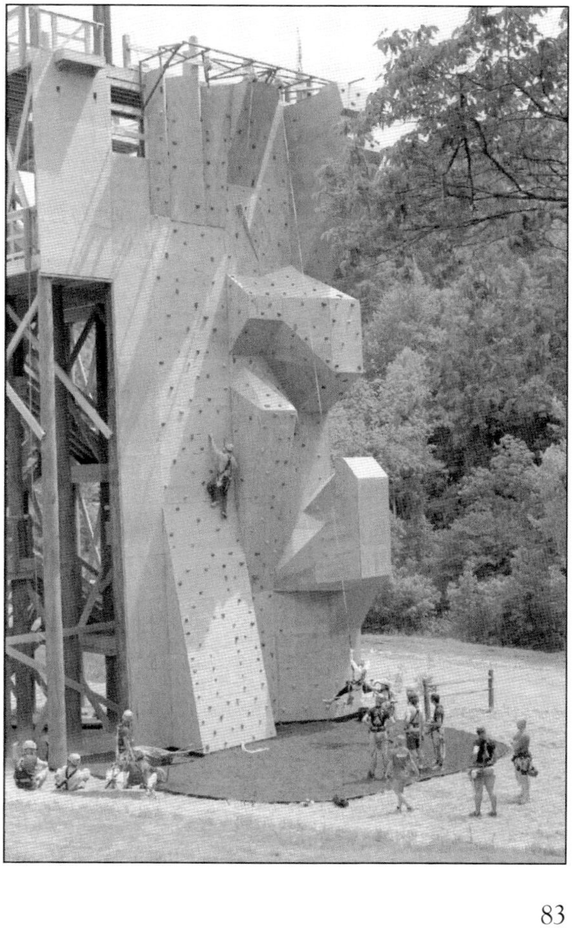

The Gorilla was opened in June 2014. Climbers are challenged on five lanes, with each becoming more treacherous than the last. (Courtesy of Stephanie Postlewaite.)

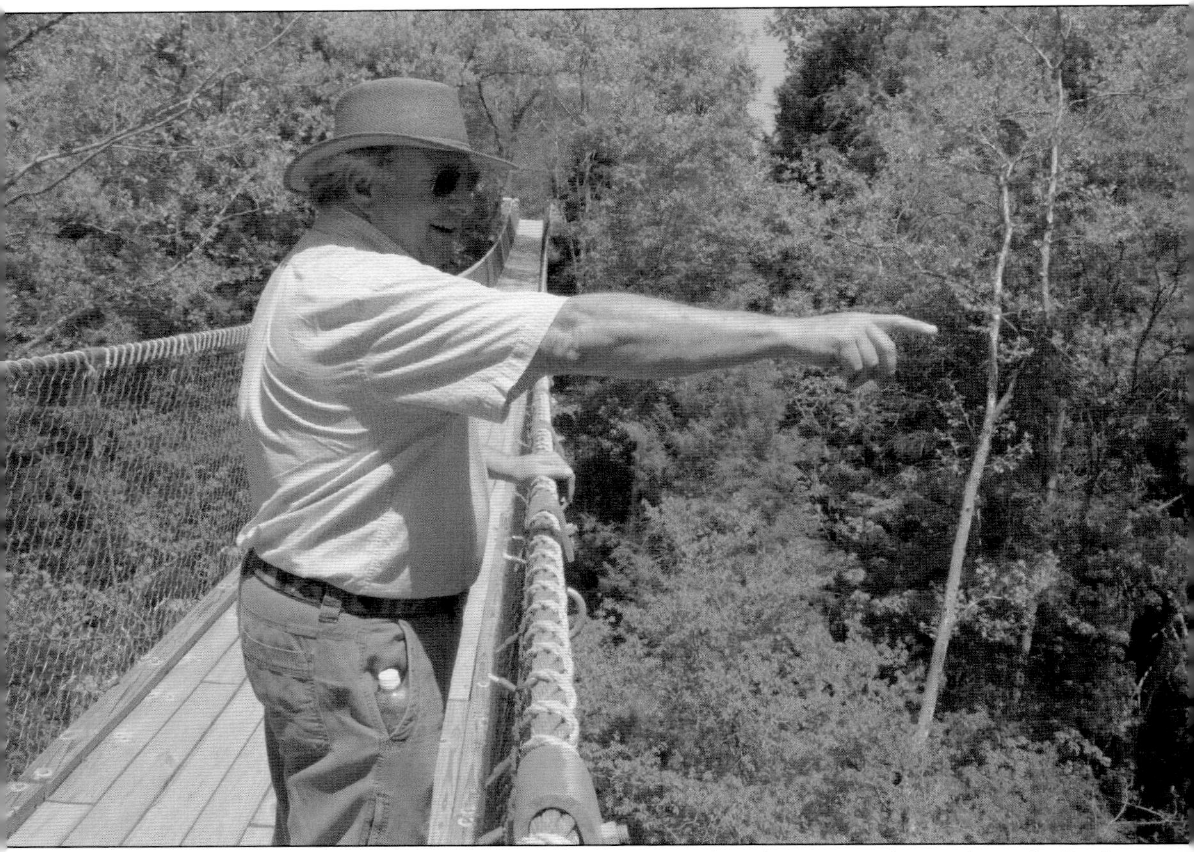

Marc Postlewaite, the founder of Foxfire Mountain Family Adventure Park, stands on the Bridge to Prosperity, the longest swinging bridge in the United States. At 355 feet in length, the bridge at Foxfire Mountain is longer than a football field. The bridge was inspired by an international organization that builds swinging bridges in Third World countries to make it possible for villagers to gain access to better job opportunities, medical needs, and educational opportunities. Postlewaite had the bridge built at Foxfire Mountain in hopes of raising awareness of the need for such structures in developing nations. A donation box at the bridge has raised thousands of dollars for charitable organizations including the Boys & Girls Clubs of America, Americans Helping Americans, and Bridges to Prosperity. (Courtesy of Stephanie Postlewaite.)

Three

Schools, Churches, and Institutions

No religious denomination has had a greater impact on the lives of the people of eastern Sevier County than the Methodist Episcopal Church. It was the Methodist Episcopal Church that funded a mission to build a community.

In 1919, Dr. John Burnett, a Methodist minister, presented a missionary plan to the church at its annual meeting in New York; the church approved his plan to create a community in the remote area of Emert's Cove. With the help of Rev. Eli Pittman of Elmira, New York, Burnett secured $15,000 for the project. In 1920, Burnett purchased 135 acres and construction on 16 buildings began. This took two years and provided jobs to many people in the area who had never held a job away from the family farm.

In late 1920, the school opened, and 100 students from the eastern Sevier County area enrolled. To honor Dr. Pittman, who worked tirelessly in New York to raise funds for the construction of the community school, it was named the Pittman Community Center. The school eventually expanded to included 1,500 acres, with 16 buildings and a student body of 240 students, operating with an annual budget of $9,000. The community included a general store, a post office, and a small medical clinic. The area was incorporated in 1974, and the name of the town was changed to Pittman Center. Today, the town has a population of 528. It is located in the foothills of the Great Smoky Mountain National Park.

Before the establishment of Pittman Center, numerous community schools and churches dotted the region. The schools were built by men in the community; many also served as teachers. The same men who constructed the schools performed maintenance on the buildings; they received no compensation, as their work was voluntary.

Among the many churches that dotted the area were Shults Grove United Methodist Church, Webb's Creek Methodist Church, Pearl Valley Methodist Church, Richardson's Cove Methodist Church, and Jones Cove Methodist Church. The church served as the epicenter of each community.

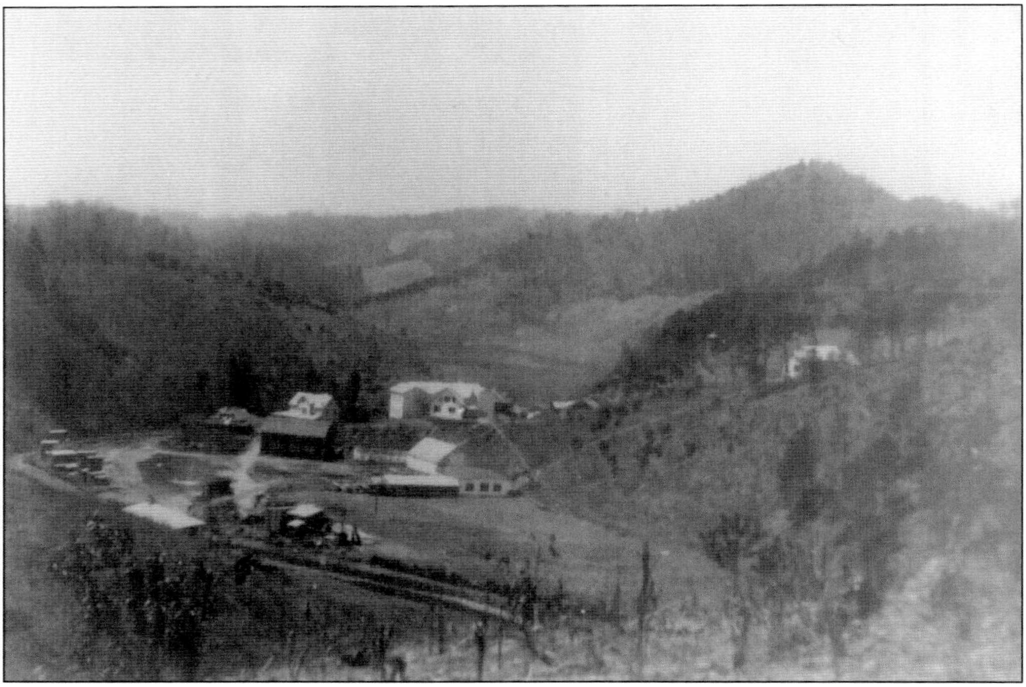

Here is Pittman Community Center as it appeared soon after completion in the early 1920s. The home of Dr. R.F. Thomas stands in the foreground. Thomas served as a community doctor in the area, often providing free medical care to the residents. (Courtesy of Glen Cardwell.)

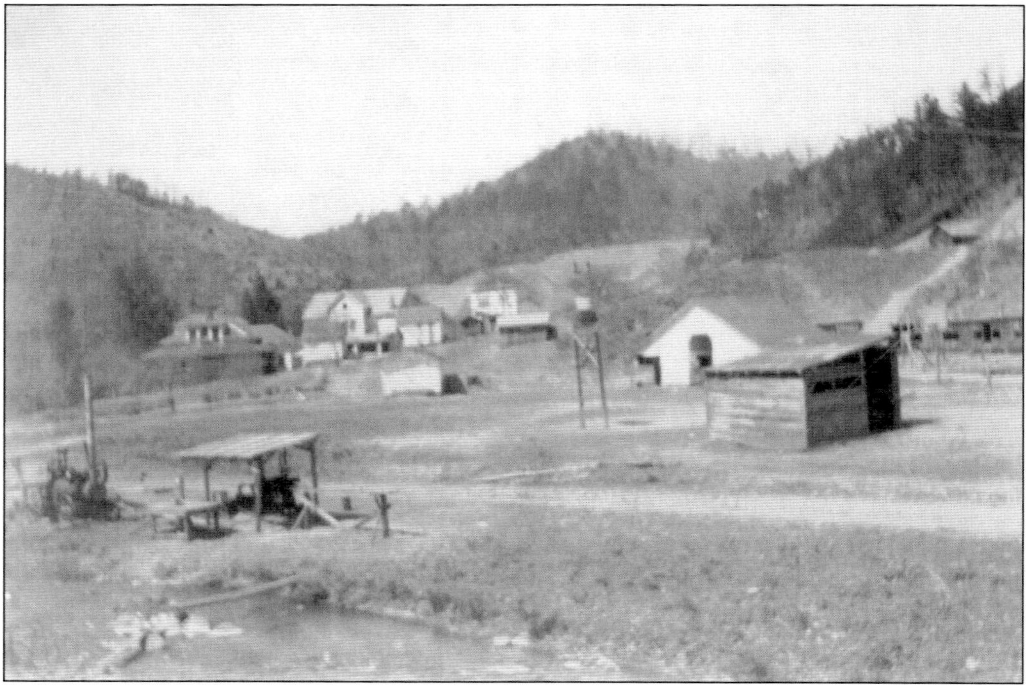

The Pittman Center School was constructed between 1919 and 1921. Before the school was constructed, the community utilized a one-room school where several grades studied simultaneously. (Courtesy of Glen Cardwell.)

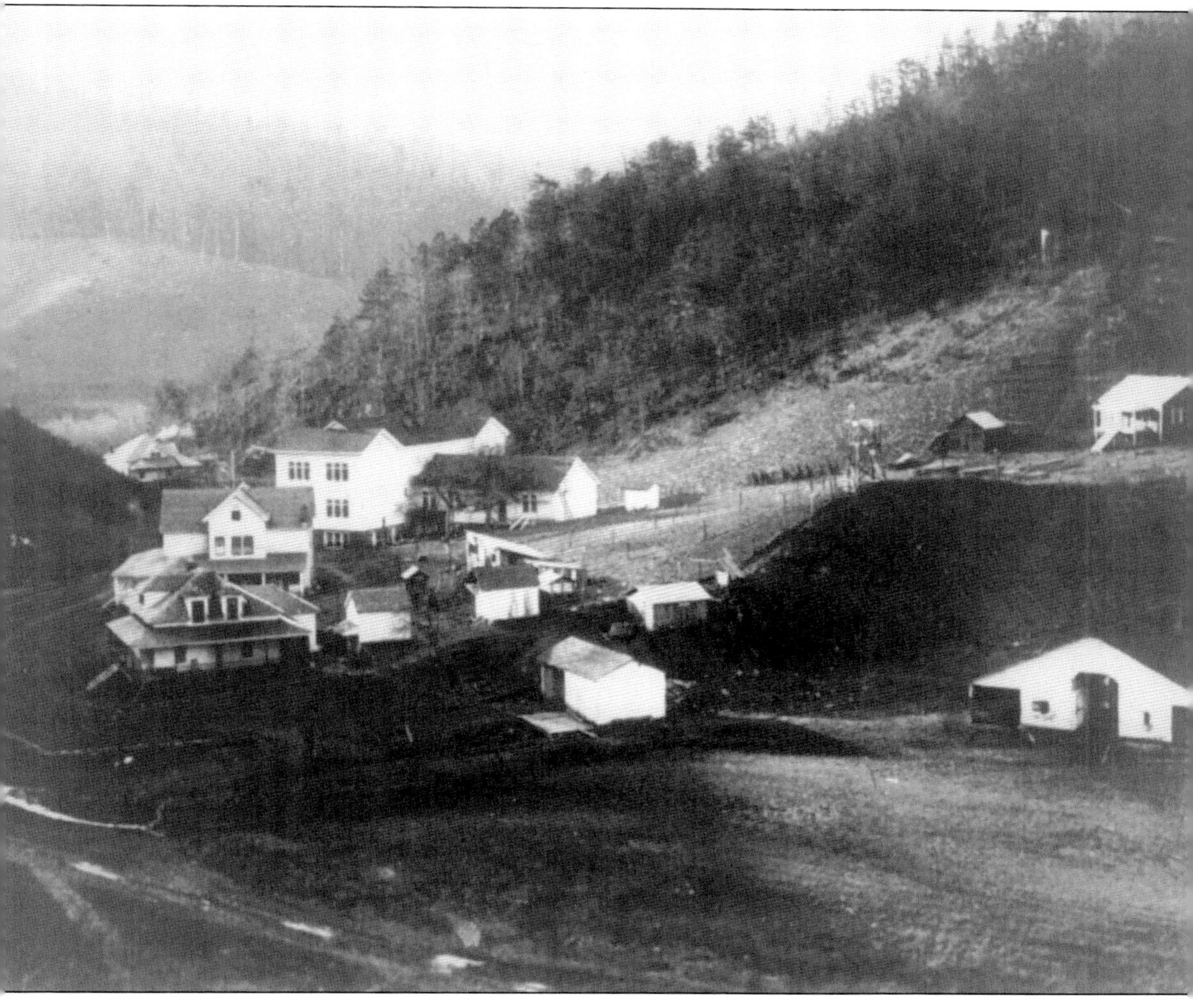

The campus of Pittman Community Center was completed in 1921. Once completed, it served the educational and medical needs of many in eastern Sevier County; it also was a retail outlet in the area. (Courtesy of Glen Cardwell.)

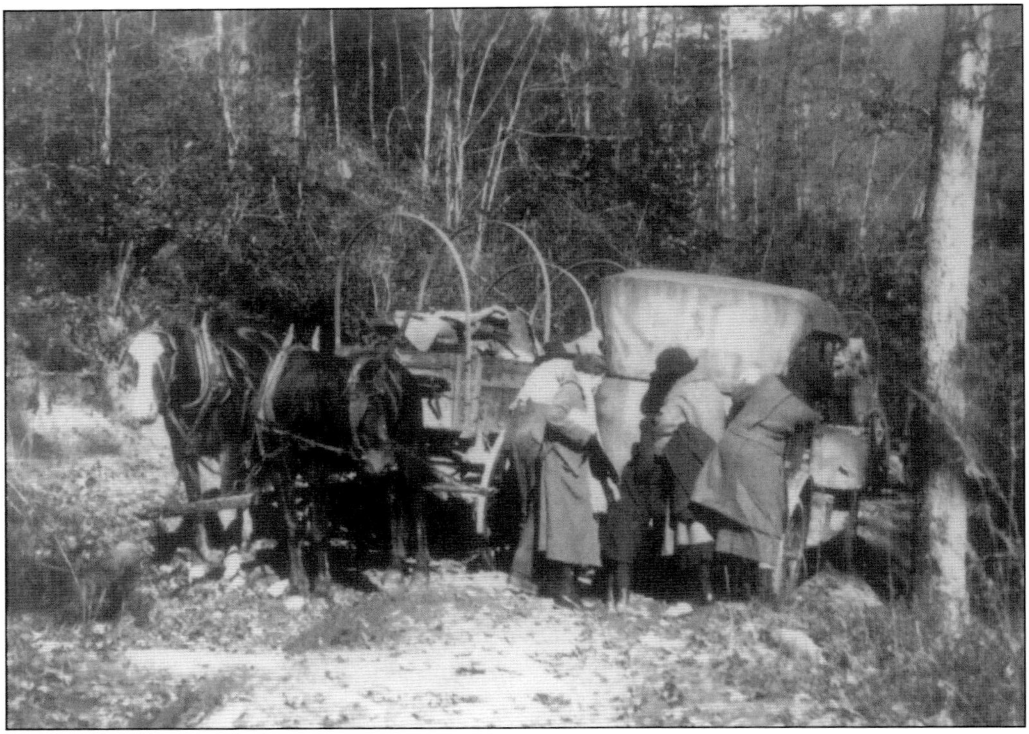

This 1920 photograph features several Pittman Community Center schoolteachers as they prepare to embark on a trip to neighboring Sevierville. The 20-mile round-trip could take as long as two days by horse or two to three hours by car. (Courtesy of Glen Cardwell.)

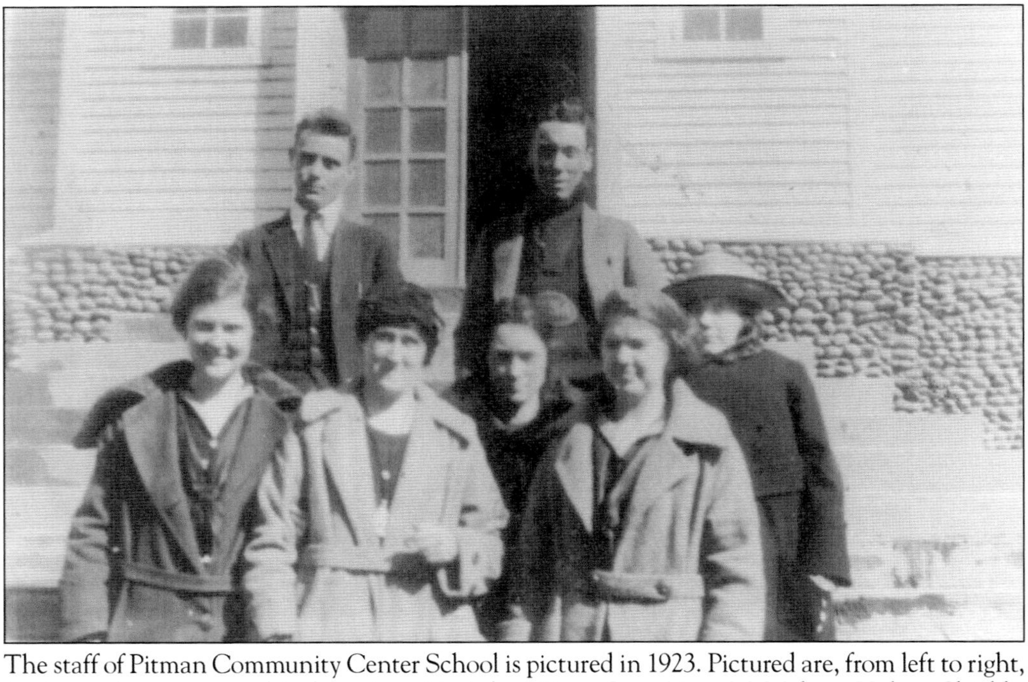

The staff of Pitman Community Center School is pictured in 1923. Pictured are, from left to right, Jessie Mecham, principal Helen Wesp, J.J. Asher, Dicia Cate, Nora McMahan, Hobart Shields, and unidentified. (Courtesy of Glen Cardwell.)

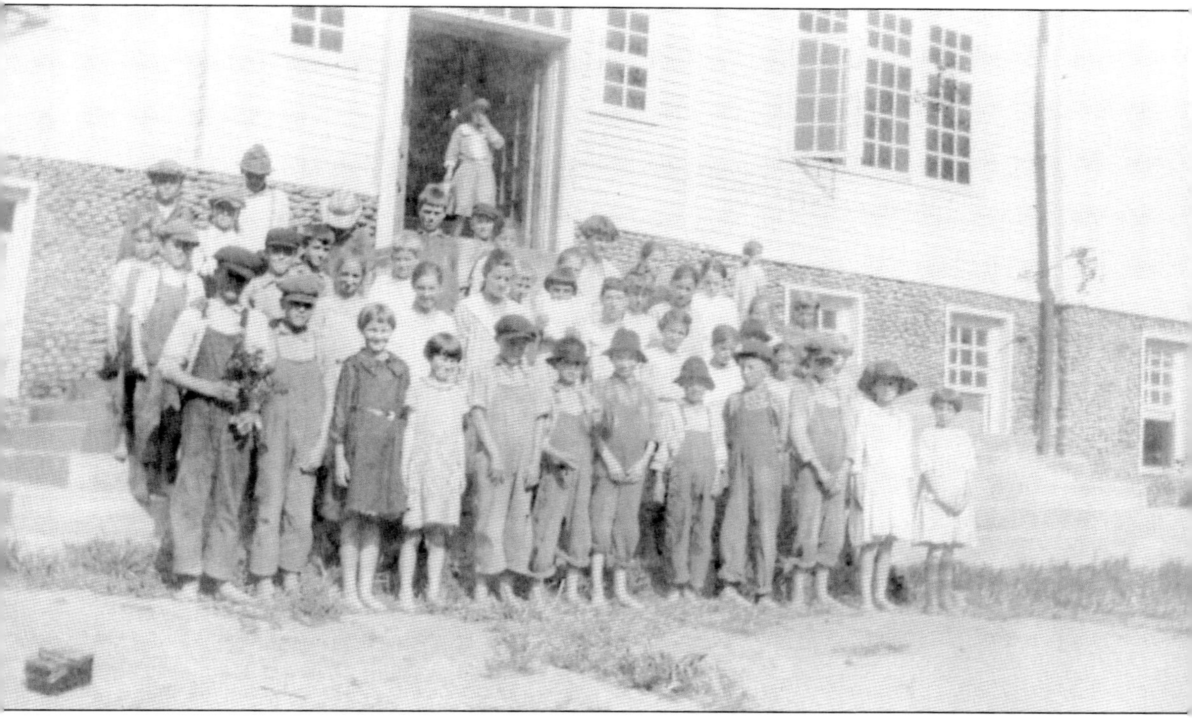

The fifth-and-sixth-grade class at Pittman Center is pictured in 1924. Many of the students are not wearing shoes. Many students did not own shoes, and other students did have shoes but preferred to wear them only when the weather was cold. (Courtesy of the Anne Handlon collection.)

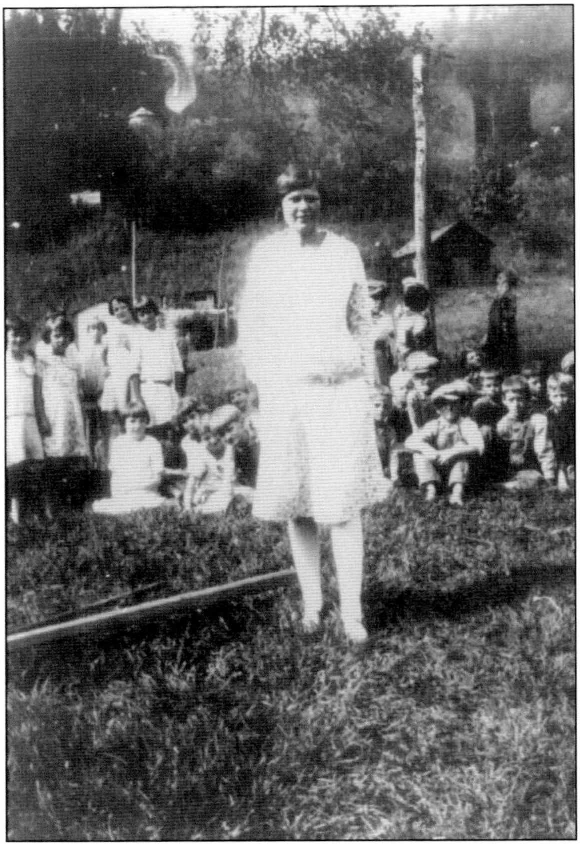

Eleanor Grace, a teacher at Pittman Center, is shown with her third-grade class in 1929. Many of the teachers came from out of state and resided at the teachers' cottage. (Courtesy of Carolyn Large Whaley.)

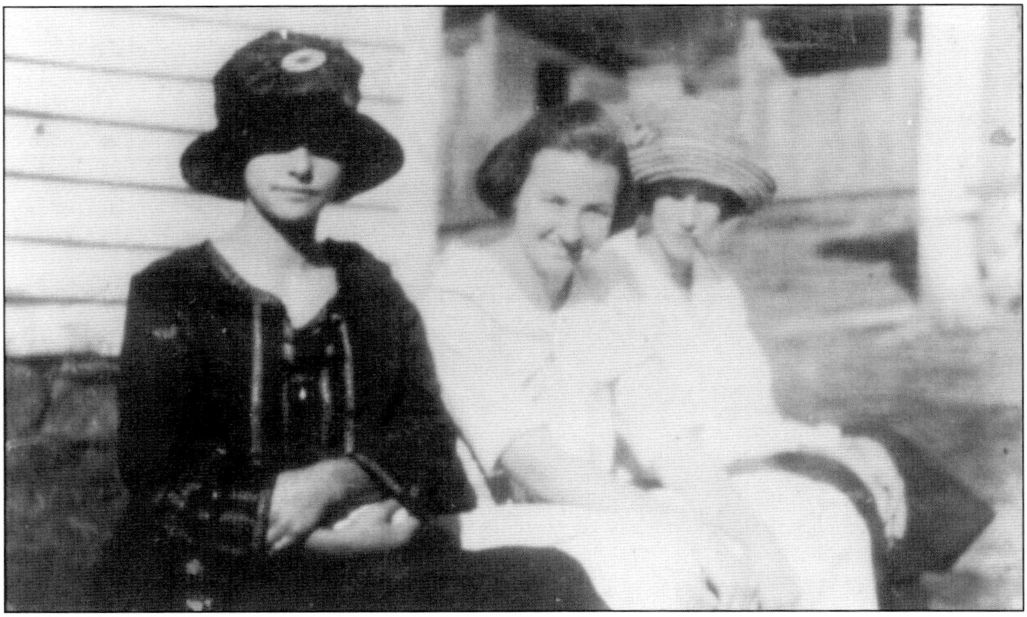

Early students at Pittman Community Center are pictured here in an undated photograph. Their clothing indicates the photograph may have been taken in the 1930s. They are, from left to right, Lizzie Lindsey, Tishie Huskey, and Ethel McGaha. (Courtesy of Glen Cardwell.)

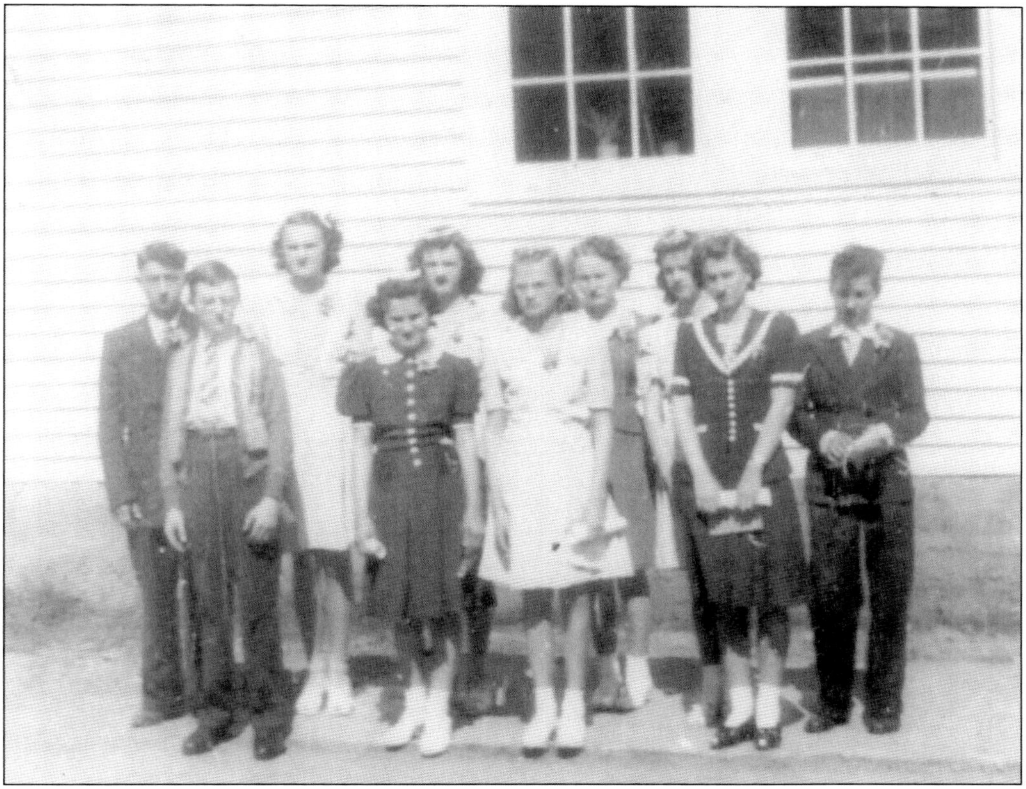

The graduating eighth-grade class at Pittman Community Center is pictured in 1944. (Courtesy of Glen Cardwell.)

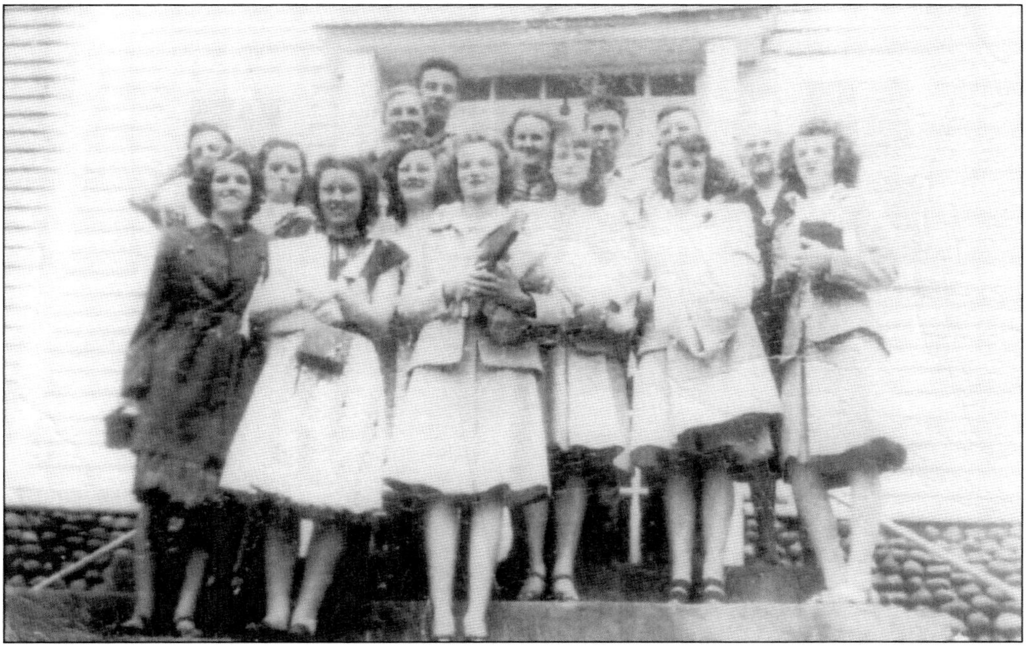

The Pittman Community Center graduating class of 1947 is shown here. Many graduates left the area to seek job opportunities. (Courtesy of Glen Cardwell.)

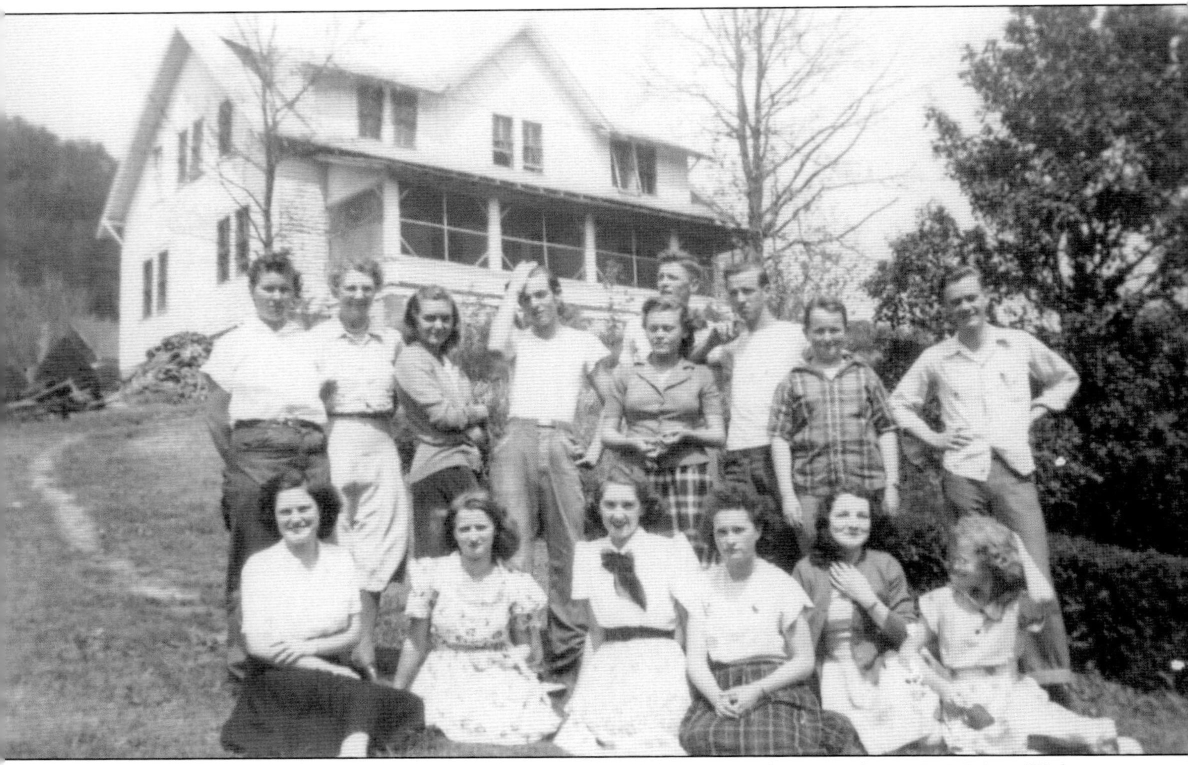

]The Pittman Community Center chorus is pictured in a group photograph in 1949. Myra Wakeman served as the music teacher. (Courtesy of Glen Cardwell.)

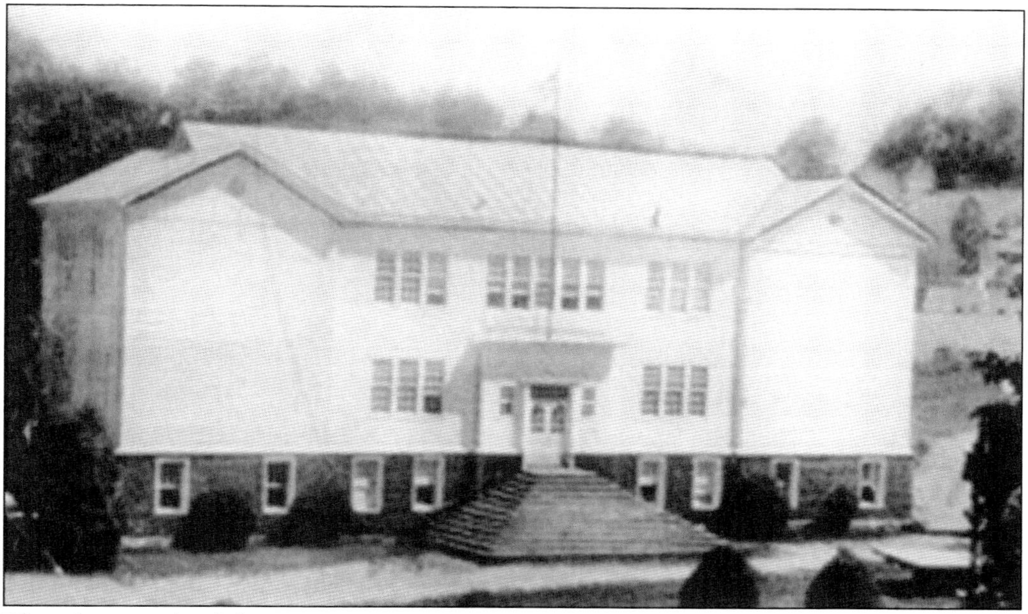

This photograph of the Pittman Community Center High School was taken shortly after it opened in 1921. The campus also included a dormitory for students and cottages for teachers. (Courtesy of Glen Cardwell.)

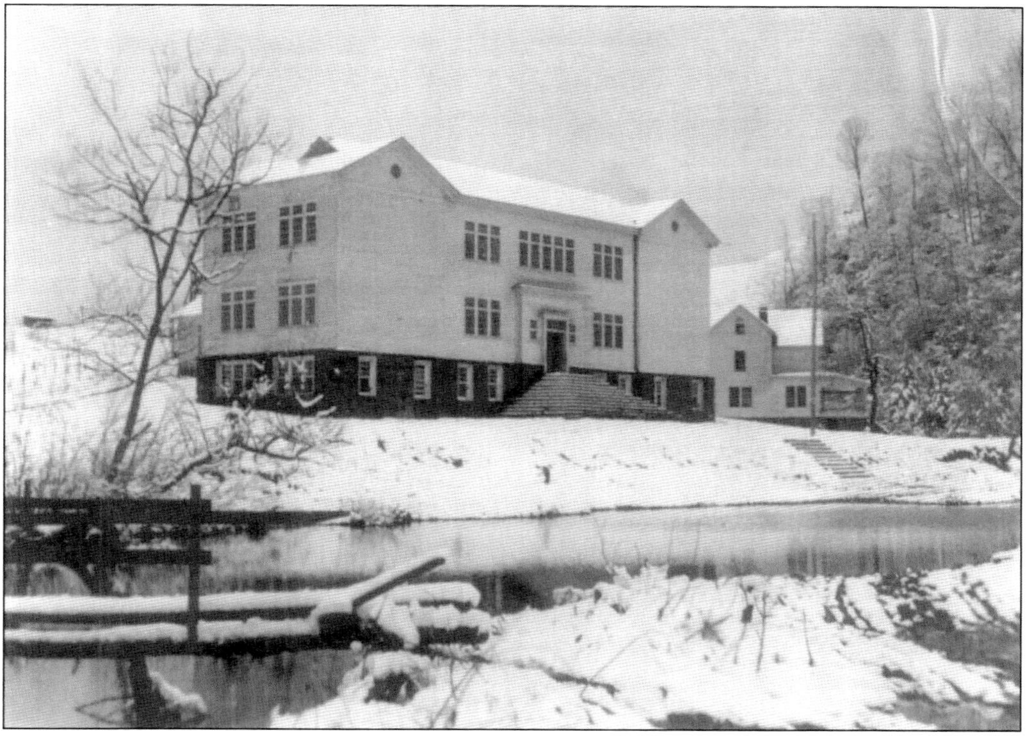

The Pittman Community Center High School is pictured here on a cold, wintry day shortly after completion. The dropout rate among students was high, as many boys left school to join the service or left town for better job opportunities. Many girls dropped out to get married. (Courtesy of Glen Cardwell.)

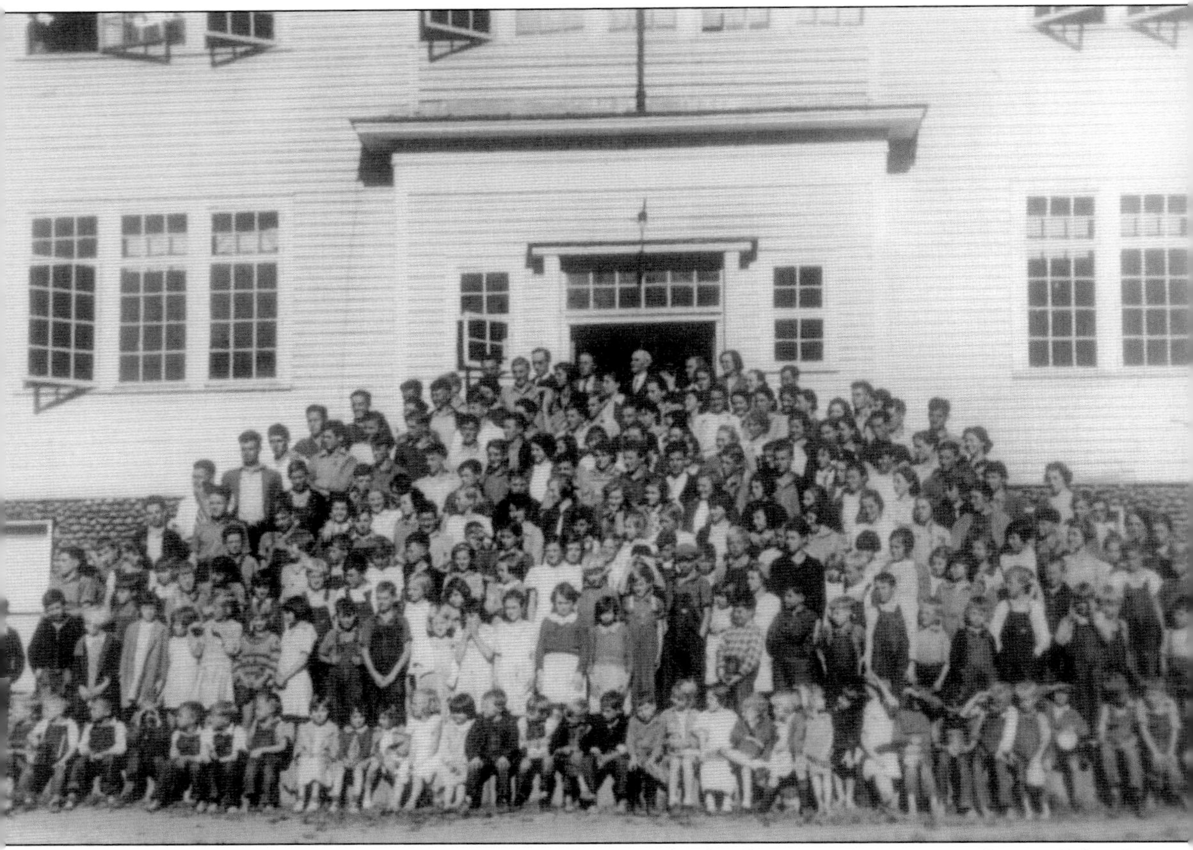

The 1937 class photograph features the entire student body of Pittman Community Center School and its faculty. Faye Huskey is the student sitting in the first row with her legs crossed. She later married Glen Cardwell, who now serves as mayor of the town. Glen is seated in the first row holding a lunch pail, which was actually a lard bucket. (Courtesy of Glen Cardwell.)

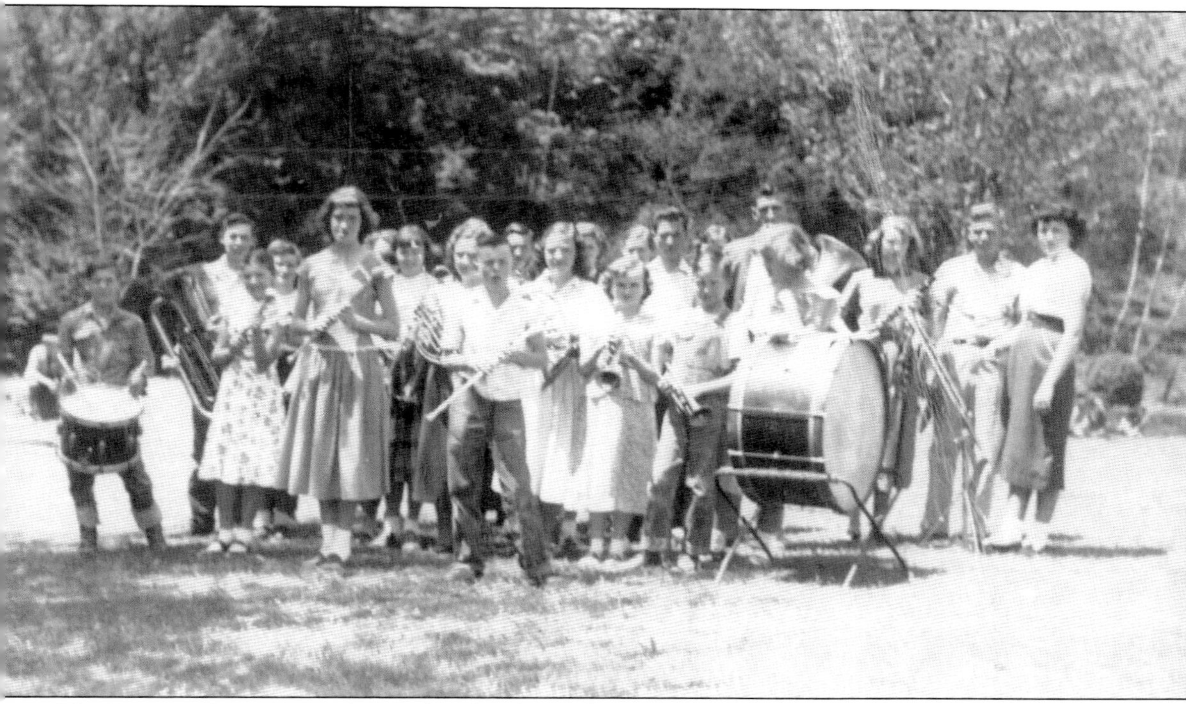

The Pittman Community Center band is shown here in the late 1950s. The band occasionally accompanied the basketball team for road games. For many students, these road games were the first time they traveled more than 20 miles from home. (Courtesy of Glen Cardwell.)

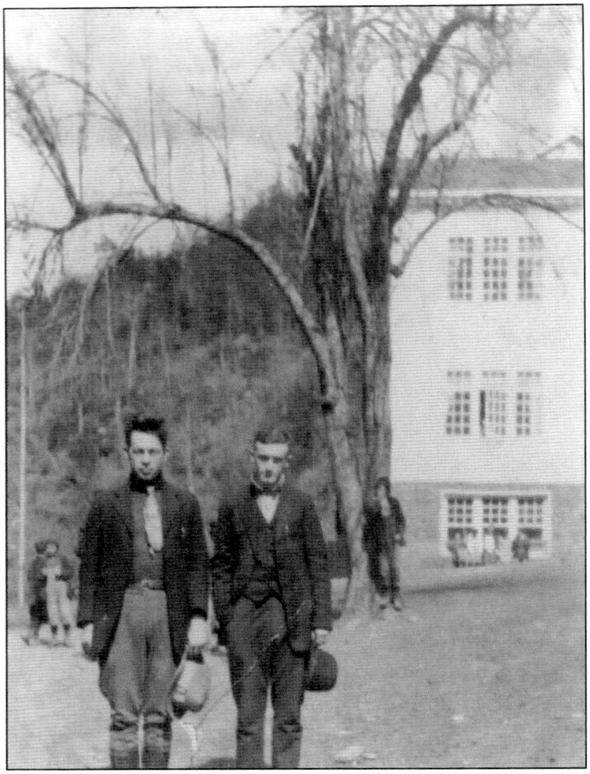

Luther Cook (left) and Garland Grubb are pictured standing in front of Pittman Center High School in 1921. The creation of the school by the Methodist Episcopal Church brought educational opportunities to many children and struck a blow against illiteracy in the area. (Courtesy of Glen Cardwell.)

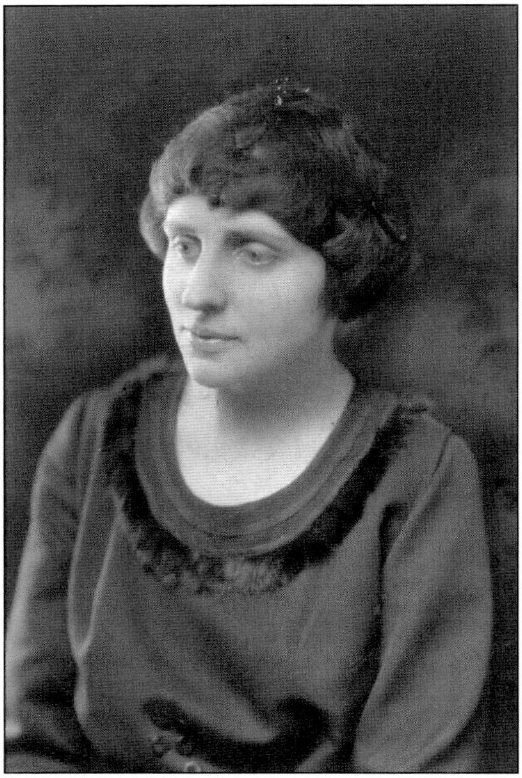

Miss Enkhauser was one of several schoolteachers to have moved to the community to teach school. Enkhauser taught at Webb Creek School. (Courtesy of Glen Cardwell.)

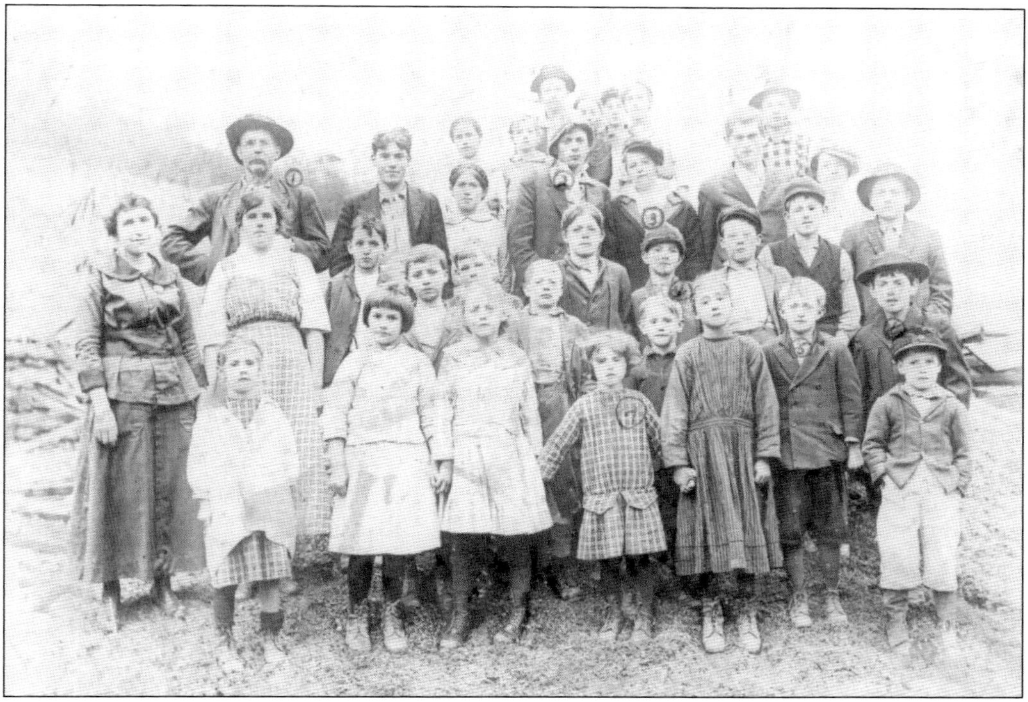

Isaac Huskey was the schoolmaster of the Webb Creek School, a precursor of the Pittman Center School. The Webb's Creek School later became the Webb's Creek United Methodist Church. (Courtesy of Glen Cardwell.)

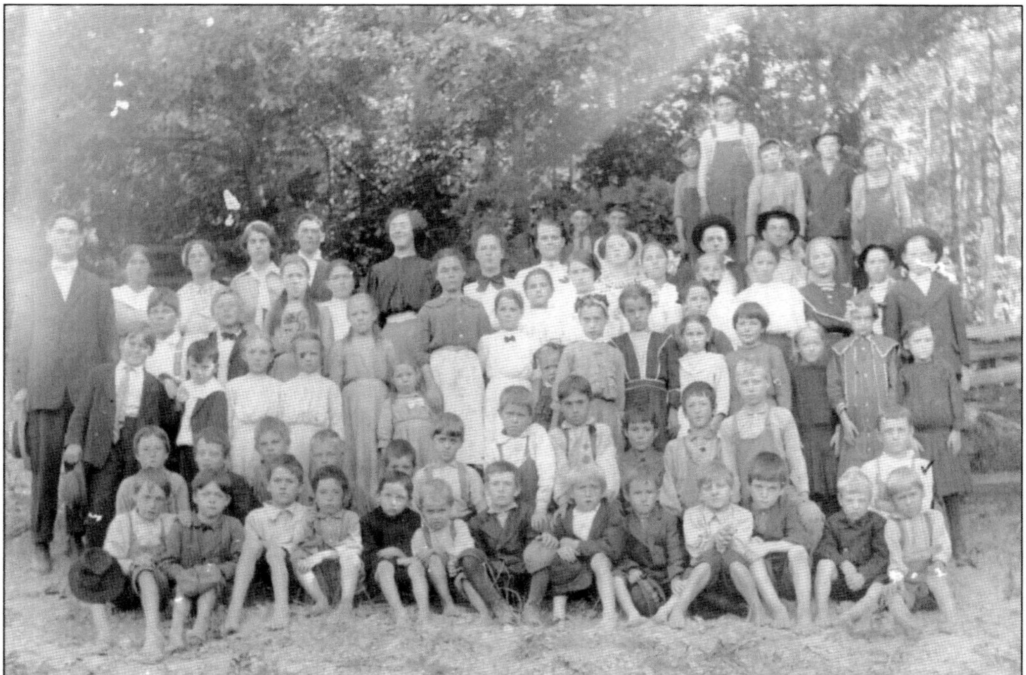

Columbus "Lum" Reagan was teacher of the Webb's Creek School class of 1908. Many of the teachers at the time were volunteers. (Courtesy of Glen Cardwell.)

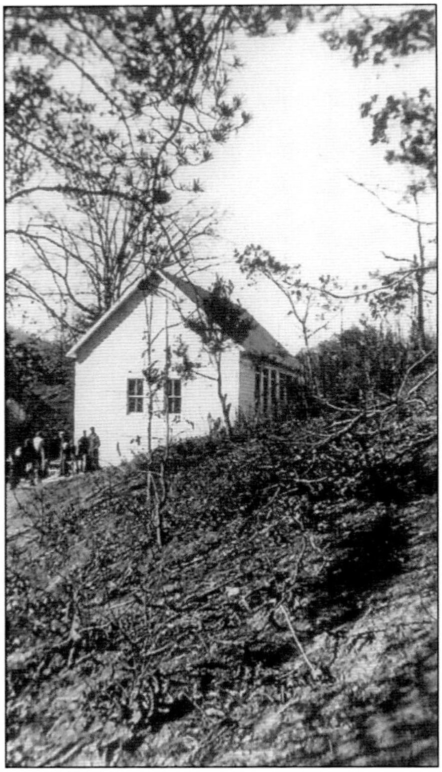

The McMahan School sits on a hillside in Pearl Valley near Richardson's Cove. The school had been newly remodeled. The McMahan family, for whom the school was named, was one of the first to settle in eastern Sevier County. (Courtesy of Jackie Underwood.)

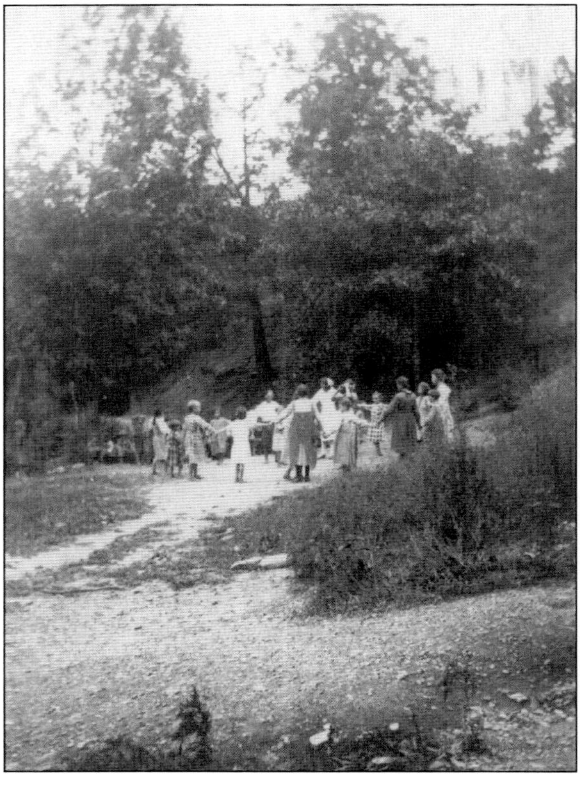

Children are pictured playing at school in the 1930s. Children had to use their imaginations as playgrounds had no man-made equipment. (Courtesy of Carolyn Large Whaley.)

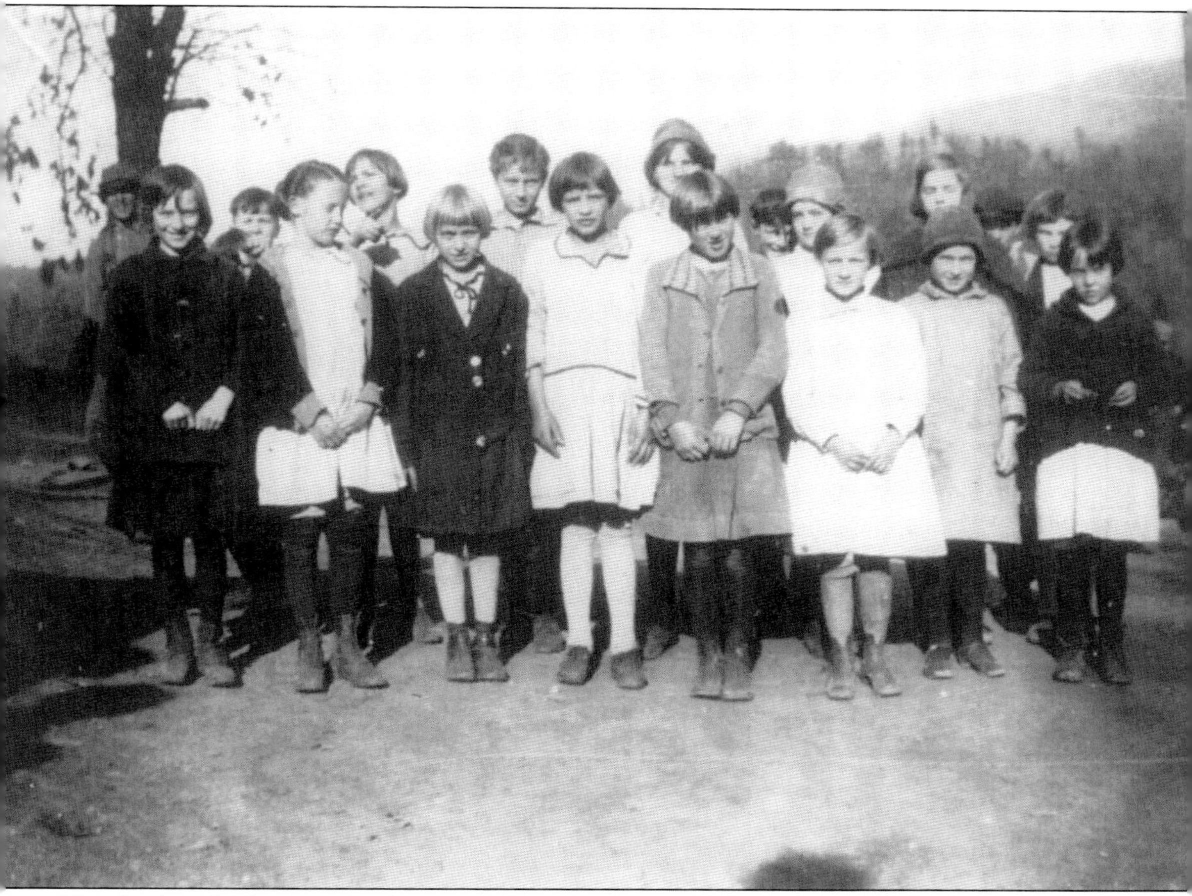

The third-grade class at Greenbrier School is pictured in 1925. Parents of the students in rural schools often helped with maintenance of the buildings. (Courtesy of Carolyn Large Whaley.)

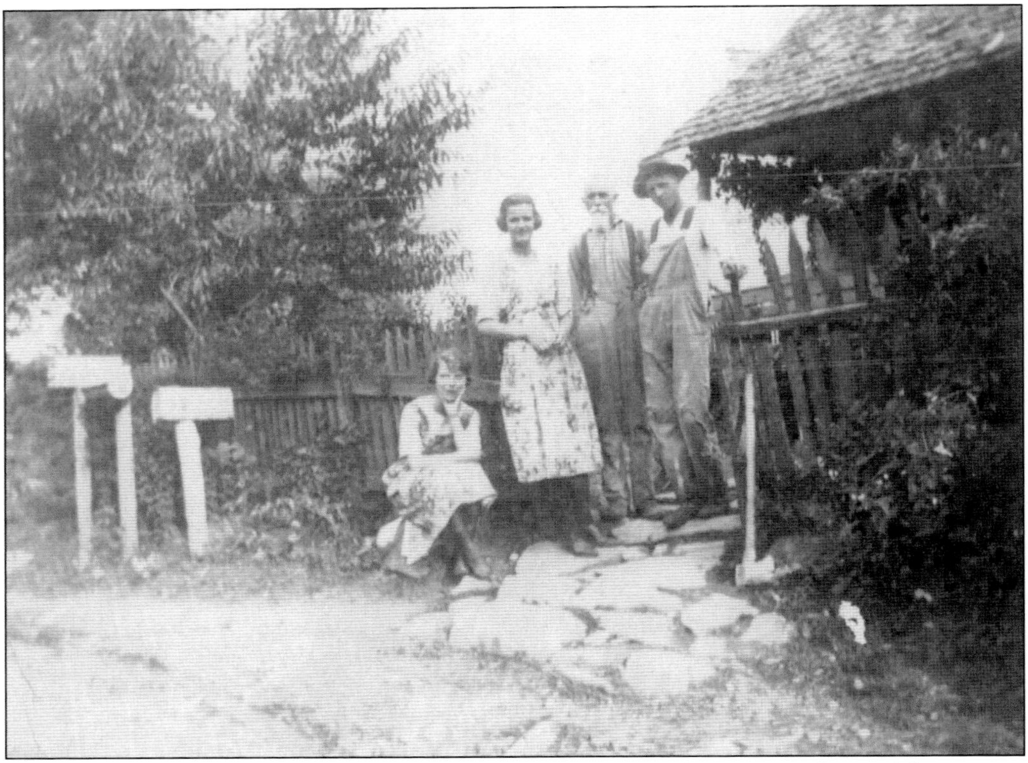

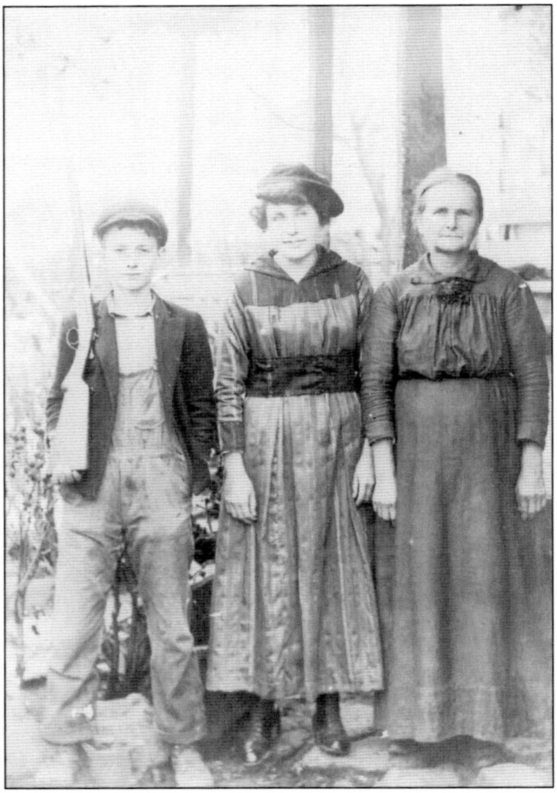

Two teachers pose in front of the home of Bud McCarter. Until the teachers' dorm was built, teachers lived with the parents of their pupils. It provided the teachers an opportunity to get to know their students better. (Courtesy of Carolyn Large Whaley.)

Carl McCarter shoulders a gun while posing with an unidentified schoolteacher and his mother Josephine McCarter. In the early days of Pittman Center, teachers lived at the homes of the students. (Courtesy of Carolyn Large Whaley.)

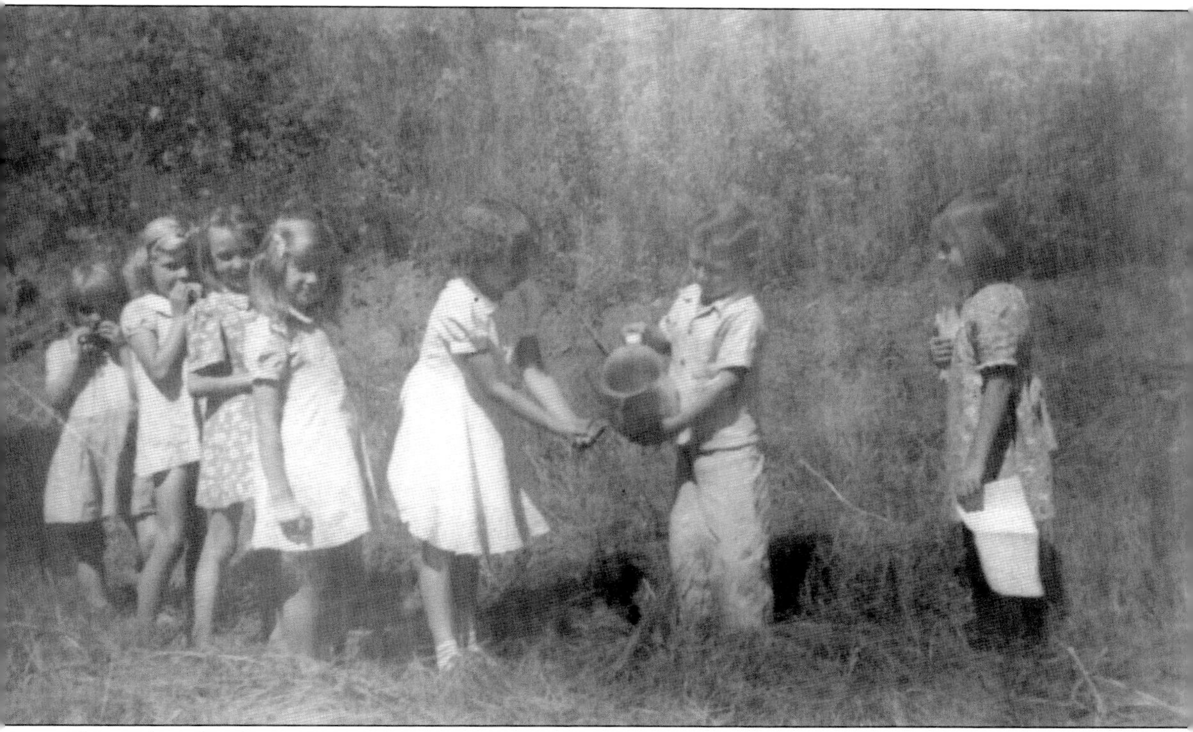

The early schools in eastern Sevier County had no indoor restrooms or indoor plumbing. Students went to the yard where they washed for lunch using a pail of water. (Courtesy of Glen Cardwell.)

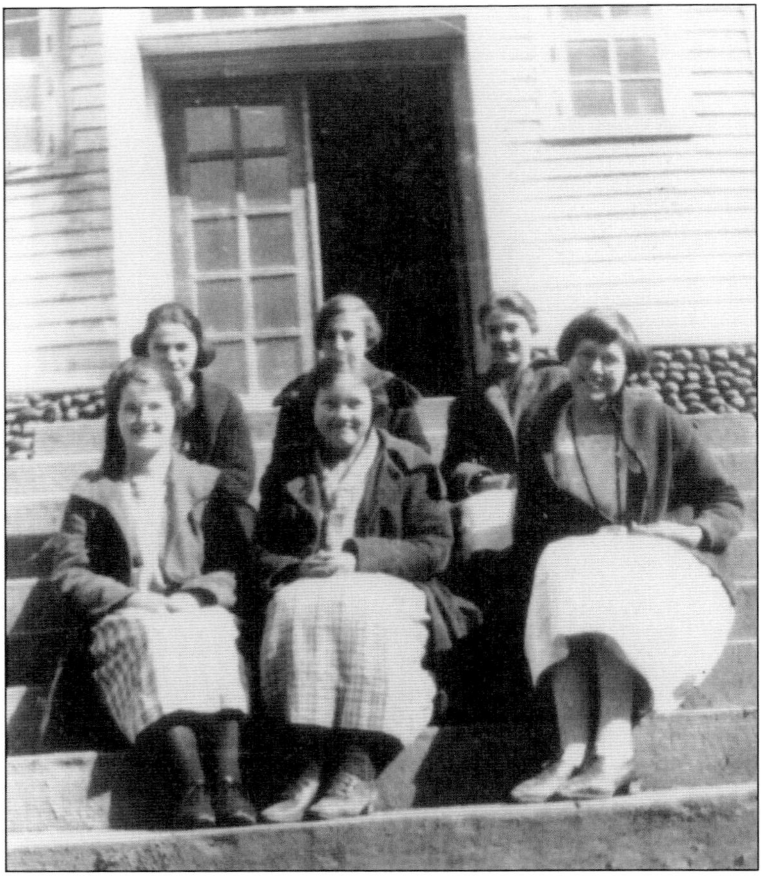

A group of schoolgirls is pictured in the 1920s. From left to right are Mamie Williams, Christine Ramsey, Roxie Headrick, Lizzie Lindsey, Lou Williams, and Eullale Ramsey. Before buses, many kids had to walk to school over muddy trails and roads. (Courtesy of Glen Cardwell.)

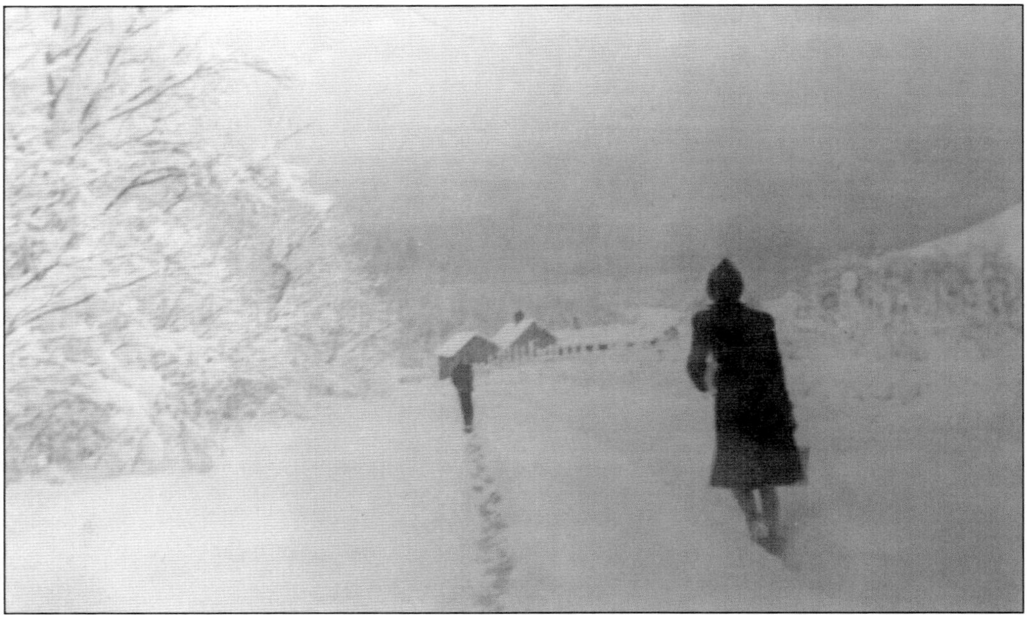

Many older people recount how they walked for miles through the snow to get to school. Cora Huskey could certainly make that claim. (Courtesy of Glen Cardwell.)

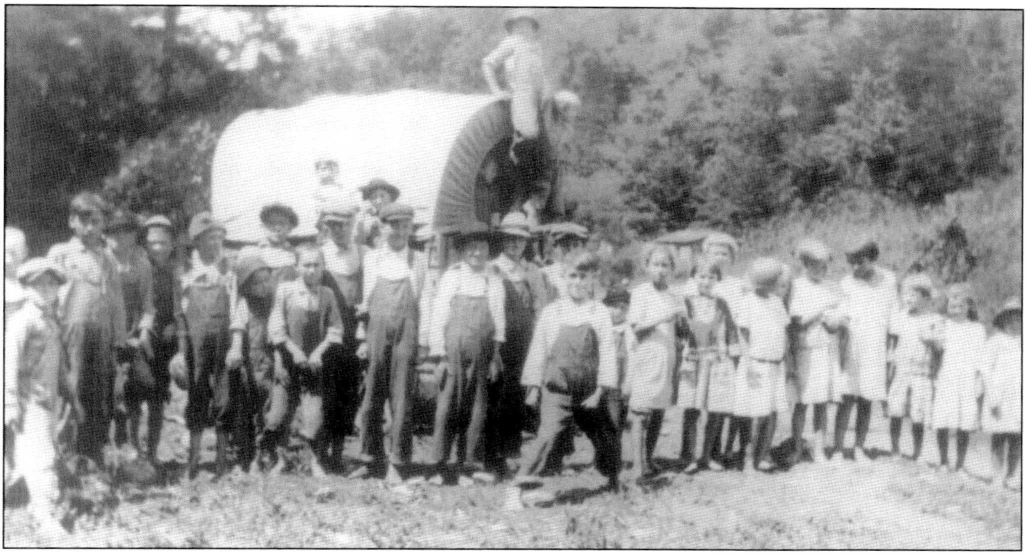

In the days before school buses began running in the area, children were taken to school in covered wagons. The wagon master or driver would ride the horse-drawn wagon from home to home to pick up children. Often, these wagons were manned by the parents of the students. (Courtesy of Glen Cardwell.)

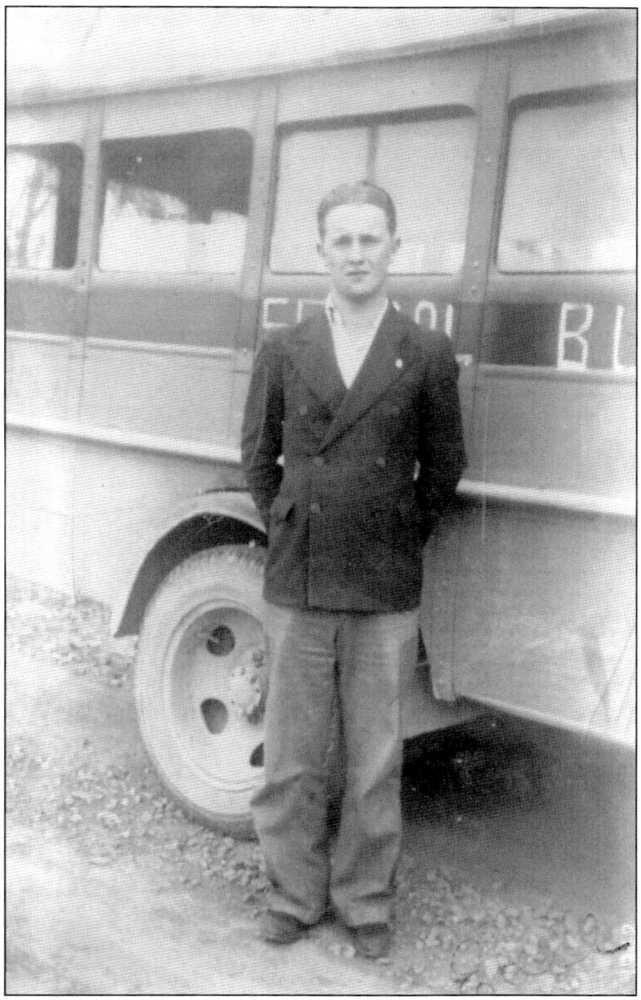

Earl Reagan stands in front of a school bus in 1930. This innovative form of transportation made school more accessible for students in the more rural areas of eastern Sevier County. Until the bus was purchased by the county, parents took their children to school in horse-drawn wagons. (Courtesy of Carolyn Large Whaley.)

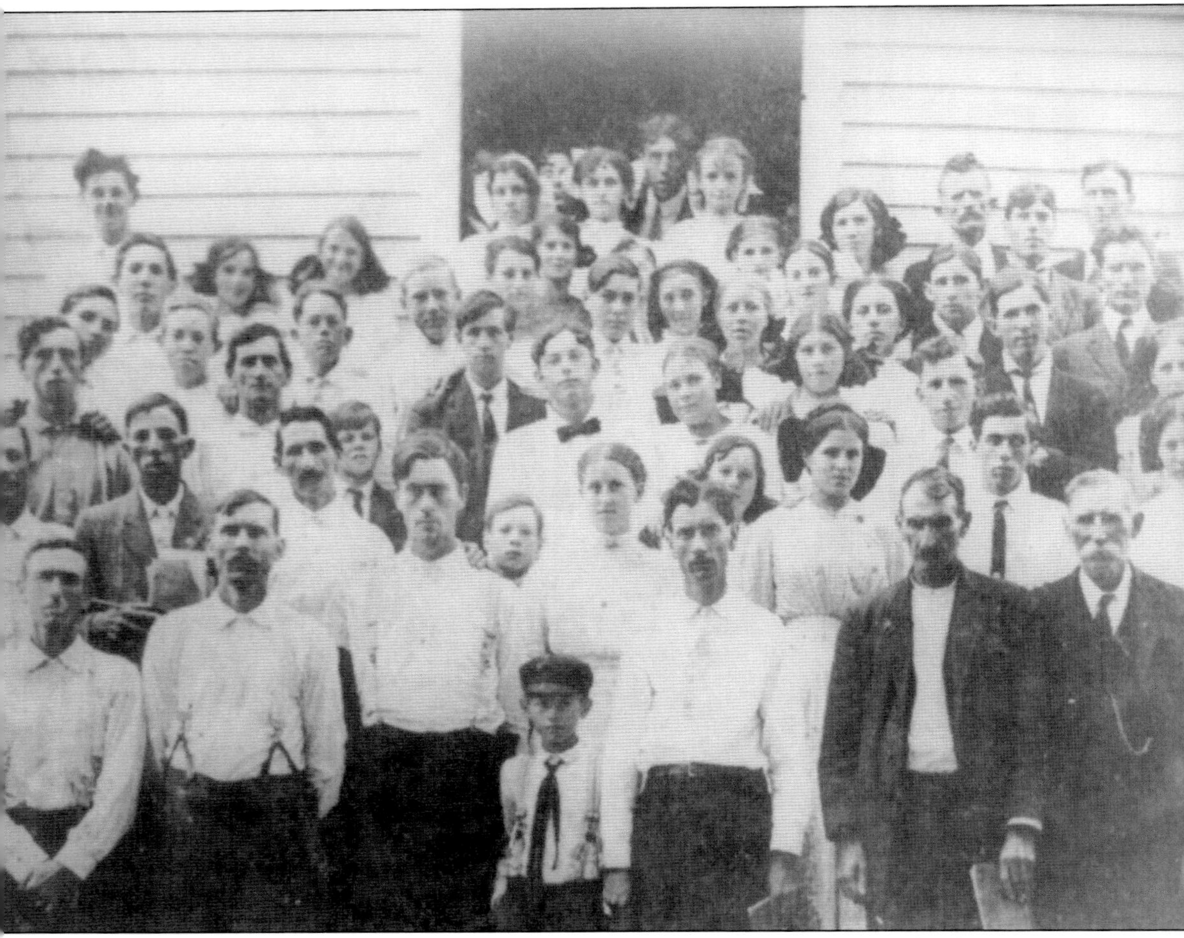

The Greenbrier Church, which once stood in the Greenbrier Community south of Pittman Center, was torn down by the government when the national park was completed. This photograph was taken in the late 1920s. When the park was built, the federal government purchased many buildings and homes and had them removed or destroyed. (Courtesy of Glen Cardwell.)

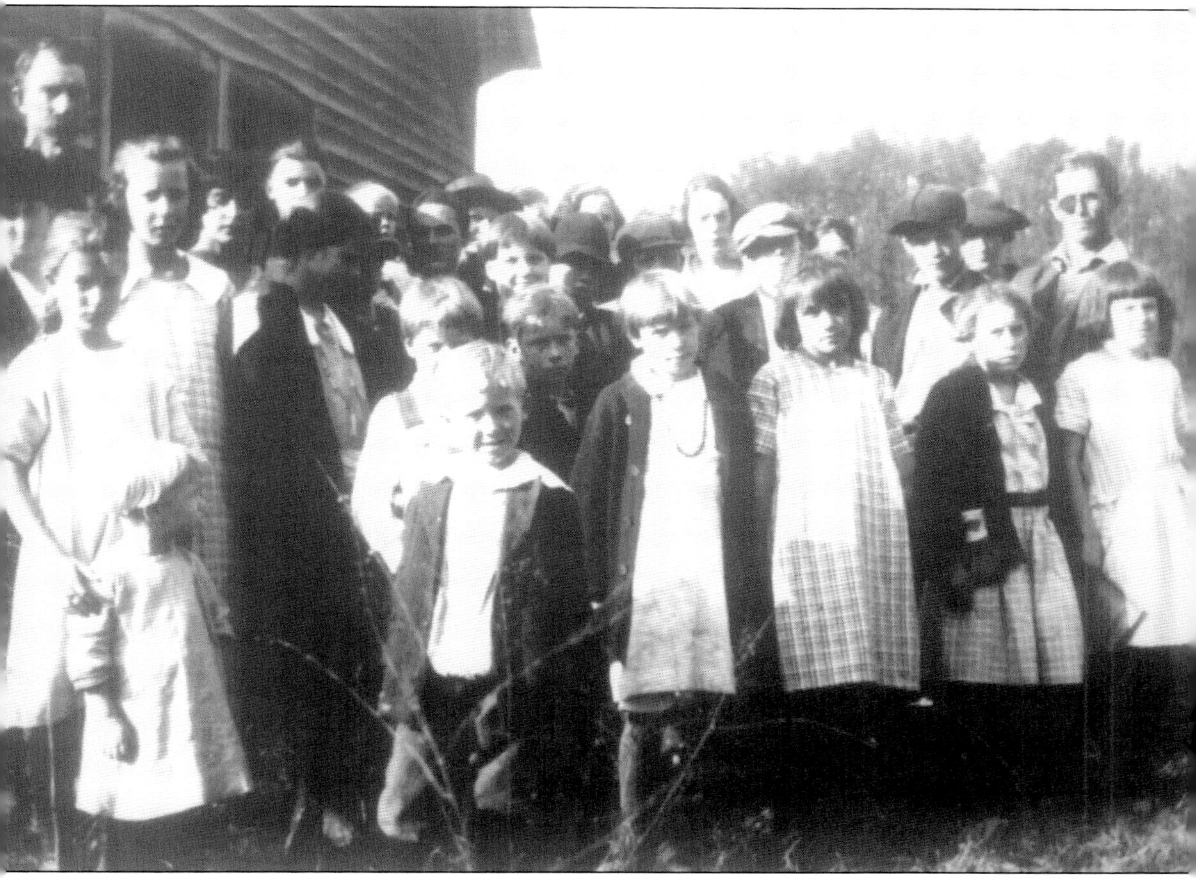

Evans Chapel Church No. 2 is pictured here in 1923 soon after the creation of Pittman Community Center. The church was one of several in the area that were torn down when the Great Smoky Mountains National Park was created. (Courtesy of Glen Cardwell.)

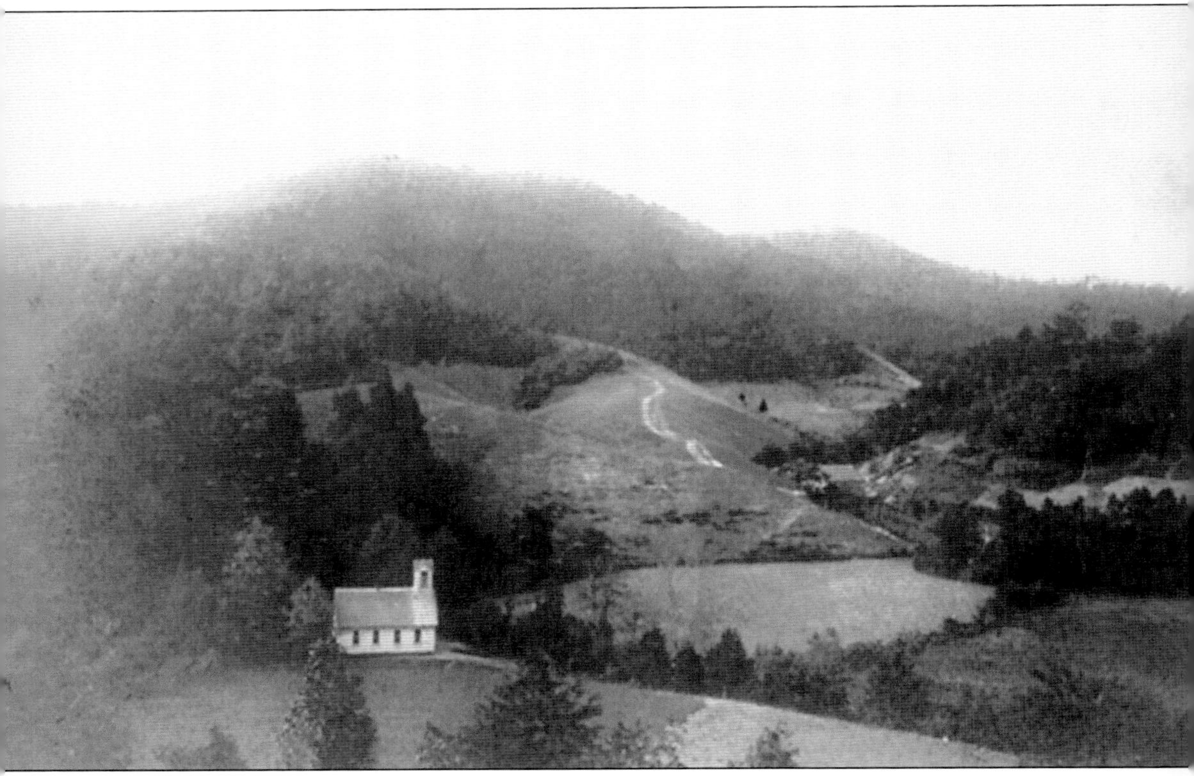

This photograph, taken in 1931, depicts Pearl Valley Church, located in Pearl Valley in eastern Sevier County. The tiny church sat in the shadows of the Great Smoky Mountains. The scenery of the majestic mountains as viewed from the church was breathtaking. A.R. McMahan donated the land on which the church was built. (Courtesy of Jackie Underwood.)

Shults Grove United Methodist Church near Webb Creek was one of the earliest churches in the area. The church is located near present-day Rocky Flats Road near Pittman Center. (Courtesy of Carolyn Large Whaley.)

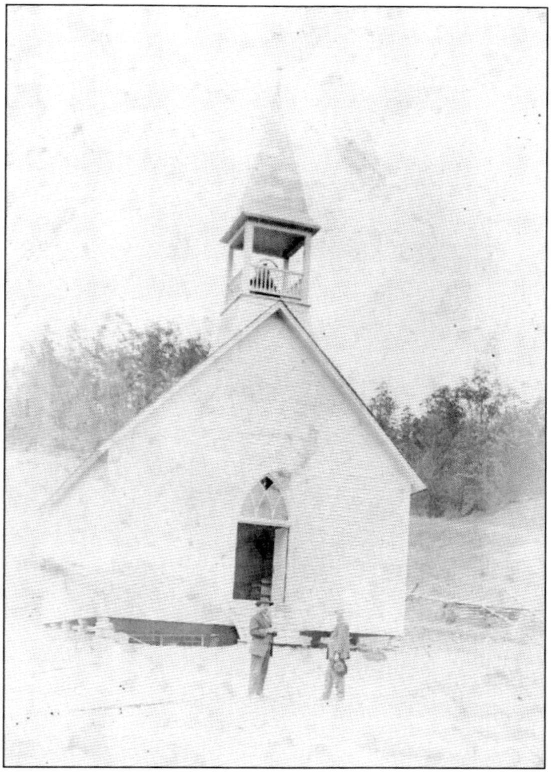

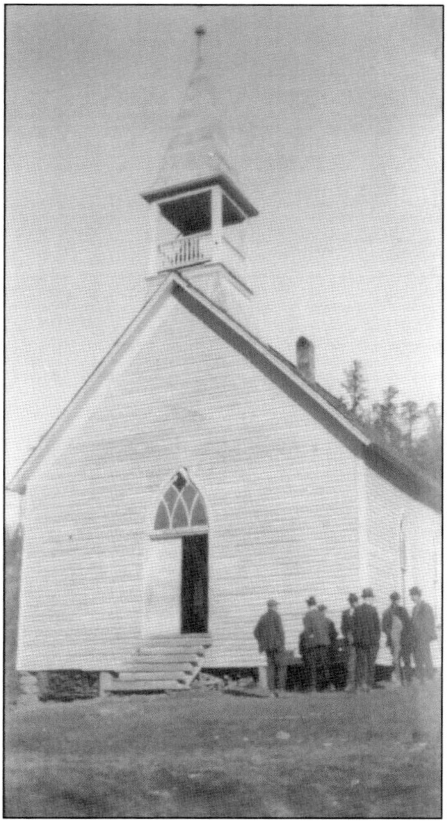

The Shults Grove United Methodist Church sits nestled in the foothills of Shults Mountain. The church was built on land donated by the Shults family in 1914. (Courtesy of Carolyn Large Whaley.)

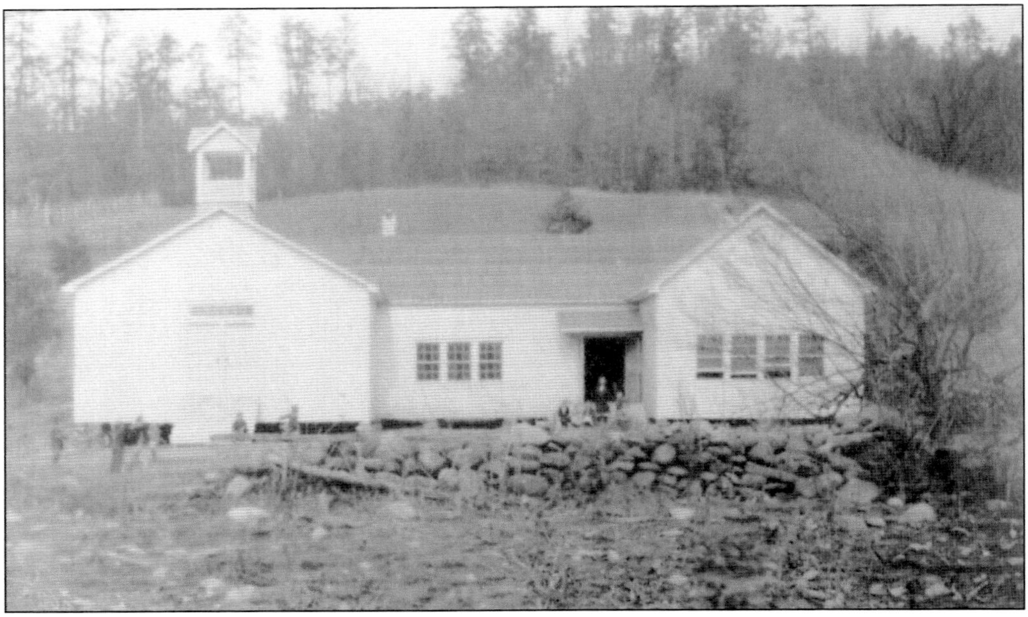

The Webb's Creek United Methodist Church is located near Pittman Center. The church served as a school until the 1950s. (Courtesy of Carolyn Large Whaley.)

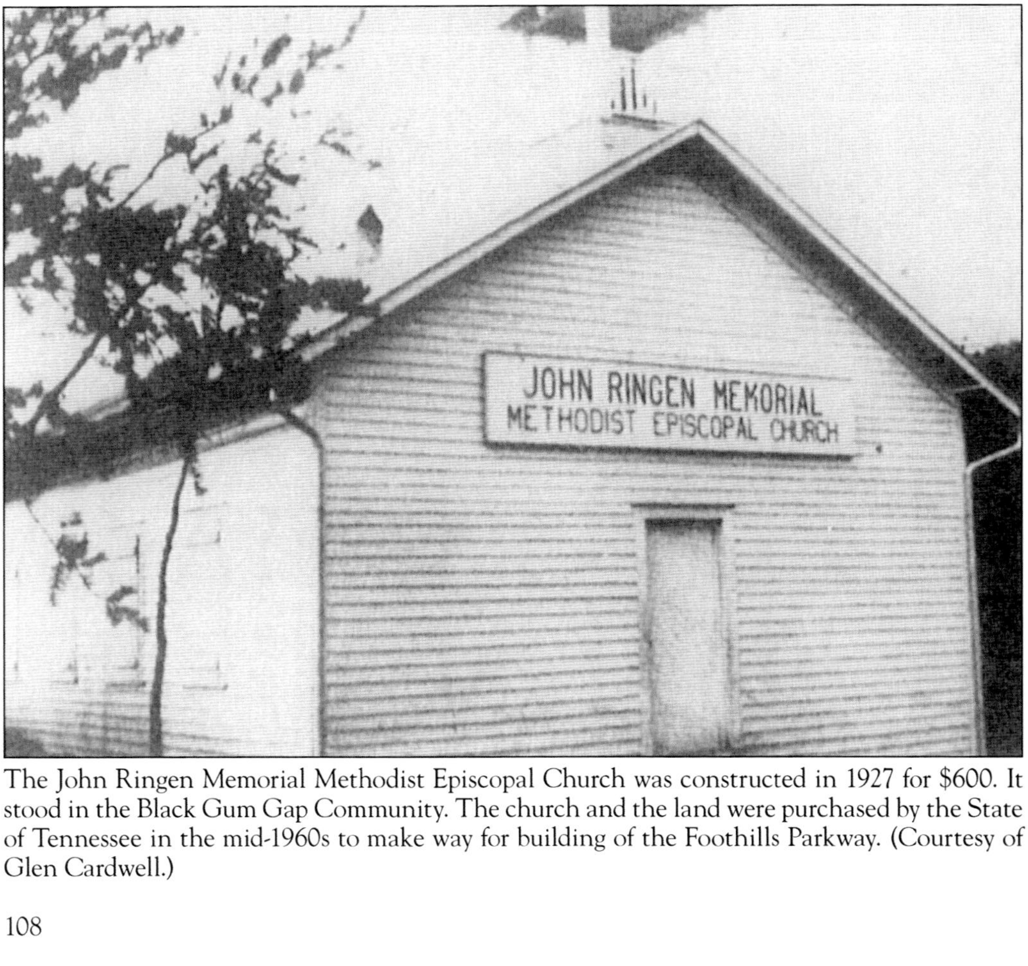

The John Ringen Memorial Methodist Episcopal Church was constructed in 1927 for $600. It stood in the Black Gum Gap Community. The church and the land were purchased by the State of Tennessee in the mid-1960s to make way for building of the Foothills Parkway. (Courtesy of Glen Cardwell.)

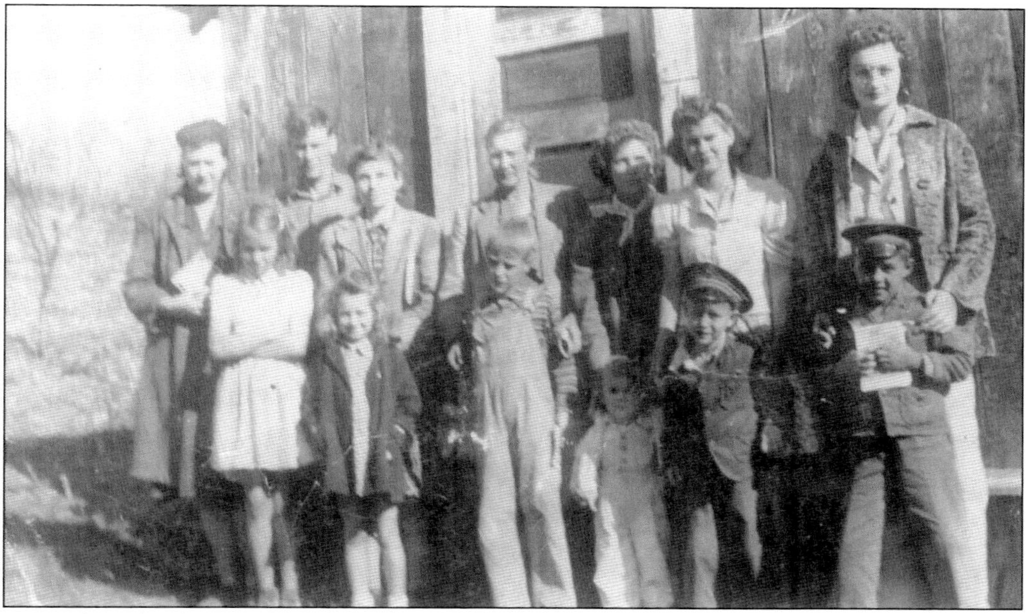

A Sunday school class is seen here in the early 1940s at Grassy Branch. In the early years, there were few ministers in the area, and the Methodist church sent preachers to the area churches. Some preachers had to visit as many as 12 churches a month. Sunday school classes were conducted by local deacons and usually held in private residences or any other building that was available. This particular group met each Sunday in the home of a man who had been sent off to fight in World War II. The minister would only come preach once a month as he had to travel. (Courtesy of Glen Cardwell.)

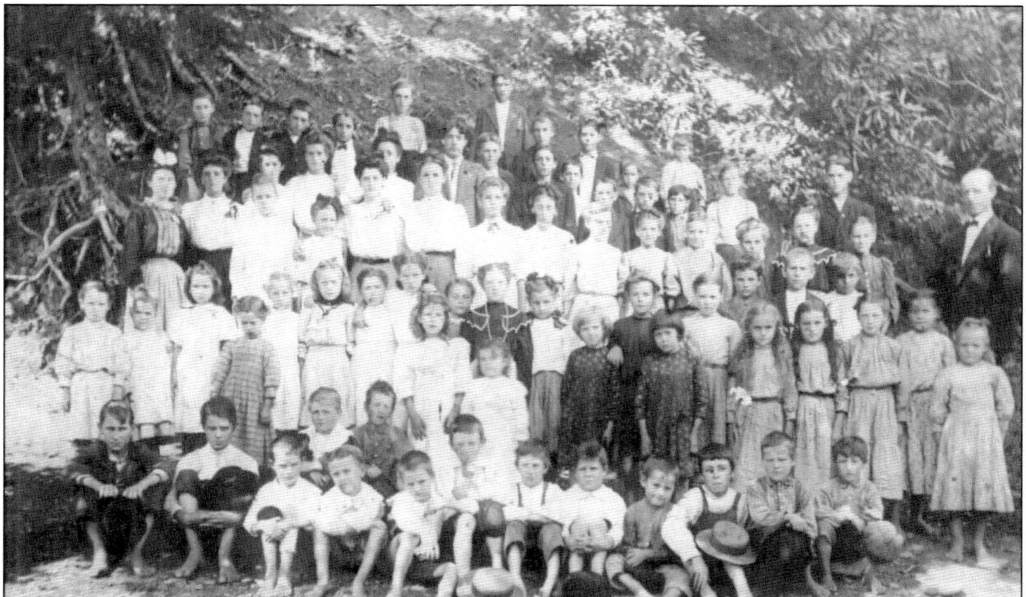

Pictured is a 1930s Sunday school class. (Courtesy of Glen Cardwell.)

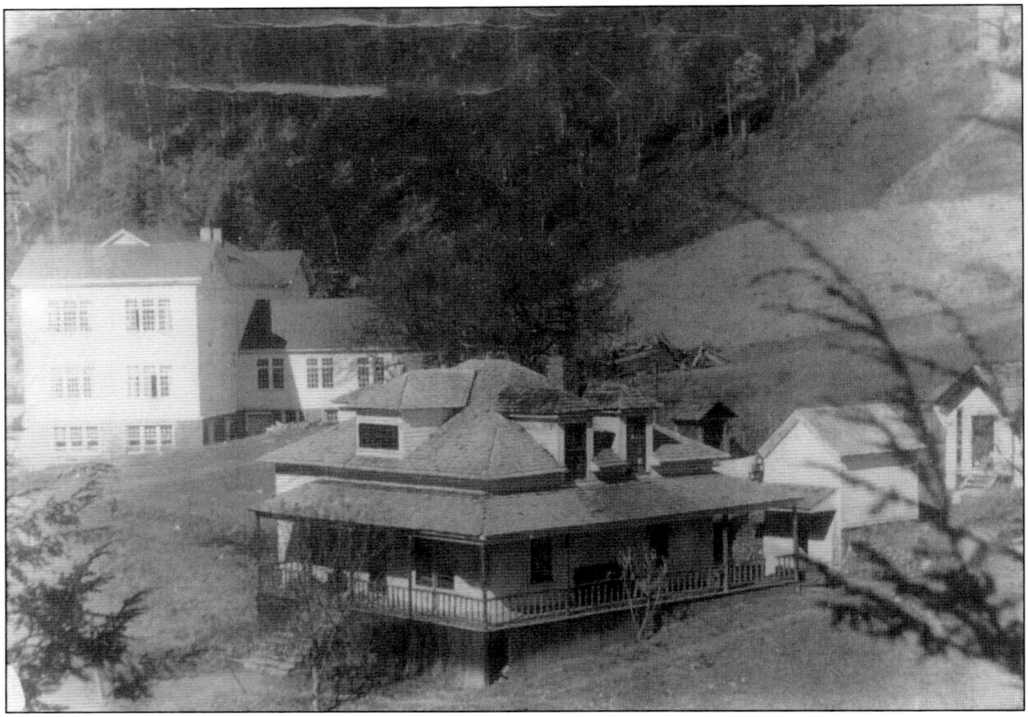

The Garfield-Scott House was one of 16 buildings constructed by the Methodist Episcopal Church for the Pittman Community Center. (Courtesy of Glen Cardwell.)

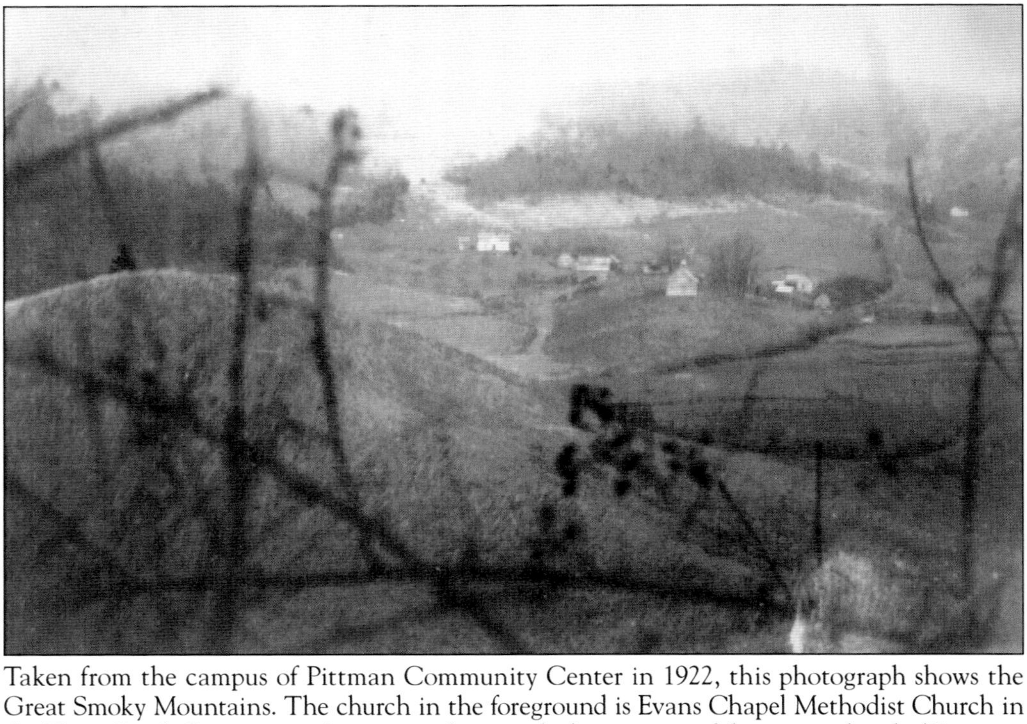

Taken from the campus of Pittman Community Center in 1922, this photograph shows the Great Smoky Mountains. The church in the foreground is Evans Chapel Methodist Church in the Tunis Creek Community. It was torn down with the creation of the national park. (Courtesy of Glen Cardwell.)

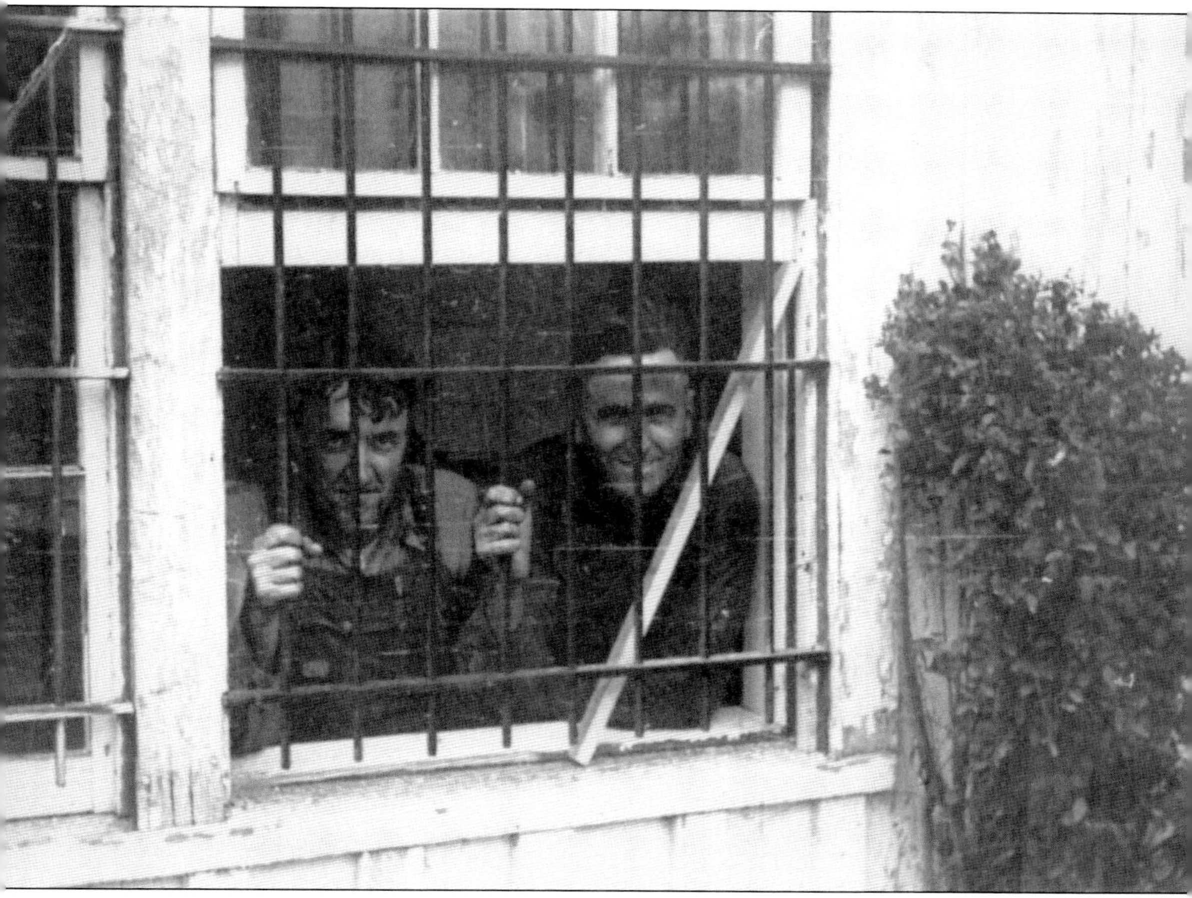

The only store in town served as a post office as well. The store had bars on the windows, and some customers would occasionally pretend to be prisoners in a jailhouse. (Courtesy of Carolyn Large Whaley.)

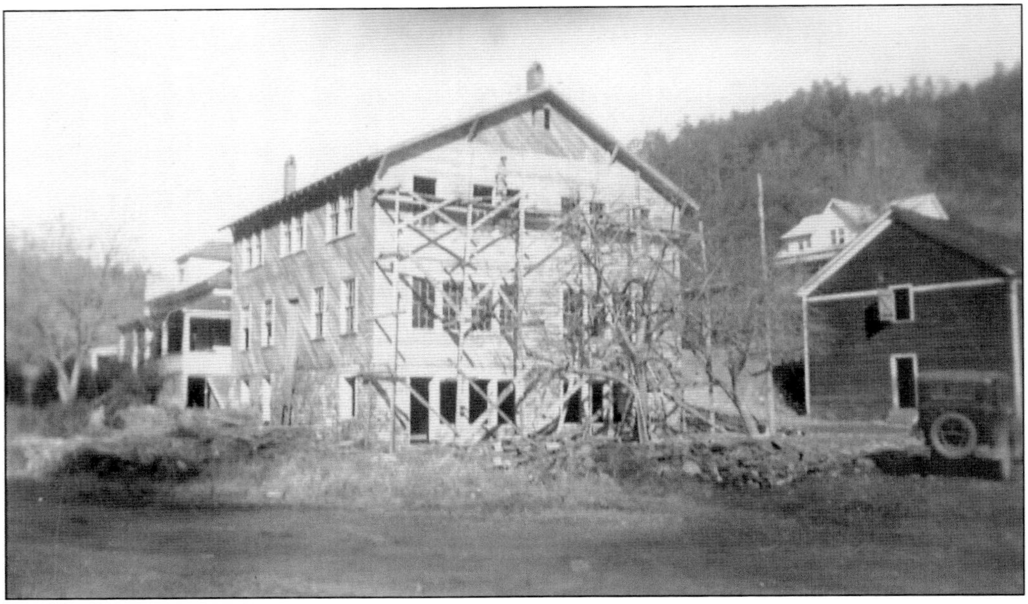

Construction began on the building that was to become the Pittman Center City Hall in 1919. According to historian Glen Cardwell, once construction began, the sawmills operated for 12 hours a day. The Methodist Episcopal Church financed the 16 buildings that formed the new town. (Courtesy of Glen Cardwell.)

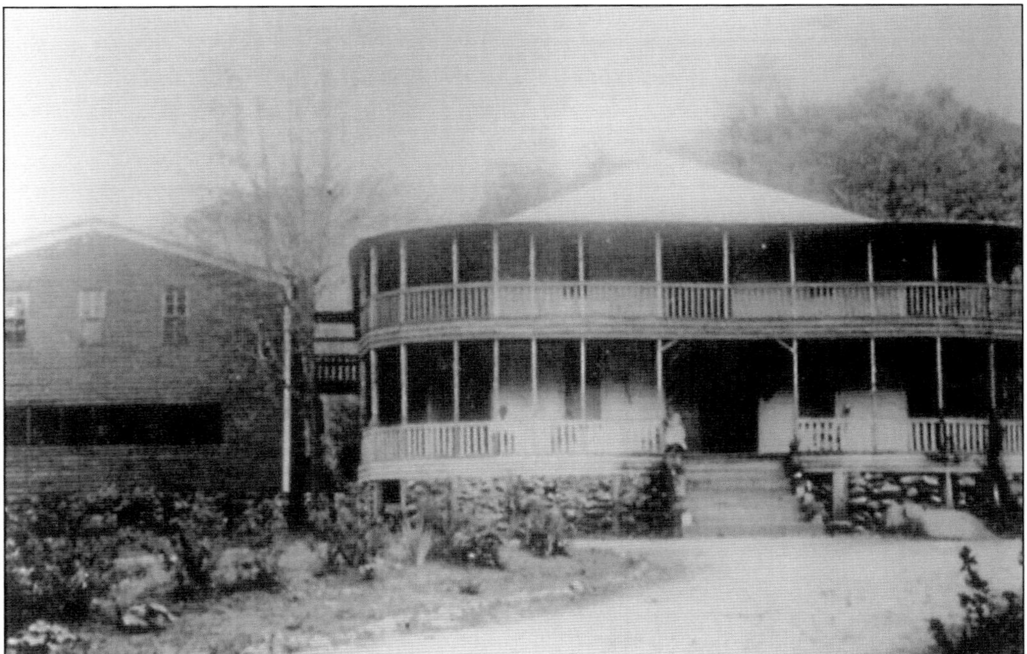

The Greenbrier Hotel once stood in the Greenbrier area, now part of the Great Smoky Mountains National Park. The hotel burned down in the 1950s. (Courtesy of Carolyn Large Whaley.)

Four

Disaster and Loss

Like any other place, eastern Sevier County has experienced its share of tragedy and loss. The first settler of Richardson's Cove met with tragedy when his family was wiped out by an Indian attack. William Richardson settled the area in 1792. At the time, Cherokee Indians occupied the area. One night, Richardson left his home to go to a gristmill. Soon after he departed, a band of Indians (historians disagree as to whether they were Muskogean or Chicakamauga) entered his home and killed his family, which included his wife, two other women relatives, and two children. The family was killed with tomahawks and a war club. The invaders left the war club before fleeing the property. Richardson hurriedly buried his family and left the area never to return. The Richardson family was buried in Richardson's Graveyard. Until the local Indians were forcibly removed from the region in 1838, there were numerous skirmishes between the settlers and the indigenous people.

Childhood illness was more common and frequently fatal in the early years of the settling of eastern Sevier County. Illnesses that children are routinely vaccinated against in the modern era were fatal in the early days. Childhood mortality and infant mortality were much higher then.

The region has experienced loss in every war since the American Revolution. Several Civil War battles were waged within a 50-mile radius, including the Battle of Dandridge, the Battle of Fort Sanders, and the Battle of Knoxville.

The biggest natural disaster–related loss in the area was the flood of 1938, in which eight people drowned in a flash flood that resulted from torrential rains that caused a massive mudslide. On the night of August 4, 1938, a cloudburst over Webb Creek created a deluge that ravaged the land, washing away houses and crops and killing the family of Alfred Ball and two visitors to the area. Webb Creek has flooded on other occasions, but never once have floods proved fatal since the tragedy of 1938.

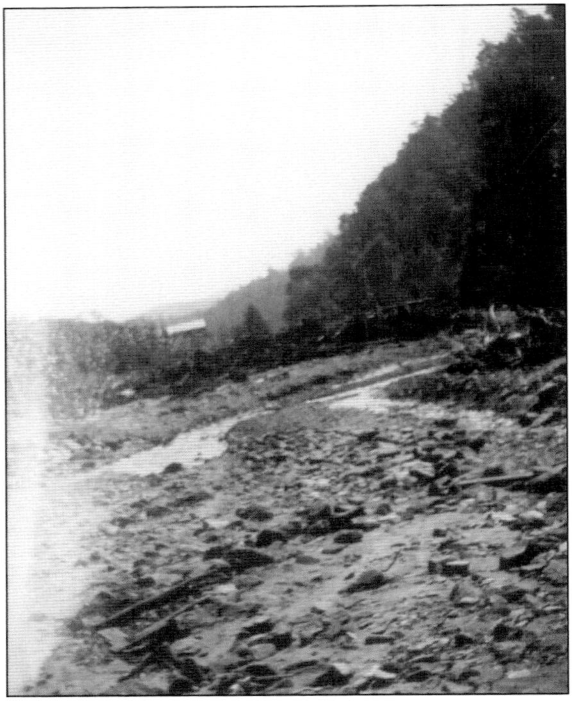

The locals remembered August 4, 1938, as a beautiful, cloudless day. It was Election Day and voters who had cast their ballots had begun returning to their homes. Later in the evening, the skies turned gray, and a tumultuous storm created an intense, swift, thunderous flash flood, which set off a chain of catastrophic events. The cloud burst weakened the ground near Webb Creek, resulting in a landslide. Throughout the hollows, the rain fell relentlessly, pouring down in torrents. The wind howled and blew with ferocity. Then came a terrifying roar that grew progressively louder as the mountain gave way and tons of mud and debris washed toward the tiny town, creating a swath of destruction. (Courtesy of Carolyn Large Whaley.)

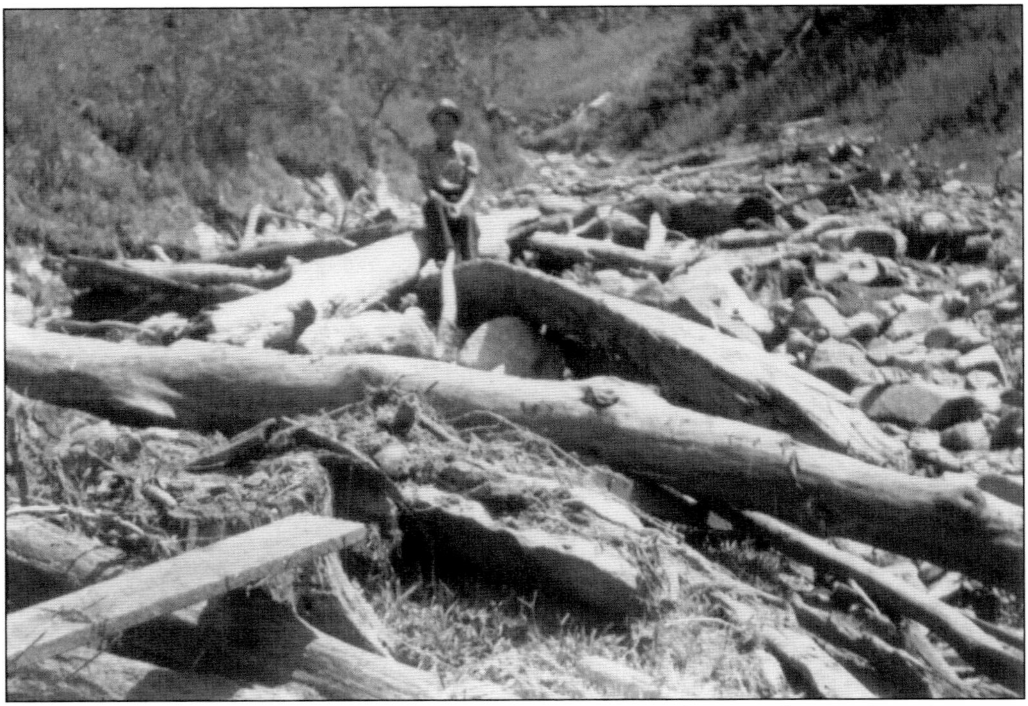

Jesse and Eula Evans lived in Sutton Hollow. They were on their way home when the storm began. As the torrential rain poured down, the couple made the fateful decision to go to the nearby home of Alfred Ball with the intention of waiting out the storm. Hours later, Ball Hollow, where the Ball home was located, was swept away in the flash flood. Nine of the homes in Sutton Hollow were washed away or seriously damaged. (Courtesy of Carolyn Large Whaley.)

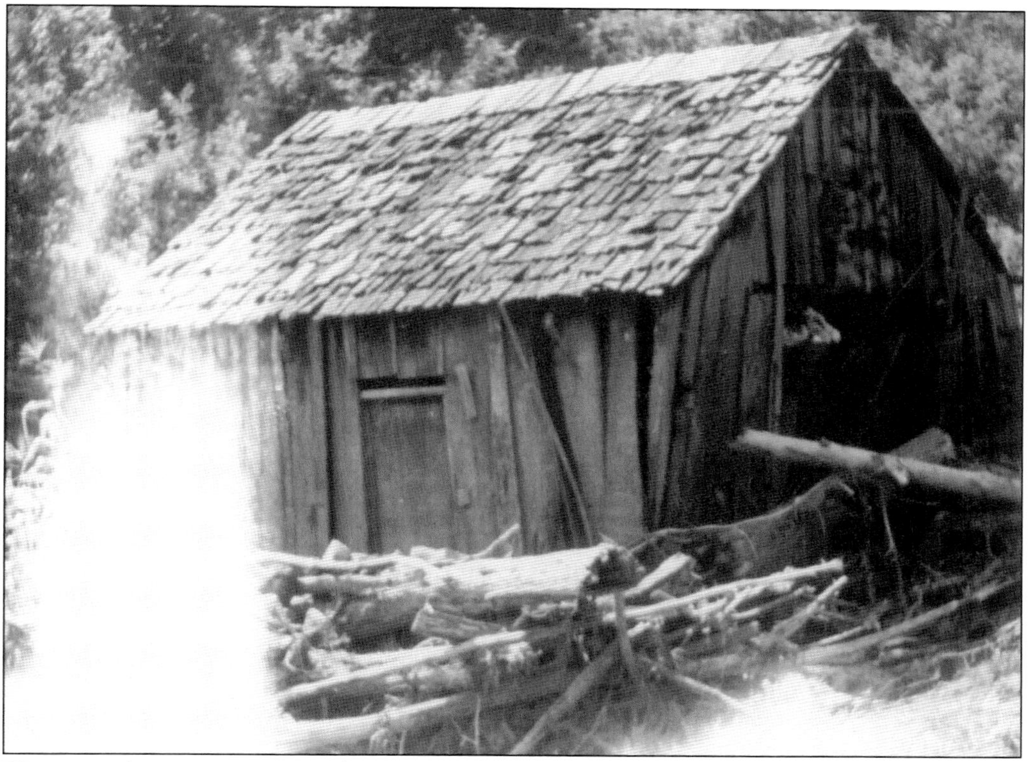

The worst damage was reported in Pittman Center, although damage was reported as far as 10 miles away in Sevierville. In Pittman Center, entire homes were destroyed. Roads were washed out, and corncribs, silos, tractors, farm machinery, bridges, and cars were washed away in the deluge. In the aftermath of the tragedy, eight people had lost their lives. In addition to Jesse and Eula Evans, the entire Ball family died in the flood. The dead included Alfred Ball, 38; his wife, Lona McCarter Ball, 31; and their children, Glenn, 11; Alfred Jr., 5; Dallas, 2; and Harold, 3 months. Jesse and Eula Evans were found almost a mile away from the Ball home and about 100 feet apart. The day after the flood, hundreds of locals sifted through the debris in search of the bodies. (Courtesy of Carolyn Large Whaley.)

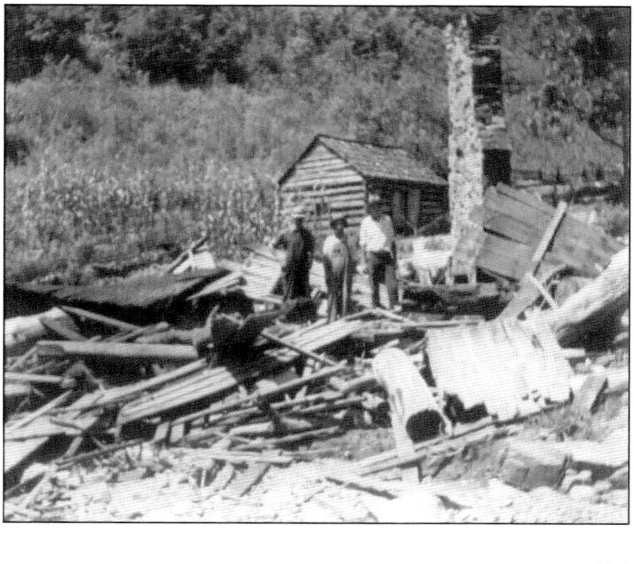

A roof and a chimney are all that remain of this home. Pictured, from left to right, are Hugh Morris, Bruce Morris, and Lawrence Proffitt. Bruce was the searcher who found the body of Lona Ball. (Courtesy of Carolyn Large Whaley.)

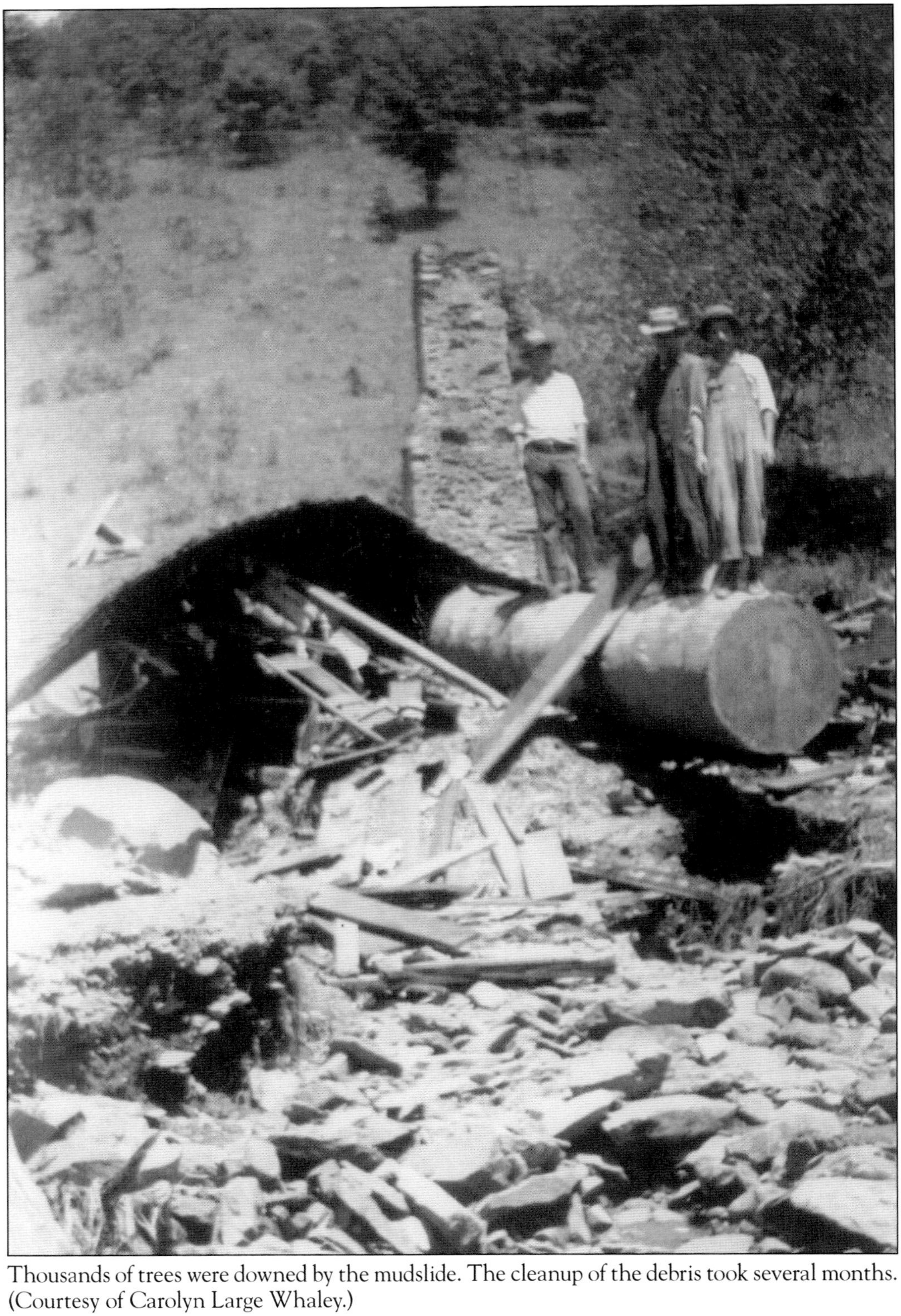

Thousands of trees were downed by the mudslide. The cleanup of the debris took several months. (Courtesy of Carolyn Large Whaley.)

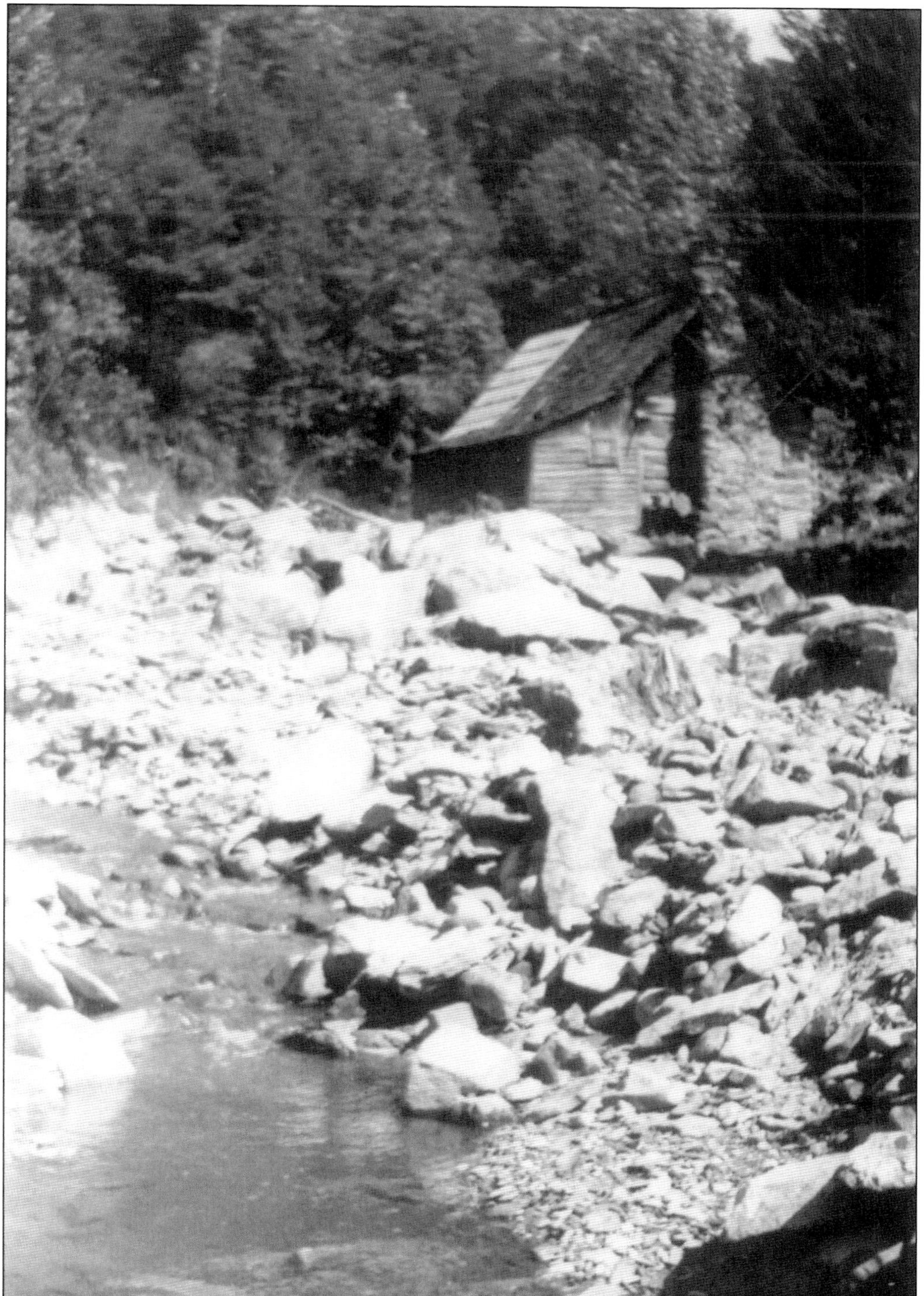

This unidentified cabin escaped damage though large amounts of debris were left at the stoop. With few tractors in the area, much of the cleanup involved moving the debris with mules and horses. (Courtesy of Carolyn Large Whaley.)

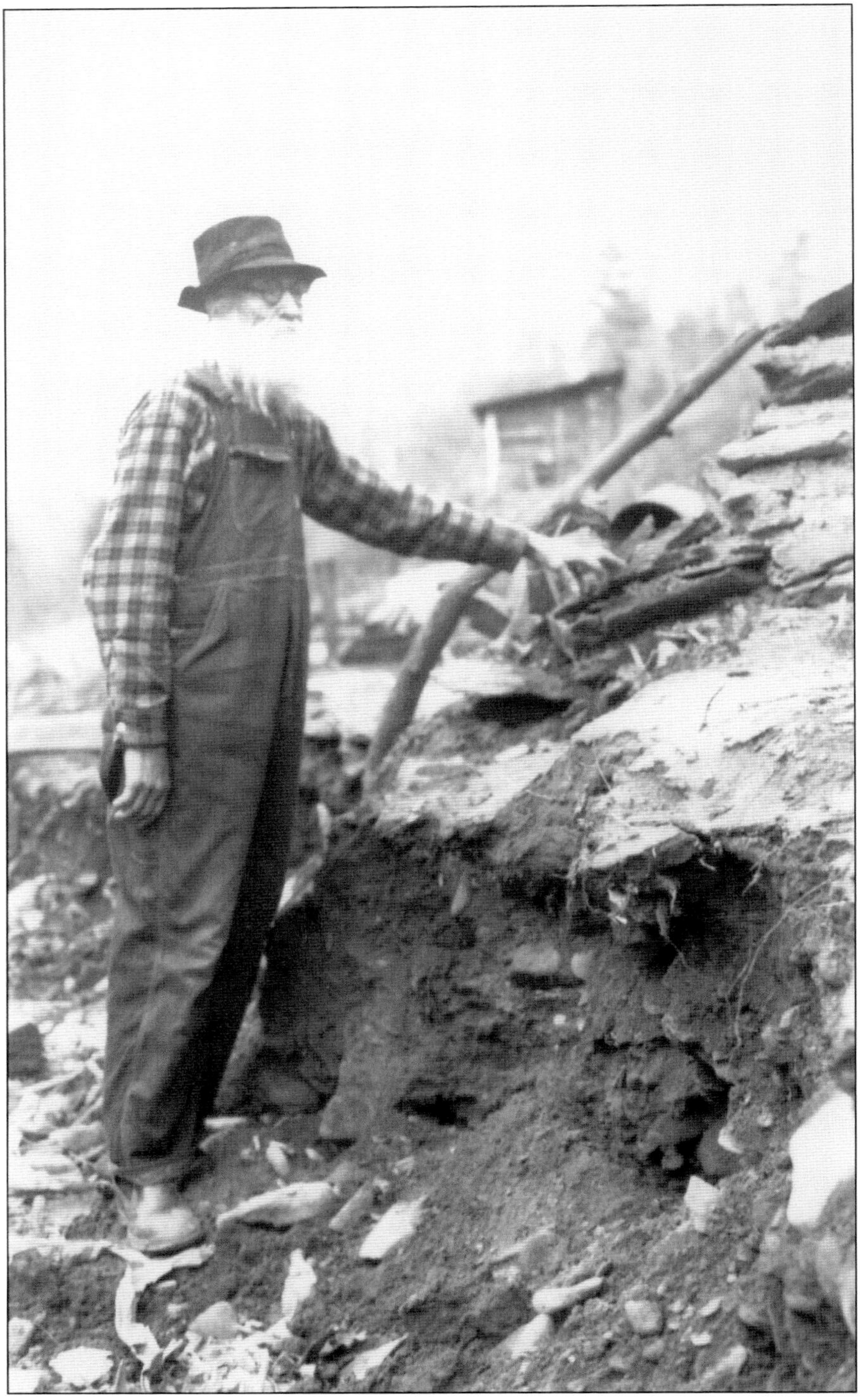

A farmer surveys the damage and debris left at his property. Experts said the destruction was caused by "a blowout" in Webb Mountain. A blowout happens when water gathering in underground chambers causes immense pressure, which makes the mountain explode. The floodwaters swept down the mountain causing the creeks and rivers to swell into raging torrents. (Courtesy of Carolyn Large Whaley.)

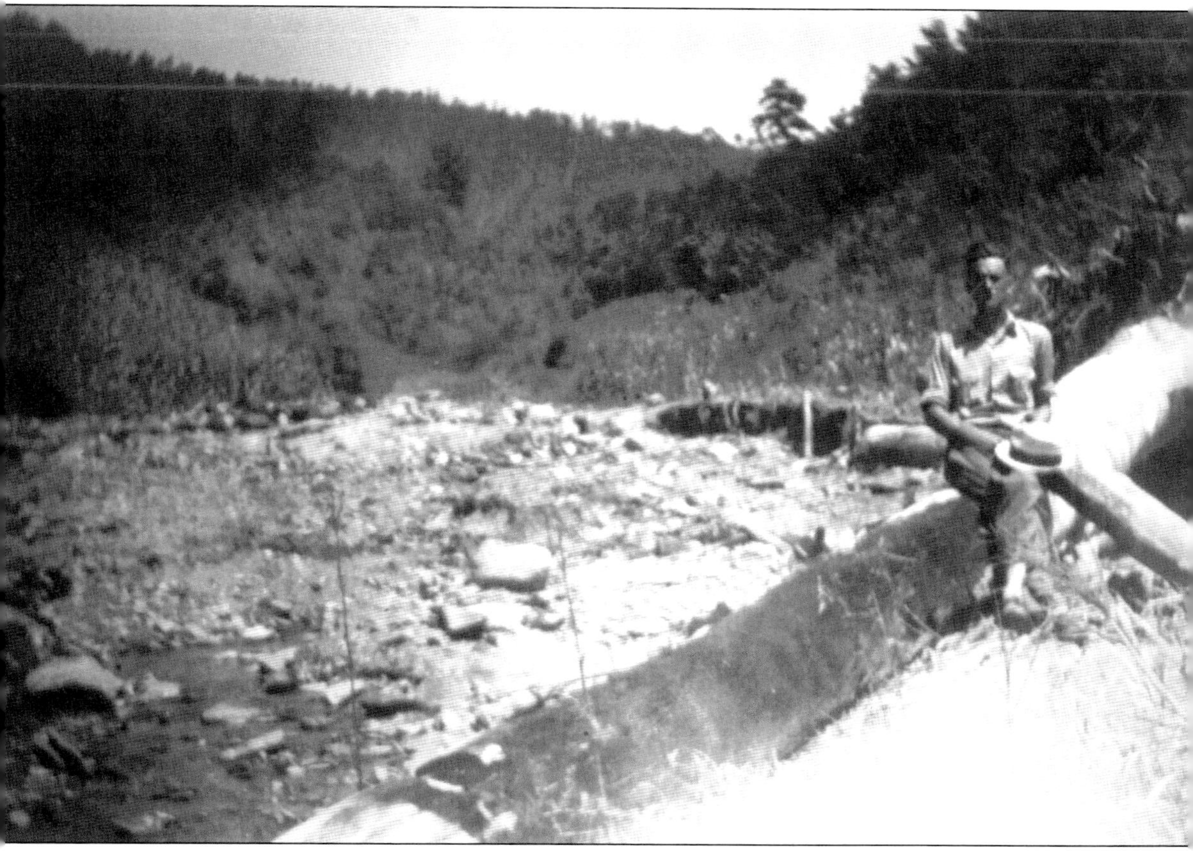

Carl McCarter sits atop a downed tree in the aftermath of the flood. Locals began to mark time by the flood. For example, someone might say, "I built my home a year after the flood." (Courtesy of Carolyn Large Whaley.)

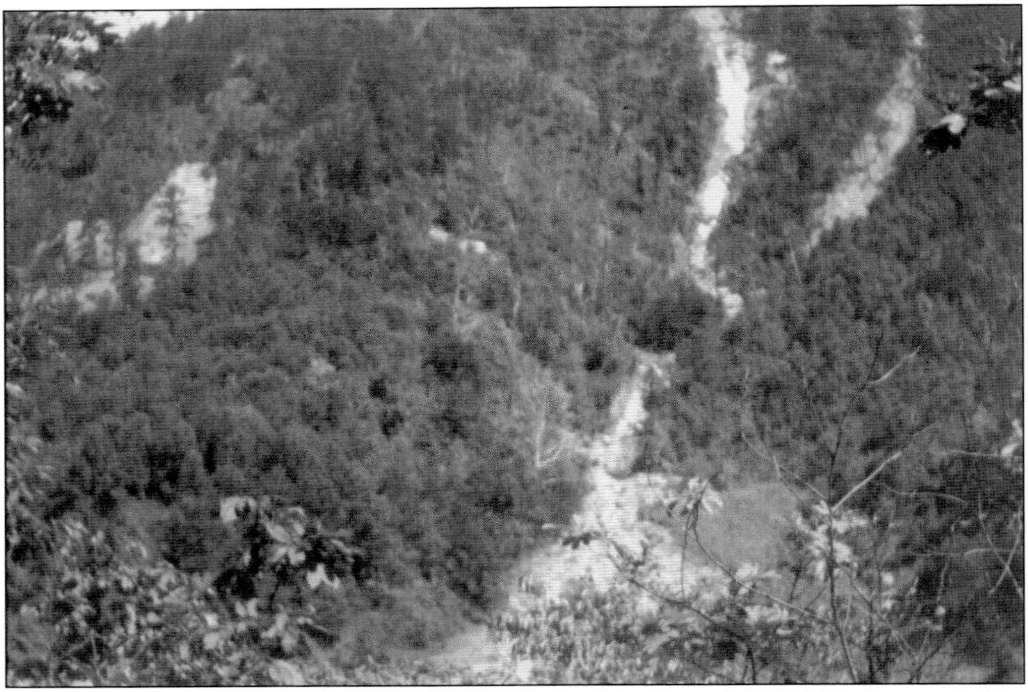

Two swaths of destruction scar the face of the mountain where the landslide occurred. The flood changed the topography of the area and left 50 people homeless. (Courtesy of Carolyn Large Whaley.)

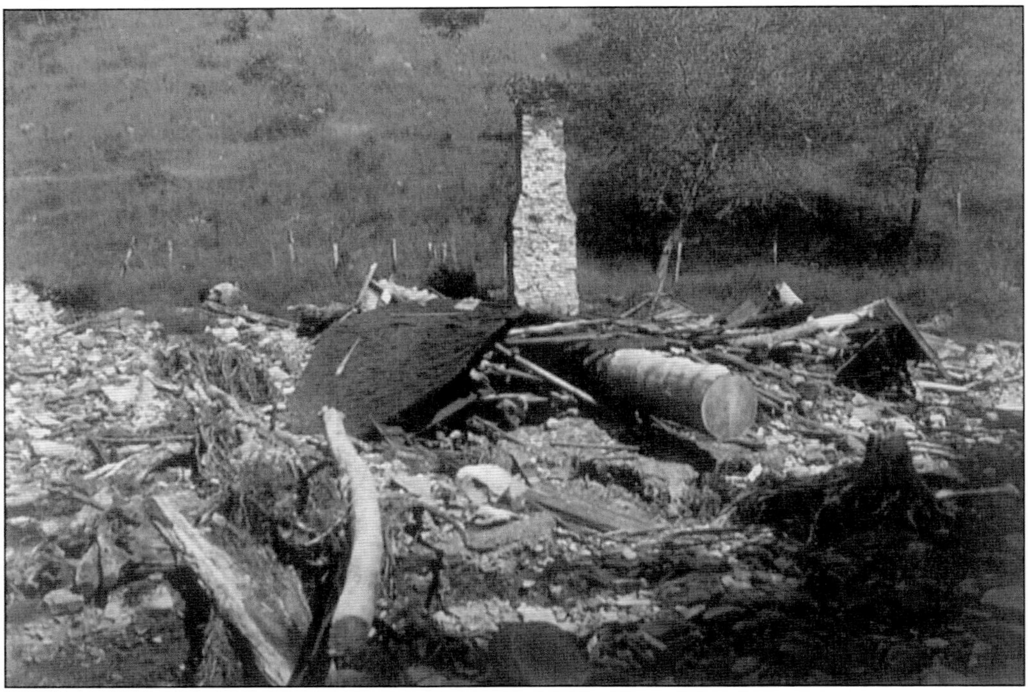

A chimney is all that remains of this home following the flood that claimed the lives of six people at Pittman Community Center in 1938. It started with a flash flood, which was followed by torrential rains and a massive mudslide. (Courtesy Carolyn Whaley.)

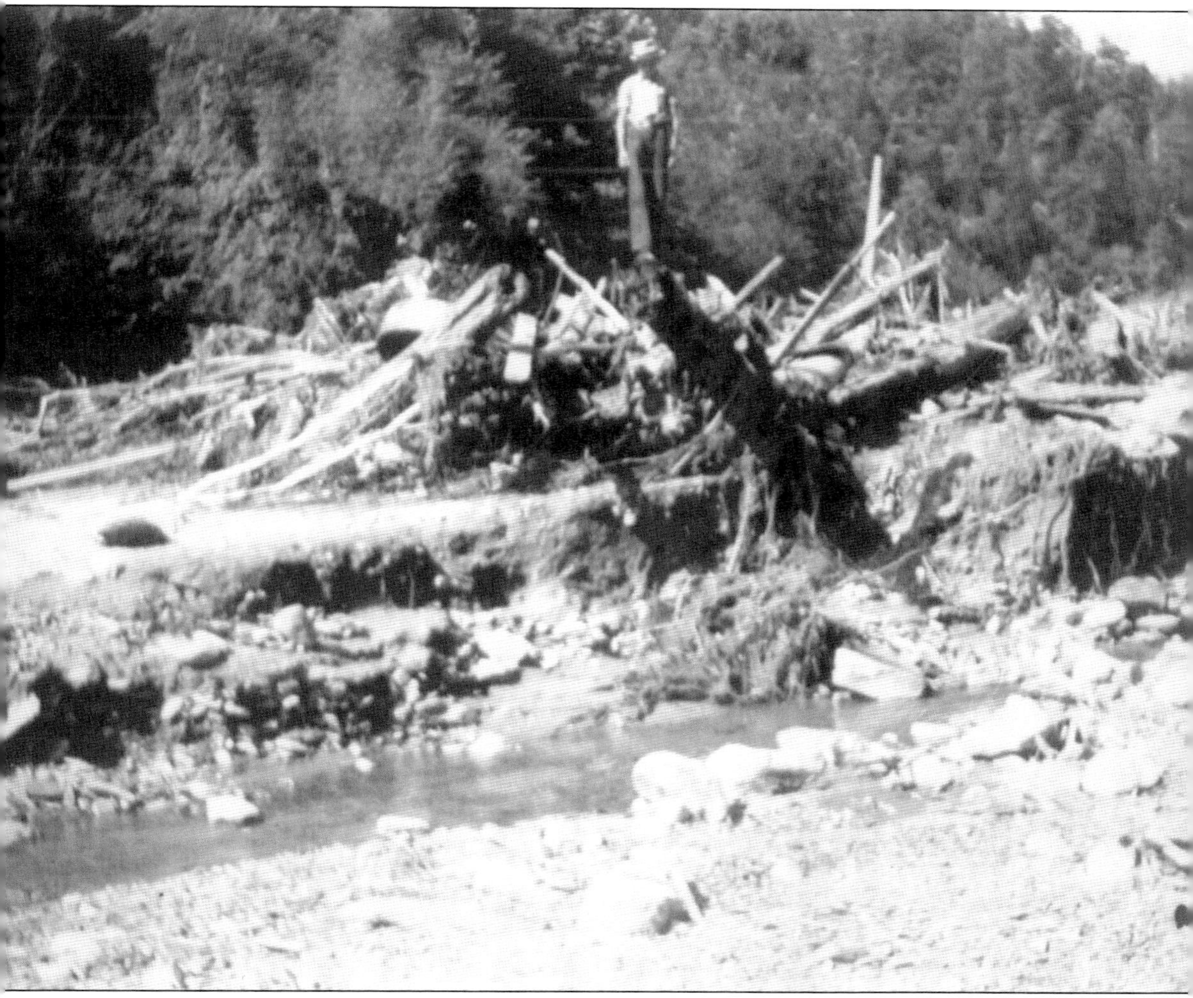

An unidentified man stands on a tree trunk in the wake of the Webb Creek flood. (Courtesy of Carolyn Large Whaley.)

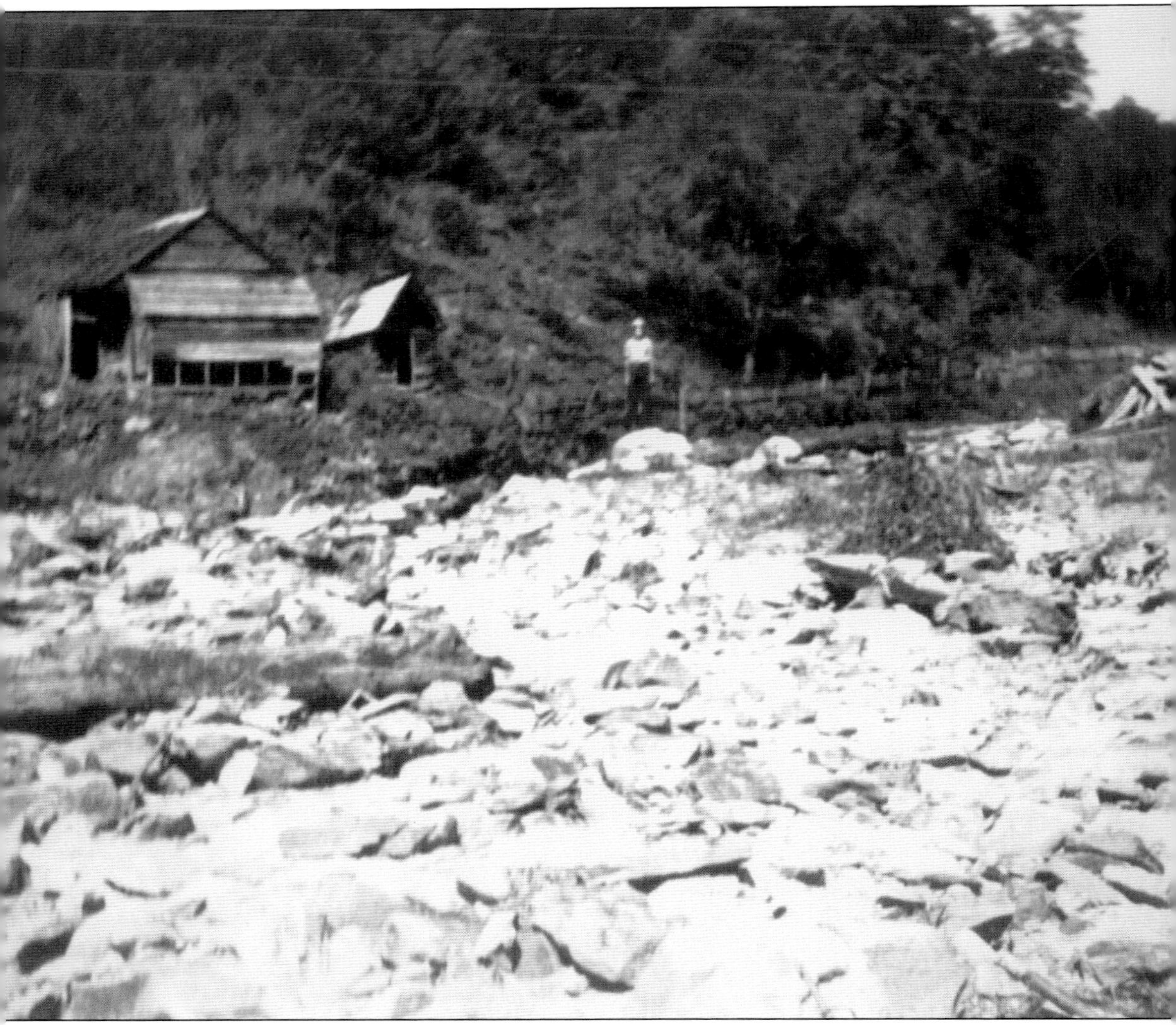

A cabin stands in the distance. This lone surviving cabin was one of the few spared in the swath of destruction from the flood of 1938. One can only imagine the terror the occupant of this cabin must have experienced as he watched his neighbors' homes wash away and was left to wonder if his home would be next. (Courtesy of Carolyn Large Whaley.)

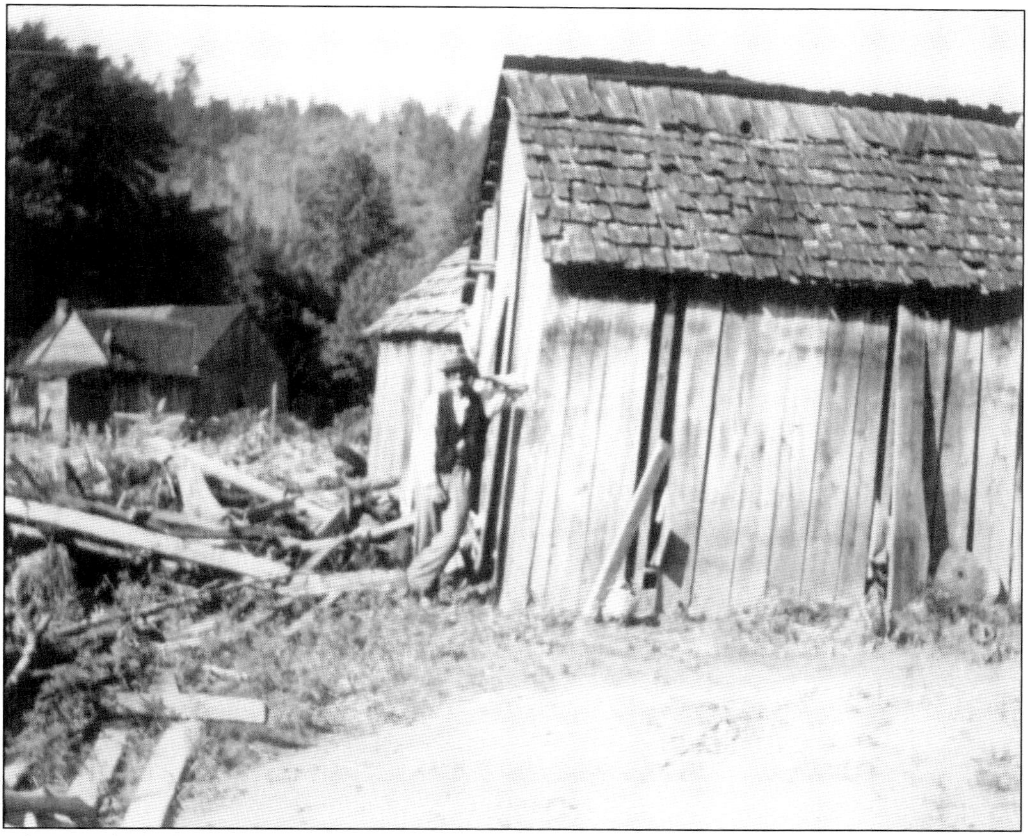

Along with the loss of homes and eight lives, the flood washed away numerous crops from many farms in the area. Because most farmers grew their own food, many worried about the prospects of starvation in the coming winter months. Fortunately, the people of Pittman Center were united in the wake of the tragedy. Many of the local farmers who had not lost their crops aided their less fortunate neighbors. (Courtesy of Carolyn Large Whaley.)

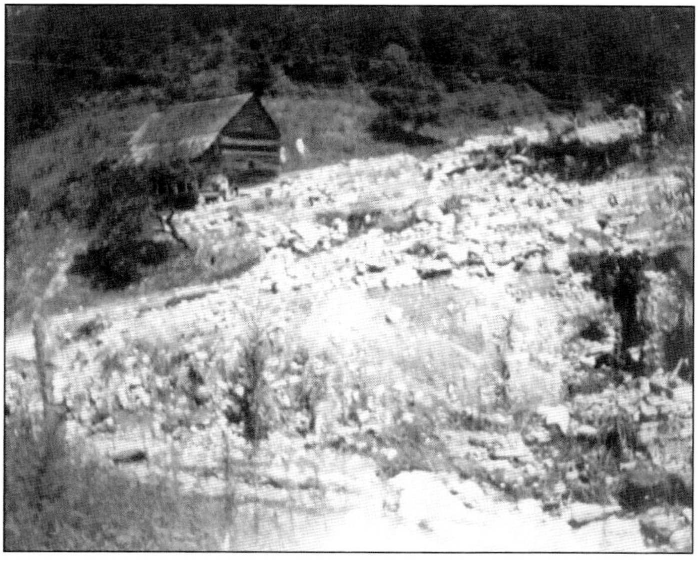

This farmhouse was one of the few in Ball Hollow that survived the tempest. More than 20 other families were not as lucky. (Courtesy of Carolyn Large Whaley.)

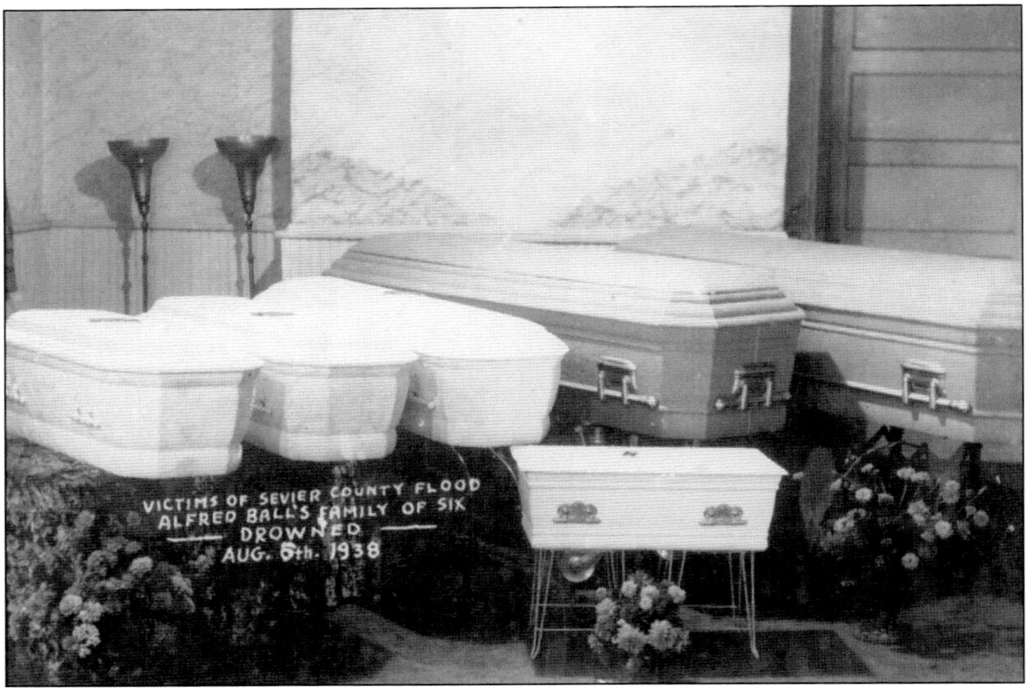

On Sunday August 7, 1938, the Ball family was laid to rest in a single grave in Clear Springs Cemetery. Jesse and Eula Evans were put to rest the day before in the Shultz-Whaley Cemetery. The coffins of the Ball family were buried side by side. (Both, courtesy of Carolyn Large Whaley.)

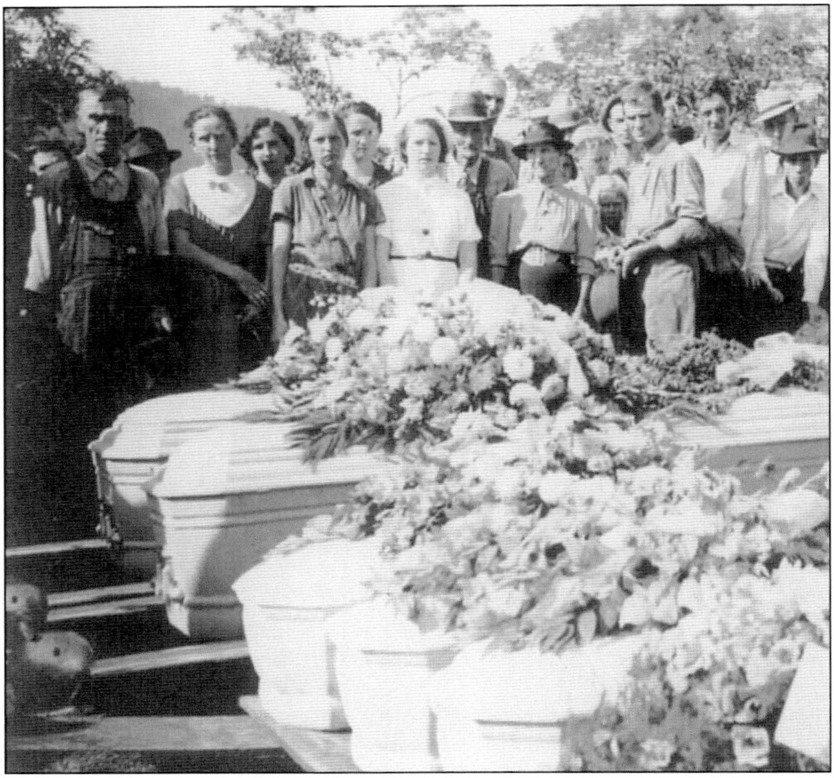

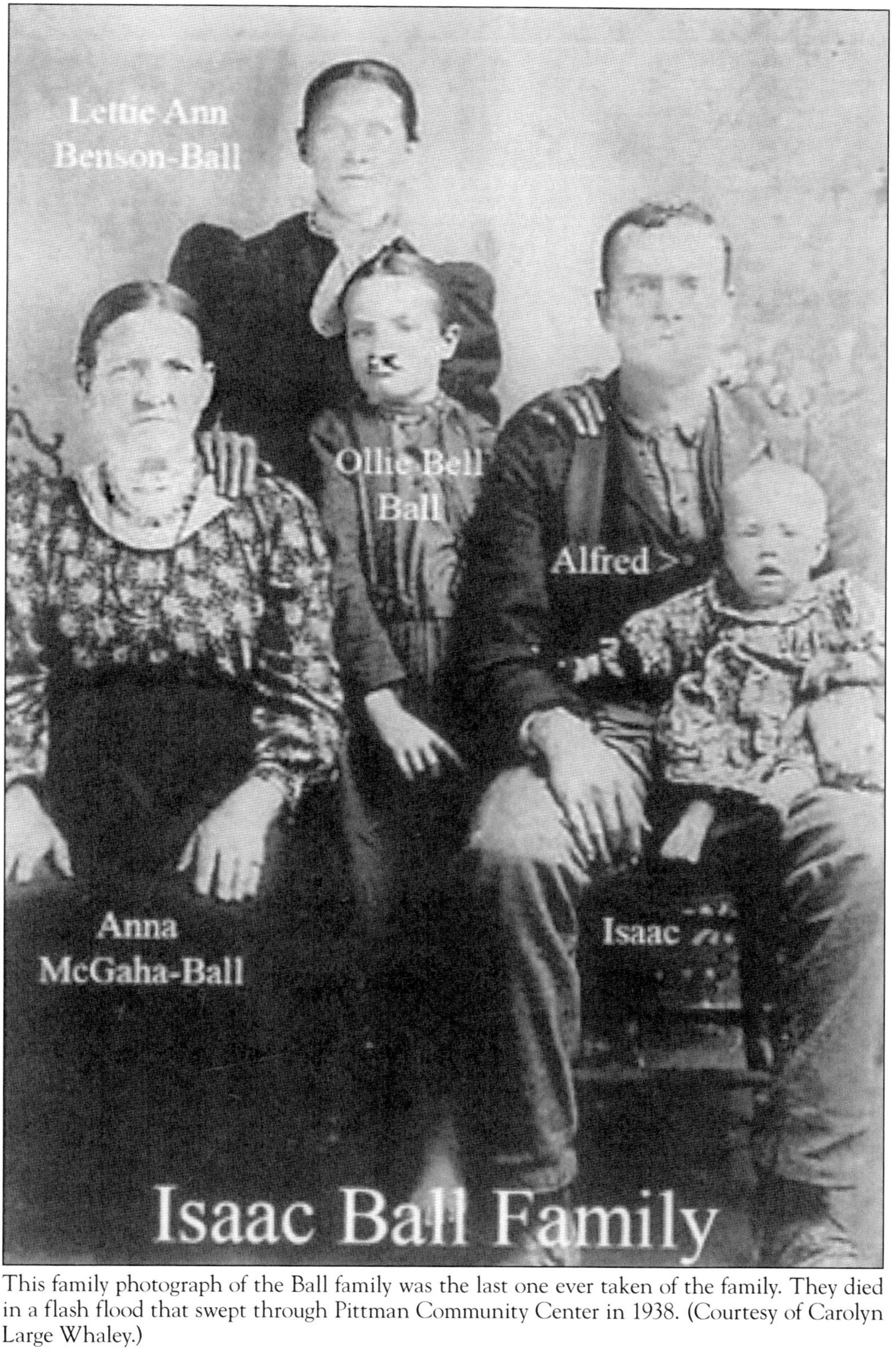

This family photograph of the Ball family was the last one ever taken of the family. They died in a flash flood that swept through Pittman Community Center in 1938. (Courtesy of Carolyn Large Whaley.)

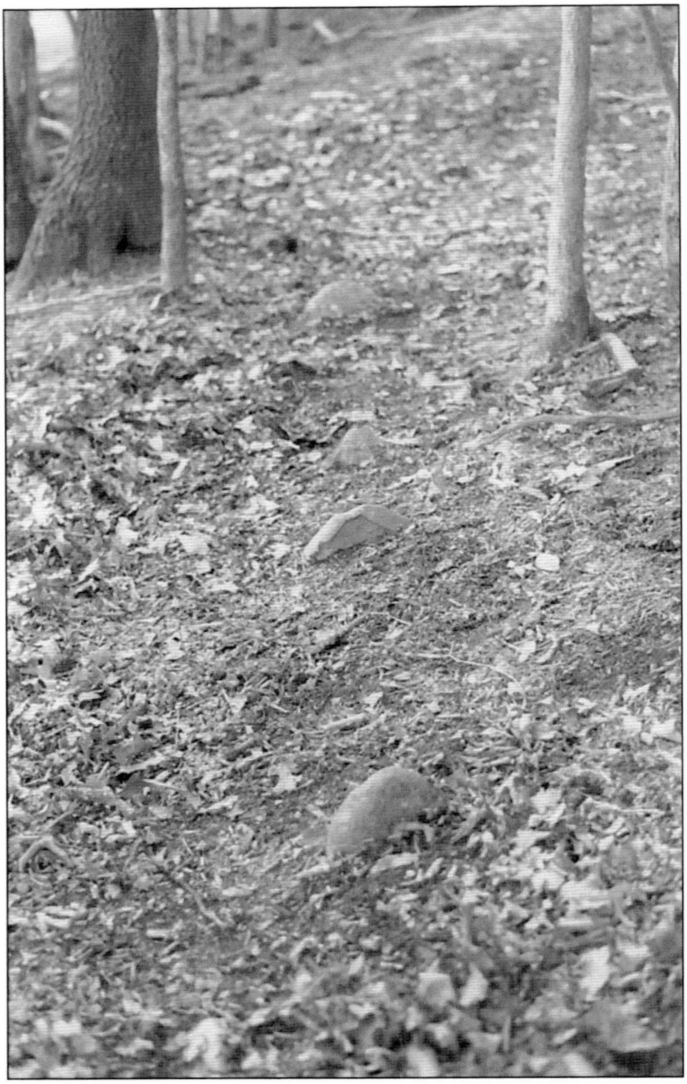

Stones mark the graves of the Richardson family. On the morning of December 29, 1792, William Richardson's frontier cabin became the scene of a tragedy. Richardson left his home that evening destined for the gristmill—unaware he would never see his wife again. Richardson did not know that lurking nearby was a band of Indians waiting for his departure. Soon after he left the cabin, the Indians entered the home and brutally killed three women and two children with tomahawks and a war club. They left the war club in the home. Richardson returned home the next morning and was traumatized when he saw the carnage. He hurriedly buried his family in what is now known as Richardson's graveyard. He subsequently left the area and went to live with his daughter in Obie's Branch. He never returned to Richardson's Cove. (Courtesy of Jackie Underwood.)

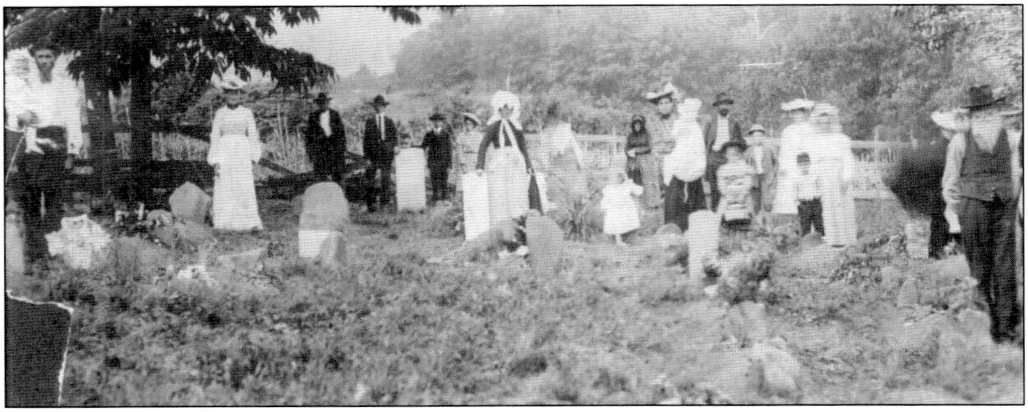

Church members are gathered at the Huskey family cemetery in 1905. The nature of the assembly is unknown. (Courtesy of Carolyn Large Whaley.)

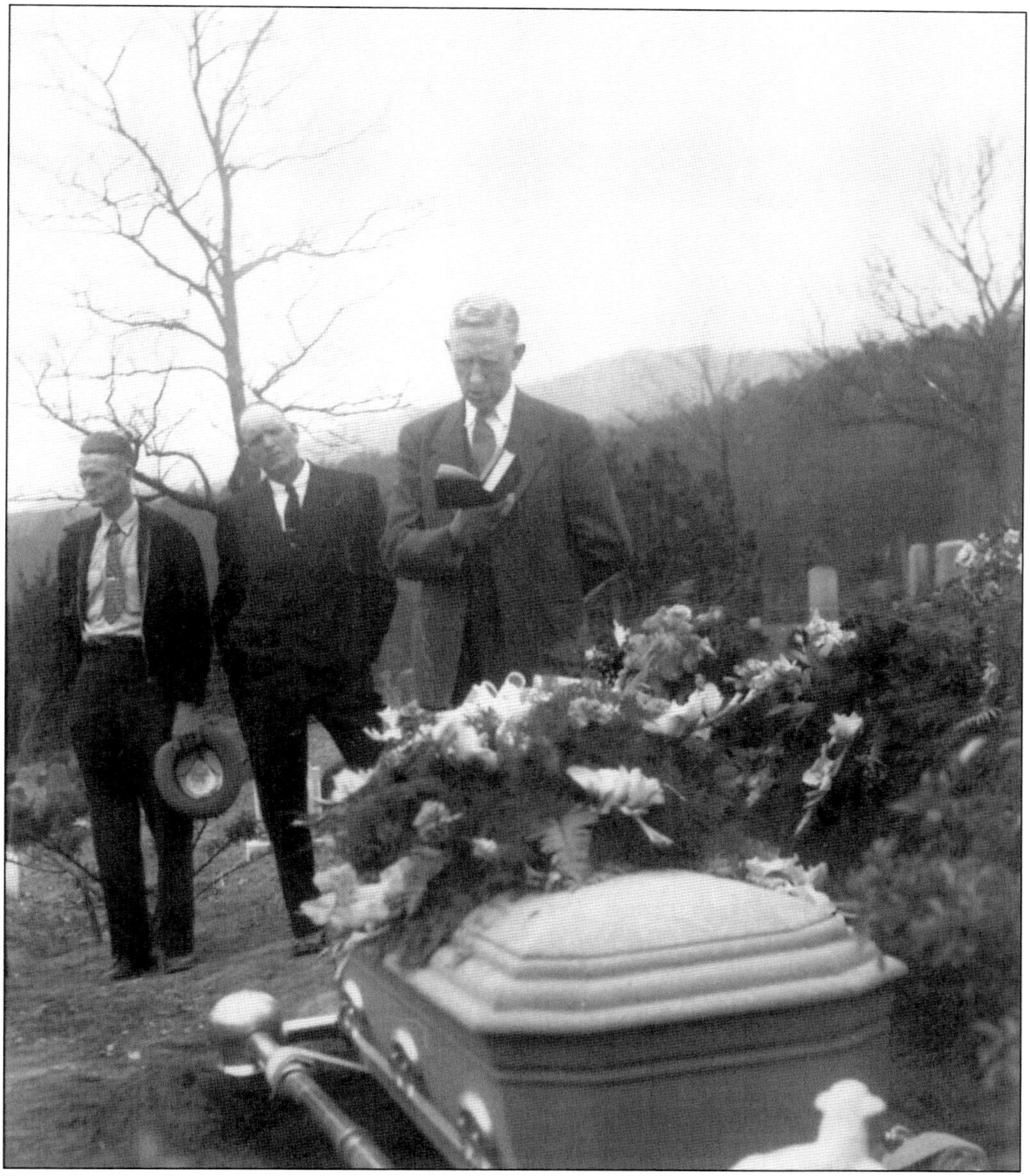

Dr. Robert F. Thomas presides over the funeral of Steve McCarter. Thomas played a significant role in the founding of Pittman Center. In the background stand Oliver Huskey (left) and Rev. Richard Watson. (Courtesy of Carolyn Large Whaley.)